ATHEISTIC SPIRITUALITY

ATHEISTIC SPIRITUALITY
(SOME STRANGE COSMIC EXPERIENCES)

Gopal. N. Honnavalli

PARTRIDGE
A Penguin Random House Company

To order additional copies of this book, contact
Partridge India
000 800 10062 62
www.partridgepublishing.com/india
orders.india@partridgepublishing.com

PREFACE

It is more than five decades since I have been experiencing, on and off, astral traveling to unknown regions and spheres all over the universe. Probably, it may be, to some extent, because of my long association with some of the so called spiritual Institutions and persons; all of which, in fact, I gave-up about a decade back, after which, I feel the intensity of such experiences have increased and I have been journeying, now, directly to the center of the universe where only a sub-atomic particle of light energy which, I presume, controls the entire universe, is seated.

Since years, some force wakes me up around three in the night irrespective of at what time I go to bed. It is the most lovable, blissful and joyful feelings I get when I wake up at that hour of the night and sit to contemplate (meditate?). Some vibrations start floating around and the entire atmosphere fills with these vibrations. I could feel as if some divine Being is standing by my side and some unique divine fragrance pervades all-round and slowly I lose myself and start my astral journey while still physically continue to sit on a chair. Though I am alone in this journey I have no fear of the unknown because I could feel the presence of that Divine Being by my side guiding me. Silence, deep and divine, encompasses the vastness of the universe. I feel my consciousness expanding to the universal consciousness. After I come back from the journey and while still in that stupor that Divine Being, by my side, urges me to write and I start writing, unaware of myself, on which I have no control, probably but for my limited English literary knowledge which is reflected in the writings.

I never wanted, for these years that my handwritings be typed, let alone published. I don't know some force intuitively urges me to publish; and hence this publishing. I neither accept nor reject any of my experiences and I can never give any rational or logical or scientific answers to anyone who may question or challenge the genuineness of my experiences. I just experience them and that is how it is and I do not know how and why it happens. With these experiences I am becoming more and more ignorant of everything which is leading me to 'nothingness'. Hence, I pray that I be spared from any questions since no answers would be forthcoming from me.

In spite of some changes from within, I seem to have not changed externally and physically which gives to my associates and relatives the feelings of ordinariness in me, which in fact, I am and may be even below the ordinariness in their values. I respect every ones' values about me.

There are many contradictions, opposites and disjointed one's having no links between the writings of different days and even of the same day, which strengthens the critics while I do not like to indulge to defend any of these writings, since I claim no personal authorship, though they are in my handwriting, but to the dictation of some force beyond me.

I dedicate this to my grandchildren, Aarna & Ronk ; to my daughter, Megha; to my son-in-law Sharath and last but not the least to my wife, Sharada.

Mysore
December 2013

Gopal. N. Honnavalli

ATHEISTIC SPIRITUALISM
(SOME STRANGE COSMIC EXPERIENCES)

I contemplate on the Central Balancing Point of the Universe, which, to me, looks to be a sub-sub atomic Light Energy. I call it as the God (Particle) [Recent findings of Higgs-Boson at Large Hadron Collider-LHC-, in my view, cannot be called as the God Particle] The one and the only one God (Particle) in the entire Universe, which is the creator, sustainer, and ultimately the destroyer of the entire Universe. However, let us just call that as a point of light energy. It is eternal, self-propelling, pure energy. It is the Ultimate Intelligence (Cosmic Central Intelligence). It has very powerful and invisible rays which keep millions of galaxies all over the vast universe in balance. One ray of this energy reaches the center of a galaxy and controls and keeps the whole galaxy with its milky way in perfect order and balance, so that that galaxy can rotate on its own axis, spherically and spin around this Central Particle of Cosmic Light Energy.

When so, one cannot imagine how much more powerful this Central Point of the Universe of light-energy is, controlling and keeping all the millions galaxies in the universe in balance perfectly and accurately. And another ray takes off from our galaxy and reaches the center of our Sun which-in turn keeps our solar system in perfect balance. This is a chain reaction-the center of the Universe sending a ray to the center of our galaxy and the center of our galaxy sending a ray to the center of the sun which keeps the solar system in balance. Our solar system is like a grain of sand on the vast arena of the Universe's beach.

May be, there is intelligence in different forms in many other galaxies. Without this intelligence all galaxies cannot remain in balance per-se. The intelligence of all intelligences is this central balancing point of light energy. I feel that I, as a point of light energy, also have the same characteristics and qualities like the universal one.

I travel as a point of light energy in my subtle body towards the subtle world through the pathway that was emitted from the central point of energy which has two tunnels each of one way. I take the one which goes out and travel beyond our galaxy and arrive at the subtle world. On reaching the subtle world I give up my subtle body and start traveling as a point of light shedding the layers of causal body which is in the form of an onion and by the time I reach the point, I become a pure naked point of light. From there I perceive the entire universe looking like a sphere on the surface of which all these millions of galaxies with their milky way rotating in perfect order on their own axis in spherical manner around the Central Point of Light Energy. As I feel that I am arriving nearer to the central point of energy, it is nowhere to be perceived, for all rays going to different galaxies are merged and a very huge, flat and wide ring of light is formed and rotating in line with the galaxies. I land on this ring and cross the ring and enter into another tunnel of a ray which is like a spoke of a bicycle wheel connecting the hub and the rim. When I arrive at the inner ring I feel the intensity of the energy and I stand as a naked point of light. The central point of light energy, I feel, converses with me, though not with sound, conveying the happiness of my meeting with it. This central point seems to be omnipotent, omnipresent and omniscient, pure, blissful, self-propelling and eternal. The exchange of communication having no language, is still perceived beyond expression experiencing the peace, bliss, strength and fulfillment. While I still desire to stay there in that state in the presence of this Central Point, I am reminded to get back and I am sucked back through the out-going tunnel picking up the layers of causal body, already transferred from the other tunnel, and subsequently my subtle body, I finally enter into my physical body. All these process seem to take only a few minutes but the time had stopped and so the thought process. It is said that the Center of the Universe from this earth is about 50 billion light years and yet I could be able to reach IT, probably, in about 50 seconds (in the time measurement of this earth). However, I had no knowledge of any of these since my thought and intelligence were withdrawn and I was beyond time, space and causation and also was beyond thoughts, words, and deeds and I was in deep silence.

—⚍—

25TH MAY 2009   04 00 A.M.

Happenings are not miracles. They are just happenings. In spite of your-self there were happenings and they continue to happen. You cannot either qualify or quantify them, because, you can never understand the happenings as they happen. Your birth is a happening, so is your death and so also the in-between, what you call as life. You are the very happening itself, though a figment on the cosmic arena of the Universal happenings. You can never know the cosmic happenings for you can never know your own happenings. So, just be yourself. Probably, then you may peep into these happenings, but not sure. Eternally all things happen to be happenings. In a way God is also an eternal happening in the concept of human being. As such, man calls the conceptual God as omnipresent, omnipotent and omniscient.

—m—

11ᵀᴴ MARCH 2009   03 00 A.M.

Yes, time, one of the man-made dimensions for the physical purposes, is actually running out, especially in my case. Why do I feel that? Is it because of the so called conditioned concepts of achievements that are not met with? However, there is a deep, very deep, urge to attain something inexpressible, though knowing fully well that there is nothing that could be achieved. This urge for achievement is not set as any physical goal, but beyond. What that beyond is? I know not. With the end of this physical body does it bring to an end of my-entity too? Is there anything like an entity of "ME" and also is this entity connected to the ENTIRITY? However, I have no knowledge of my entity or entirety. Once again, these are conditioned concepts. In these conditioned concepts, my life goes in a circle, but the speed has slowed down and one day it comes to a stop, a dead stop, and the dead wheel falls. In the process, somehow, deep within me, I feel that "I" shall never be stopped nor shall I fall. I feel, I would continue to be "Me" to myself and yet I shall not be "The present me". The present me is the result of all the process of life not only of this phase but also the left over of the last phase combined with physical, mental and the so called spiritual acts, talks and thoughts, ever changing, but at the same time never changing in certain aspects. Change! What is it? It is: 'It-is-not-what-it-was', either wholly or partially but superficially. Within, it is always never changing but ever the same. And probably, this ever unchanged status of the entirety is also "Me". The entity is only a hallucination and illusion created by the self-ego to recognize itself as one with the entirety. It is the entirety that is without a second one and that may be the ultimate reality.

—m—

19ᵀᴴ DECEMBER 2008   04 00 A.M.

Everybody wants to be "Somebody". But nobody wants to remain as "Nobody", which they already are. This inner crave to be 'Some-body' is only a hope that one day he will be somebody. The most important question is, is he a body (Person) at all? No. He is not a separate entity. Slowly, this "no-body" melts and nothingness of this' no-body' remains. In this nothing-ness there raises "some-body", not to his self recognition, but because of his status of nothingness, and to the recognition of 'some-other-body'. This 'some-body' also, one day, starts melting and becomes 'no-body' and ultimately this 'no-body' also vanish to nothingness and finally nothingness becomes the only Reality. Nothing ness is the power of the cosmic energy. Energy and that power cannot be separated while the energy is an in-put the power becomes the out-put and yet the energy and power cannot be separated from each other so the cosmic energy and the functions of the Universe as an output, cannot be separated, as they are both entity and entirety and all pervading. So, the entity can also be called as the entirety and the individual as 'I-am-That'. 'I-am-That'.

—ᴍ—

13ᵀᴴ DECEMBER 2008   03 00 A.M.

A strange feeling started to creep into me. I was becoming a stranger to myself. So, there was a 'Myself' and also a stranger within me. I was witnessing myself becoming a stranger to myself. Everything almost became unrecognizable. I didn't know how I was becoming 'not-myself', unrecognizable both mentally and physically too. Some Energy was gripping me, though lightly, and I could feel the transformation taking place within me. Transformation of myself to become a part of every function of the Universe. I was everywhere at the same time. There was reflection of myself in every particle of the Universe and also its functional energy, though at various degrees. I could feel that the kind of energy in every function of the Universe was the same but differed in degrees according to requirement for its function. I was there in the Sun, the moon, in the entire galaxy and the entire universe which is far beyond the human comprehension, but still there was a 'ME-PERSONALITY' comprising of both the witness and the witnessed. I was both the witness and the witnessed and also in the functioning of the witnessing. I could feel the divine smell, all pervading, and also the Bliss encompassing the whole of me. Slowly, I lost to myself and there was neither

ME nor IT. Nothingness became the reality. I don't know how long I was in the state of nothingness. Time had stopped; probably everything had stopped. There was deep, very deep, SILENCE in this nothingness. I was both that silence and the nothingness, and thus I 'was not I' and was not knowing what 'I' was, there was vacuum and that vacuum had the highest degree of Energy and the vacuum was functioning and I was also that vacuum. It, this vacuum of nothingness, was beyond time, space and causation. In the process, ignorance, complete ignorance of everything became reality. When I came back from that state, there was a very strong desire to go back to that state and remain there eternally. Is it possible? I don't know. I am totally ignorant of everything including of myself. I wish I am lost permanently and eternally to that State of Being.

—m—

12ᵀᴴ December 2008   03 00 a.m.

It is said that 'Time is Life, do not waste time so that the life is not wasted'. Now, what is time? It is a hypothetical dimension coined and fixed by man with global understanding and standardizing for the physical use, such as scientific, historical and other measurements. In reality there is no such a thing as 'Time' and so with the names of days, months and years. But what 'Life-is' is only a conjecture. There may be lot of nomenclatures, social requirements attributing certain qualities and to escape from the dominance of the intellectual, sociological, economical and even the physical strong holders to ultimately survive. To make such strong holders to fall-in-line for the others to survive, nomenclature to the life is attributed to.

I feel that the man is surviving in the way he is now, only because of his power to speak. Had this faculty been absent in man as in the case of other species, this Universe would not have been existing to man as it does now. To think of this faculty not being in man, is something beyond the imagination. From the power to speak, writings—first through the symbols and subsequently through the scripts of the spoken languages—have been born. With these two faculties-speaking and writing-man developed his society and all things started to develop and the man is now standing at the edge of the Universe to destroy it and is in the process of destroying his race and as well of certain other species. Man has become an enemy to himself. And is this reality to be called as Life, irrespective of whatever the other definitions are? Definition is not life.

—⟋⟍—

11ᵀᴴ DECEMBER 2008   03 00 A.M.

It is the intellectual egoism that creates an Entity-ME—separated from all other functions of the Universe. I am a part of this entire Universe and at the same time a separate entity too. It becomes, therefore, impossible to understand the functioning of this Universe. Am I really an Entity? I do not know. 'Knowing' has three parts, the knower (me), the knowable (the object outside me) and the process through which these two are brought at one level of functioning. I feel that I am not that 'me' which I am supposed to be. Then, what is the real 'me'? I do not know. It becomes impossible for me to know that 'ME' in me is, let alone knowing anything outside of me. In a way there is neither inside nor outside of ME. In fact there is no ME at all. It is so called awareness of this Universe that creates ME and others. Intellectual division may not be the reality. Then what reality is? Once again I do not know. Not knowing anything about anything is, probably, The 'REALITY'. This knowledge of ignorance does not create duality. Ignorance, true ignorance of this Universe is the Real knowledge. Ignorance of ignorance, probably, is the Ultimate Reality. Awareness of ignorance of all things of the entire universe may bring to the real awareness of the Cosmic Energy, which is both the Cause and the Effect of the Universe. The fact is, that this writing is not by me though physically it is. Some force cajoles me at 3 a.m.; some days and I become only an instrument to write. I resist, but it compels me. Then I completely lose myself and I am lost. Writing goes on without my involvement. When I get back from this strange state to the normal state of being, and read what has been written, I wonder with aghast as to who wrote this, for sure, I do not have the capacity or the intellectual ability to write the way it is written, it is beyond me. All things stop and so do I. I stop functioning at the gross awareness level and start functioning at a different level while I do not know what that different level is. In fact, to me, there are no levels at all. I stand at the same level at the same platform, but the background changes with the scenes of different screens painted and draped, dropped and lifted, as and when required, giving a feeling—an hallucinated feeling—that I am changing, going from one stage of scenery to another. I strongly wish that this stops and forever and this 'I' be completely annihilated eternally.

—⟋⟍—

23ᴿᴰ SEPTEMBER 2008   04 00 A.M.

There are no Questions, so there are no Answers. All questions are burnt-out and the questioner, the question and the questioned have become one and so the answer, the answered and the answerer. These three are being one, have completely burnt-out to nothingness. And nothingness seems to be the Reality. Ignorance seems to be the Reality. Even these too become hallucinations and illusions, because the awareness of nothingness and ignorance are from someone who is aware. But he is not there to be aware of nothingness and ignorance. The entire Universe and all its functions are inseparable, while so, the so called the one who is aware, the processes of being aware and the subject of awareness are inseparable per-se, and in-turn inseparable from the Universe and its functions. There are no cause-effects, no time, no space in the functioning of the Universe. Space-less-ness, time-less-ness and cause-less-ness have no existence. They too have burnt out. I am aware of these burning-outs, and I am equally aware of nothingness and ignorance. The only one that remains is this 'I', which also is slowly burning out as, 'being-aware' of is being burnt-out. One may call all these as intellectual jargons and intellectual somersaults. This awareness should burn-out and it is slowly happening; and so in-turn these writings too should come to an end because the writer, the writing and written subject all being one and is becoming nothing from which ignorance grows. The awareness being and becoming to nothing-ness, man is sucked into the black-holes of ignorance and thus the awareness of himself may become a black-hole of ignorance and nothingness within himself. And that may be the ULTIMATE REALITY.

—m—

17ᵀᴴ AUGUST 2008   03 30 A.M.

The desire to reach becomes very strong when not reachable, keeps the human race functioning. In the process the desire for God becomes the strongest, but equally elusive. God is elusive because the God we want is not available except as a pre-conditioned concept in our mind influenced since birth by the religion, the culture, the caste, the geographical region, the peers, the teachers and so called holy books and epics. And also by such institutions (and god-men) who are selling this illusive God, very dearly, to gullible man, since the beginning of the human race. Never, never we can come across the God we want, since that God is only a thirst created by our own selves. Then what is the way out? There is neither any way nor the out-let. To forget to attain, to 'know' and to give up God completely is the only way out, I think. It is like a mirage in a desert. We are in the desert since the inception of the human race. We are made thirsty and we see mirage of water at a distance. We create a desert mentally, walk towards the non-existing water-pond, which always shifts, becomes elusive and yet human nature being what it is, he runs and runs and ultimately dies out of exhaustion becoming more and more thirsty. Had he stayed back without looking towards the mirage, probably he would not have had the thirst. However looking to the people running, those who are sitting also get up and join the runners. Mass mentality, mass hysteria, self-deception and auto-suggestions make the man to join the runners. But, he who sits back and seeks a small shelter untouched by the runners after mirage can overcome the thirst. Slowly, but surely, the thirst evaporates and he does not require water, anyway the water being only a mirage.

—⁂—

30ᵀᴴ July 2008   03 00 a.m.

I do not find any reason to live this life any longer. Slowly life is ebbing away from dusk to night. Before long this life comes to an end. But, is it the beginning of a new one? I hardly know. But for the birth of my daughter, I achieved nothing. May be there was nothing more to achieve. The very thought of achieving pre-supposes a goal. There is no goal. No goal, nothing at all. Tired completely, tired both mentally and physically. But, spiritually I am not tired, because it has not started yet. It is unknown. It is only a slippery ground. It is not there at all. May be it is only a pre-conditioned conceptual thought. And yet there is something still wanting, something still unfulfilled, something dis-satisfied. I wish the Cosmic Force hits me and be done with me. Waiting for something to happen cosmologically, is once again a conditioned conceptual thought. Something, most likely does not happen at all, as there might not be anything to happen. 'Happening is only a thought with reference to the desire that is produced by the conditions that prevail in unique ways. I feel that the entire Universe is conditioned to the way it is functioning. It is an unchained and disjointed thought that wants something other than 'what-is'. 'What-is' in reality is not known. When so how to know 'what-is-not'? Even these thoughts are already available in the 'Cosmic thoughts stores'. We only draw these thoughts, however subtle they may be, by just desiring a still subtler wave of thought, which in fact, as giant antennae, pulls a thought from that perpetual cosmic thought stores. We draw it, meddle with it, use it and when not in use it gets back to that cosmic stores, maybe in a changed shape. So, millions of times thoughts are shaped to each entity's requirements, while these very same requirements are conditioned. But thoughts are not the ultimate answers. Maybe the thoughtlessness is the ultimate answer.

—॥॥—

15TH JULY 2008   03 00 A.M.

Whenever I get the inner urge to contemplate (call it as meditation if it is so) which mostly happens in the early hours in the morning between 03 00 and 05 00, I sit down and slowly start losing myself. In the beginning I will be aware of my losing to myself and then this awareness too looses itself and I go totally blank as if I am on general anesthesia. Even during my partial awareness I become a stranger to myself and in-turn everything looks strange and becomes something unknowable. All knowledge becomes zero. Ignorance, total ignorance of everything including of myself pervades and becomes Reality to that awareness. That very awareness of ignorance seems to be 'ME' and maybe it is the Reality. Last night when I was about to go to bed I could touch the vibrations of the divinity having its divine smell (like *dhoop* without smoke). I could inhale it which gave my lungs a wonderful and blissful comfort. Slowly I became aware of losing myself and yet the divine vibration and smell was lingering and touching me from within. Everything was fleeting, not a moment or a movement could be held firmly to look at them. Awareness of fleeting moments became hallucination. Even awareness was a fleeting moment and thus the awareness itself became a hallucination or called as an illusion. Illusion was real, so also the hallucination and to me every other thing was not real including my own awareness. In the end everything became unreal. Then, what is real? I don't know, though the unreal is a relative term from some reference point. What that reference point is I am ignorant. May be that very ignorance itself is real; but there is no way to know. The only way to know is 'not-to-know'. Ignore the urge 'to know'. The desire to know is a seed implanted since birth by conditioned concepts I gathered both internally and externally from various sources. My very thinking of this is conditioned. Hopelessly and helplessly I am conditioned to all these concepts. So called freedom is also a conditioned concept because there is no such a thing as freedom in the absolute sense. As such God is a conditioned concept. Neither have I conceptual God nor a conditioned God. But the word God conditions me with concepts.

Godlessness may probably lead to God.

—⁓—

9ᵀᴴ JUNE 2008   03 00 A.M.

It is long since this type of writing is done though the experiences were happening at these hours. All experiences simply remain as memories. Memory in a way is gross and much distorted one than the experience itself. The experiences are dead but their existence continues as memory. How do these experiences, in a way, would help to proceed to fresh experiences? Not much, I feel. Every experience is a new and unique one, rather in a new way it happens, though the core of the experience may have the same object of becoming one with the functioning of the Entirety of the Universe to rather loose the Entity of oneself to the cosmic entirety and to merge with the cosmic conscience that is ONE without a Second. I do not wait for the experience to happen. It just happens no matter what I do either to avoid it or welcome it. At that point nothing exists, except my awareness of experience and slowly this awareness also melts away. I remain no more 'I'. I will have no way of knowing what is happening. Happenings do happen in spite of my-self. May be, memory of these experiences have no valuable claims, may or may not influence fresh experiences. In the end I feel I stand to be an ignorant person. As the experiences make impressions and reflect as memories, I stand to lose, since I grow to become still more ignorant. Ignorance grows with every experience but for these writings. I feel, subsequent to these writings it was not I who wrote these. Some other energy must have done these writings, though the handwriting always remain to be mine, and I had no part whatsoever in writing any of these, although the physical pen and my hand have been instruments of that energy.

When I pass out of the physical body, like an umbilical cord, a thin wire connects me to the physical body. I travel with terrific speed, even far beyond the speed of light which in a way has no relevance since it has no reference point, and be everywhere in the Universe at the same moment. Many galaxies I enter and pass through and become one with them in a jiffy. I feel I am a part of everything that is happening in the Universe. I pass through Earth, stars, moons, suns and even black-holes, which in fact are not black-holes but mere space. I feel I contain myself in everything in this phenomenon of this Universe and they in turn contain in me. I feel that they are not separate from me; we are the same with different degrees of functions. Even the degrees of functions melt out and I become themselves and they me. Then neither they nor I, in reality, exist to each other and this awareness of oneness also melts-out and I am completely lost. Only when some force pulls me back or pushes me back, I become aware of myself. To loose oneself to oneself creates both bliss and fear. The fear may be due to conditioned thought of death—rather physical death; while with every experience I die and am reborn. Rebirth from such a death does not make much difference to my earlier existence. I continue to be my old-self at least to the outside world though I loose something of my old existence every time, which, in-fact, leads me to higher ignorance. These experiences fortify and build ignorance and this ignorance turns out to be the reality. That is my reality, no matter what I exhibit. I wish to become the Entity of ignorance in totality without awareness of ignorance even and to be ignorant of my ignorance. I desire to remain in this state eternally.

19TH MARCH 2008   03 30 A.M.

I felt, rather was aware, that there stood someone all of a sudden who was though visiting me frequently. Very deep silence encompassed me. Everything stopped and everything including my own self became irrelevant for those moments. How long I had been in this state, whether for a few seconds or minutes could not be measured, but the impact of that moment had been very deep and strong and can never be explained. This very writing stands only as a memory but not as the experience itself. As usual at this hour, I was sitting alone in my chamber and IT came suddenly and the whole atmosphere was vibrating and yet very calm and deep silence had penetrated everywhere, which could only be experienced. Everything had stopped, the time, the thoughts in me had come to a dead stop. Nothing seemed to have existed at that moment. I had got into this state of 'being' many a times before; it came and comes uninvited and uninformed and so it goes leaving behind a trail of inexplicable joy and bliss and fragrance to last long. I lose myself to be a being in that state. It is beyond the rational explanation, beyond any human comprehension. Even while being in that state, a thin energy thread is connected to my physical body like an umbilical cord so as to pull me back to the physical existence lest I escape beyond the physical existence. This may be because of the hidden fear of death-physical death—that has been conditioned into me and conceptualized by me. I am sure this thread, one day snaps as my physical body is already withered and in the last lap of existence. When it happens, it makes no difference either to me or to the world. It will be an insignificant function of the Universe, which is happening every second with full force significantly. I could smell it, feel it, even touch it, but I cannot say when it fully consumes me, though before long. I wish it does before I realize it. I desire that to happen especially when I am in that state. Then, probably, I become a part of the entirety, rather the entirety itself, annihilating 'I-ness', as I have been in that state

—w—

20ᵀᴴ FEBRUARY 2008   04 00 A.M.

To me, at least at this point of time, the entire Universe looks to be a hallucination, for the reason I cannot know about my own self let alone anything outside, even the one besides me. Nothing could be known or understood in the way as it-is. Everything becomes unknowable. So it brings me to the realm of ignorance. In the process of reaching this realm of ignorance, somewhere along the line, I lose myself to myself. 'I' stands nowhere. 'I' becomes a non-entity. In this non-entity status my consciousness becomes the Universal consciousness, where neither the Universe nor its functions, nor 'I' will have any meaning. They just remain as they are. No desire arises to know them. Maybe I am one with the entirety of the Universe and its functions. Now, somehow, in spite of loss of this entity, a small question from this state of entity arises-'is this Universe necessary?' Why, how etc. arise, but no answers are forthcoming. It is conditioned habit of this entity, probably reserved only for the human species, to raise such questions. Answer-less questions. When I reach that status where no answers are forthcoming the questions melt away, as non-existing ones. While the questions are projected by an entity, the entity expects the answer from the entirety. But when the entity does not have any questions, so does the entirety will have no answers. It is the ego of the entity to recognize itself as an entity while the reality being that no entity exists as an entity in the Universal entirety. This entity is only a grain of sand on the vast shore of the Universe encompassing everything. When one reaches that realm of entirety everything loses its meaning, the concept of time, space, and cause, finally vanishes untouched by anything while the pure bliss with deep silence occupies the wholeness of entity in the entirety. But once again the entirety pushes back the entity to its egoistic position of recognizing itself as an entity, for the entity to remain itself for ever with the consciousness of the egoistic entity, otherwise the functions of the entity for which the entity was created by the entirety becomes dysfunctional, which in fact is a part of Universal function of the entirety.

Once again the ignorance becomes the only reality of this entity.

When the status of ignorance of ignorance is attained then the Reality reveals. Ignorance of ignorance is not the knowledge of ignorance or the awareness of the ignorance. While of now, I am aware of my ignorance and as such I am not completely ignorant. I wish I reach that stage of ignorance of ignorance and lose my egoistic entity to that entirety.

—⚏—

16ᵀᴴ FEBRUARY 2008   04 00 A.M.

Is it possible to turn back the time or at least create the physical condition of the past—journeying to the past-say bringing the physical condition of the body as it was about 50 years ago? Maybe or may not be. Some *Yogies* say it is possible. But I don't know. Even if it is possible, is it worth to spend one's energy to go back rather than to go ahead to reach the so called goal (hypothetical realization of God)? Some say when you attain certain spiritual status everything is possible only to oneself but not to others because everyone has to find out his own method to reach his goal, which many a times change/shift from time to time depending on the mental condition of the individual. As for me, there is neither a goal nor a way.

—⚏—

12ᵀᴴ JANUARY 2008   03 00 A.M.

I can feel His presence, but He is not likely to appear before me physically in the way I have the conditioned conceptualization of Him. I feel, He is not physical but only energy, self-propelling, perennial cosmic energy which is found everywhere in the Universe. It looks Universe itself is that very energy, functioning according to the individual projected capacity to draw the required energy. I feel that energy manifests itself as this Universe in all forms and objects, animate and inanimate. There is hardly any difference between these two since that energy though qualitatively the same but of different degree quantitatively. This energy emanates from the center of the Universe pervading equally all over. The whole Universe is in the form of spherical circles having only one Centre and our planetary system is one of the small speck on one of the trillions circles with spokes like, and all such spokes connecting to the center of the Universe—unimaginable, un-understandable and un-comprehensible. With awe and aghast the experience of traveling to the unknown spheres of the Universe stands only as a memory. While experiencing, I could feel that I was in direct contact with that Center of the Universe drawing that cosmic energy without any external symptoms of that energy occupying my whole being. I submerge rather become that very energy itself, when thoughts, at that time, annihilate and the pure and divine atmosphere emerge. I feel, I can draw that perennial energy, hold it in my fist, inhale it, and even drink it too, ultimately becoming that Energy itself. But none can know that I am with that energy, lest they name it otherwise and try to exploit me. But nobody can exploit it since I am not using it for my or others material benefits. While that Energy is functioning in me, time stops, space has no existence and cause & effects phenomenon are meaningless. Even my Soul exists not. 'I' the entity becomes the Entirety. This happens, generally in the early morning hours. And this writing, probably, is the result of activation of that Energy in me.

—m—

01ˢᵗ JANUARY 2008   03 00 A.M

Sleep has taken vacation from me. It hardly stays with me unlike what it was earlier. It is like an infant troubling its mother. It wants me to be awake during the nights while it desires to come to me during the day when I refuse to entertain it. This body is almost worn out like a long used vehicle. Petrol—the soul energy might be there but the worn out parts make lots of noise and results in the slow movement of the vehicles, though qualitative energy of the petrol remaining the same irrespective of to which vehicle it is put into. It is now almost coming to a stop and the road is leading to a scrap-yard and that removed petrol is poured into another vehicle to run. This is how the human beings life too and I am one of them. The wonderful part is, I am aware, for sure, that this body of mine walking towards the pathway leading to the dead end, stopping further journey. I cannot go back. It is a very peculiar one—way path. In fact, there is no pathway at all. Every step creates a pathway to that extent and that very step rubs off the one that was already treaded. The pathway is bare, open with no direction whatsoever and you don't know in which direction to go. It can go in any direction since all directions are the same. In fact, there are no directions either to look ahead or look back the way taken by you. You are directionless, you don't know where you are, you don't know whether you are really on a journey, whether you are really what you thought as 'You'. You have no way to know anything about yourself, because you are not 'You'. A very little intelligence creates the egoistical hallucination within and creates a 'You'. There are no meanings and means about you. All means and meanings are the reflections of your intellectual hypocritical hallucinated waves created and conceived for others consumption.

—m—

14ᵀᴴ DECEMBER 2007   04 00 A.M.

Except for thought, which to a great extent also is conditioned, probably man is totally helpless about himself. May be, man feels he has control over everything, as he has, to some extent, control over money and material. Most of the times all his controls over these two also go hay-wire, hopelessly and helplessly. Materials are not his creations but of nature. He manipulates them to his advantage and usage, while the money is his creation to value himself. Human world runs on the value of money that man has created. This man created money, on the contrary, values him and controls him. Day in and day out his status differs and defers according to his created money value that he holds under the false thought of possessing it while all the time it is the money which possess the man. Take away the value of money, then the society stops and decays and man goes back to stone-age. Fittest will survive, then he becomes the man hunter and a cannibal. He is helpless even in that situation. In a way he is helpless in all situations. From his very birth to death he is helpless. He is not an independent entity. And yet somewhere deep within, a feeble voice says that he is eternal and he can choose his path. I feel, there is neither path nor any choice. Path itself being a concept, journey too becomes a concept and yet there is something hiding, something non-reachable, something powerful, something that wakes up man, something that hits him to think of IT. IT is not something that a man can hold and say 'This is IT'. IT is neither 'This' nor 'That' nor 'Something'. IT is nothing. But IT is everything. IT is beyond knowledge beyond rationality, beyond everything that man thinks he holds. Ask for IT, IT comes but you cannot receive IT. IT is always there by you but you can never see or hold or even physically feel, but can only perceive IT. IT touches you like a passing air wave blowing on your face. Its touch is momentary. You cannot hold IT. IT passes on without waiting for you. You feel Its energy, Its movement and its intensity. You may try to extend Its presence; slowly IT may come to be with you, always with Its bewitching smile. You can feel that smile, that bliss and that beauty. You actually see your own reflection in IT. Your whole being encompasses that WHOLE—that which is without a second one. IT is pure and original and always remains so to eternity. You can never, never make IT other than what IT is. In it's presence you become silent, from silence to ignorance you go and lose your identity totally. You are not you were when IT is there. When 'you' is there, IT is not there. When 'you' is lost, IT comes to fill up you in you and then 'you' ends. You and THAT cannot co-exist. When you in you are completely lost, IT becomes 'you'. Then there are neither you nor IT as two separate entities. IT is the only entity with the entirety. You are no more there. With this, you go through the process of losing yourself naturally and ignorantly. Nature and the entire creation is just something beyond your comprehension. Nature has no knowledge either of you or of itself. It just functions, that is the nature's nature but for the energy which created the Universe, the nature and everything, seen and unseen, gross and subtle, has limitless intelligence. IT is a perennial energy making its presence everywhere and always. Ask for IT with all sincerity, IT comes to your presence when you in you are lost.

Many a times I experienced Its presence before me, when 'me' was not there. It is the memory of the experience that is there. When IT is there and experiencing IT, you are not aware. It is only when you come back to yourself then it comes back to you as memory but not the experience itself. I have very strong desire to be with IT always even if in the process I am lost with no hope of survival or having no way to come back to myself. I want to be with THAT eternal force eternally.

—w—

12ᵀᴴ DECEMBER 2007   04 00 A.M.

Slowly, but surely my life is ebbing away. Time keeps its nuclear microscopic accuracy and can never be called back or be halted. Its nature is to move forward at its own precise pace irrespective of what happens to life. Time being only a human conceptual dimension, in the real sense, has no existence at all, except in the minds of men. The nature of everything, whether animate or inanimate, is to have a beginning and also an end within its own course of journey. The end though looks so, physically, in actuality it has neither a beginning nor an end; and therefore has no journey at all. As my physical body had the beginning and journeying while withering, decaying slowly, so it would have an end to its shape and form and yet 'I'—the inner personality-stands firm eternally journeying from one phase of physical body to another according to its own created path. The created path may be called as 'Karma'—the effect of cause. But one can never understand in its entirety, as an entity of this Karma. Though it looks mathematical, it is not so. You can never predict the exact nature of the result of cause—the Karma—, its duration, its intensity etc. It becomes hypothetical, disjointed. Nor from the result you can trace back the exact action, its intensity, its nature, its duration etc. All these looks disjointed and disoriented. There is no sincere effort to find out these. It is a mere attribution for self-justification, self-satisfaction and to keep away from the unsocial behavior. It is an auto suggestion.

But is there any other way to find out the reality of these so called Karmas? To me, I have no capacity even to comprehend, let alone to know about anything of anything. Everything ends in ignorance to me. The more I try to understand the more ignorant I become. Yes, ignorance leads to naturalness, without any sort of attribution to anything. 'ME' to me looks a myth. I can never know anything about myself, let alone to know something beyond me even that which is next to me. Hearing all spiritual talks, doing all rituals, everything creates and leads to self-hypnotism, lulls the brain and ends in sleep and yet, somewhere within me in some corner, a feeble voice is heard urging me to know what is beyond the physical end—to know it with authentication, with confirmation and with authority (not conjectures, not probabilities, not explanations) by experiencing 'IT' here and now. But no, it can never happen. Even if it happens, the question of returning to explain the experiences would be beyond the physical expressions. Anything said that tries to make others agree would only lead to intellectual insolvency, intellectual slavery, emotional blackmail; a mental burden, dissipating self-energy. Is there then any other way to know? I don't know. But at the same time I can neither agree nor disagree to anything on this behalf, for I have the courage to say I am ignorant and would rather remain ignorant as an independent ignorant person than as an intellectual bankrupt slave to the utterances of others, however sweet and solace it may be for that time being. It is not the vanity to reject; it is the simplicity to my own self. I am firm of my ignorance and like to remain so, at the same time fortify and increasing the strength of my ignorance so as to become the very personification of the ignorance itself.

Yes, I can see the ludicrous expressions on the faces of people hearing about my way of disposal towards my life. But to me my life is not mine nor of others. It is the ignorant entity of this entirety called me that neither has its own standing nor depends on the standing of others. Ultimately I have no identity of my own self let alone of others because I am with that Ultimate Intelligence.

7ᵀᴴ DECEMBER, 2007   02 00 AM

While time is only a conceptual dimension generally accepted by human beings at large, it does not make difference in human life. Life is also a concept reserved for human species since no other animated objects would have this concept of time rather any concept, except the basic physical needs at that point in time which also are the needs of the human beings. There is nothing that anyone can understand of this Universe. Man is sitting on a merry-go-round, but not aware of his spinning along with the earth because he is too small, a speck on the surface of the earth to see the earth spinning and going round the sun, but he could see the sun and all its satellites, the planets etc. sitting on the earth, but not the earth itself in its entire form. For that he should go beyond the earth to space and so about himself. He cannot see himself for himself. He should go out of his own body to look at himself. Even then, I am afraid, man can never see for himself in his entirety as an entity. Apart from his physical dimension, he has his own inner dimensions, the measurements of which are not standardized unlike the physical dimensions. Mind, once again a concept, differs from man to man and from time to time in the same man and as such it has no fixed dimension. Probably, it is only an immeasurable, intangible and intrinsic energy having its own positive and negative polar. The energy of thought waves run perpetually so long as this body is surviving, as it were. Physical body do survive even after the so called death but in different chemical forms. Decay starts, but microscopically life burst out in the form of different bacteria, germs, worms etc; from the so called dead body. The original DNA remains the same even in that state of death. In that DNA the original energy remains the same, so in a way there is no death at all.

Anyway, I feel that my physical body's time is running out. Earlier it was withering slowly but now it is fast and may be faster after sometime, and before long one day it will have a direct fall and then stops. Somewhere along this life's line I realized that in spite of the so called physical death I do stay eternally but with all my concentrated resultants of my thoughts and actions which to a great extent influenced the birth of this physical body. Probably the thoughts have far more actionable results (Karma) than the physical actions or the words attributed by the physical body. It cannot be measured for it is subtle and incognito but very dynamic in making the entire personality of a man. And so the saying 'As you think so you are'. Understanding of anything is a thought process. But somewhere along the line this understanding slows down and comes to a stop and it hits the man like a sledge hammer. He stands there with aghast as an ignorant person. The only understanding that he would come to, slowly but surely is, that he can never understand about anything of anything. This ignorance lights up in him. He becomes a pure energy devoid of all influences both external and internal. He looks from outside a dead man moving around. But from within that light of ignorance is ignited and bursting. He becomes aware of his ignorance of everything and nothing more is desired or wanted. There remain neither positive nor negative Karmas left out for him. Everything looks very natural as they are without any attributions. In the process, he becomes a stranger to himself. He will not be aware whether he is 'He is' or he is not 'He is'. He loses himself to himself. He is no more himself or other self, losing this entity he merges with the entirety, but he is neither, in that state of being, would be aware of his entity or entirety. But mostly he stops speaking, he looks empty and his sight will be looking at the empty space. May be after sometime he loses even physical pain also, because he will not have any physical existence; rather he will not have any existence at all. I once met a person of this type in *Sri. Ramana Ashram at Arunachalam* (TN). I just touched his feet for a fraction of a second, lo! I had electric shock, my whole body trembled and fingers burnt. But he was not aware either of me or of himself. He was lying on a bed. He was in that state of ignorance of everything and of himself too, for long. Maybe that was the state of Reality. To reach that state and be in that state eternally is the hope of me.

5ᵀᴴ Ocober; 2007   04 00 a.m.

Nothing would satisfy me. There is something, something indefinable but the sure feelings of unattained dissatisfaction. Life is ebbing away very fast. There is nothing that I could do other than to watch its ebbing away. Helplessness sets in permanently. Nothing can be done other than to just watch every day passing on. Sometimes an hour, even a minute, becomes a burden. There is nothing left for me to desire. Even God has become a desire—less one. God is slipping away. Emptiness engulfs me. The entire life looks to have gone just like that in a jiffy. The only one meaning of my life is my daughter, who probably became a reason for my birth. Otherwise it was a chance that I was born among many children to my parents. No choice. A choice-less birth, choice-less life and choice-less death. The entire universe looks to be, functioning choice-less. I am aware of this choice-less-ness as the Reality. Even God comes to man and goes out of him choice-less. No choice to take anything other than what is offered. Either you take it or reject it. Rejection too is choice-less, because offer being choice-less. Pessimism, optimism also the so called pragmatism are choice-less. You only call them under different names. Names make no difference to 'what-is'. 'What-is' is choice-less. Is there anything other than what is offered? No, that is all that is there, maybe here or somewhere else. In the process, helplessness, choice-less awareness and also not-knowingness make permanent home in you. You have no choice other than to surrender. Not knowingness about anything of anything is also a choice-less awareness, which is the only Reality. So, I am choicelessly aware of nothingness—not knowingness, emptiness, desire-less-ness and this choice-less knowledge of complete ignorance is rather the choice-less Reality.

—ɷ—

29ᵀᴴ September 2007   04 00 a.m.

Emptiness is full. Only when it is full, the Cosmic Energy rushes in and there remains only the Cosmic Energy without allowing any other thing to occupy. Is it possible to attain full emptiness? Nothing can bring full emptiness. Probably inaction can act to bring the full emptiness. Slowly I am emptying it out. But when will it become full? I can't say. Maybe when 'I' is killed, the entity goes and the entirety evolves. Is not the entity a part of entirety? I don't know. Complete ignorance of all things including the so called the point of central Cosmic Energy (call it as God if you so wish). Is IT the reflection of real ignorance? Then what is that state of being in real ignorance? Only when you are in that state, even for a few seconds, it brings you the knowledge of ignorance. However when you are in that state you do not know anything, but when you come out of that experience the impressions made thereto comes back as memory. It is in the memory of the dead past the present lives. In fact there is nothing like present or future they are all conjectures. Even a millionth of a second cannot be held to say that 'this is the present', while future is still to be born. It is the past in the form of memory which I feel, is the reality. In the abstract sense there is no time dimension at all from which the past, the present and the future are measured. It is only a dimension of relativity. The past is also a conditioned concept and so the future and present too are. They are simply the extension of the past and as such I can say for sure that I was neither born, nor am I living, nor would I die. 'I am' in reality is not I am. I don't know for sure whether 'I am' is 'I am' as I think 'I am' or 'I am' not 'I am'. Nothing can be known. Total ignorance is my knowledge, my religion and my spirituality too and 'I am' so.

15ᵀᴴ September 2007   04 00 a.m.

I am really desperate. Desperate of what? I know not. The only thing is that I am aware of my desperation. I feel that time is running out. What time is? In the absolute sense time is nothingness. I want to change. What is change? Change is something other than 'what-is'. 'What is' is also not known. I really want to know whether I am 'I am' or there is no such a thing as 'I am'. In this desperation there lies deep in me a permanent indescribable peace, silence and unknowable bliss, divine feeling not comparable, not conditioned, not of concepts, not measurable, not valuable, beyond human intelligence, a timeless, a space-less and limitless, dimension. In this dimension 'I' is completely lost. 'I' is enlarged to entirety, the entirety of the Cosmic Energy which probably might be having a central point and yet can never be pin pointed as the gravity can. One's gravity depends on others. The gravity of Earth depends on the gravity of Sun. Sun's gravity depends on the gravity of galaxy; galaxy's gravity depends on the gravity of the Milky Way. One depending on the another and in-turn, each depending on each other. Nothing can exist by itself. In reality there is no such a thing as a separate entity. The entity is a part of entirety. Entirety is the only entity. It is pervaded by the Cosmic Energy the nature of which is one of kind but of different degrees. Different degree of Cosmic Energy brings the hallucination of being of different kind. In fact it is one. And yet the whole cannot be understood or perceived, as a cell on the skin of the elephant trying to perceive the entire elephant and yet the elephant is not complete even without this micro-cell of its skin. It is impossible to the greatest scientists to know why a particular cell acts in a way it does and why not in some other way. The some other way being unknown, it becomes a hypothetical conjecture and maybe a concept. The only answer probably is, 'that is how that particular cell is conditioned to act in that particular way'. Conditioning in everything is holding the entire Universe as one entity. This very conditioning being unknown, it is impossible to know or to imagine in any other way than 'what-is'. That is all about the life. Nothing, nothing can be known about anything of anything as it is. The reality is unknowingness of the unknowable. Nothing can be known and nothing can be understood. All knowledge is superficial and for the material benefits of the human being. Acceptance of ignorance is true knowledge. Knowing is to know the 'not-knowingness' which probably may be called as Realization.

—m—

17ᵀᴴ AUGUST 2007   03 15 A.M.

May be I am conditioned by my knowledge that I picked up along the way of my life. This very writing is conditioned to my thinking, talking, reading, experiencing etc. Experience is only a memory. While experiencing the awareness of that experience is not there. It is only an after thought. Past memory is reality. Future cannot be experienced. The present too cannot be experienced. In totality only the past remains in the memory. Experience is a process stored as experience is experienced. One can never hold even for a fraction of second and say that this is the present, which just slips away. When it ticks it becomes past. Future is not ticked. I feel that the past is the only reality, which in fact, is once again a hallucination of the mind in memory. In reality there exists neither the past nor the present nor the future. I am not living in the present because I am a bundle of the dead past so I am dead already. The only life in me is my memory of the dead past. There might be many things that I have experienced in the past. But, only those which are in my memory, come out. So, though I have experienced certain things, if they do not remain in my memory they do not exist to me and they are dead to me and I am dead to them thus a part of me is dead in the unremembered experience and the remembered experience being of the past which is already dead completes my death to the present. I think the 'dead-me' is the reality, because the dead experiences live in memory only. If a memory fades or dies, so the experience too. And slowly memory fades and to live, the dead past has to be projected from the left over memory. In the end nothing remains, then emptiness becomes the reality, but we are afraid of emptiness since we are conditioned to fear the emptiness. So the future is imagined from the past dead experiences. In imagination we live, otherwise we are already dead. When we learn to die to the past, to the present and the future, we, learn to live in emptiness. Even the awareness of emptiness is not emptiness. Even the memory of emptiness is not emptiness. It just happens and nothing remains there and a total vacuum is created and only then the Cosmic Energy rushes in to occupy the wholeness of emptiness and probably, this may be called as realization. This sucks everything and with force. Force of entry of Cosmic Energy also creates emptiness. Vacuum yourself if the Cosmic Energy has to enter into you but how to do that? I do not know. It just happens as it did several times to me though for very short spells and I desire to increase this spell.

—ɱ—

16ᵗʰ AUGUST 2007   05 00 A.M.

It has become very difficult to really understand the 'Life' and yet the urge and the urgency to know the completeness of life, is becoming intolerably painful. Is it possible to know 'what the life is'? I am afraid not. But yet I strongly, very strongly, desire that before long I go to oblivion, I should 'know'. Probably, the very urge to 'know' is conditioned, because I have been told time and again that there is 'something to know' and I have, without my knowledge and before I could realize on my own, allowed myself to this conditioning as to that 'there is something to know' which is beyond everything and that is incomprehensible. Comprehension has its own limitation based on the individual capacity to stretch his thought and mind, although man thinks that his mind can stretch to infinity, while the infinity is beyond his comprehension. Time, though hypothetical, is running out and before I could know that the time has arrived I would have gone and I would have no way to know it. One can never know the arrival and passing off of this phase called the 'death'. It is not pessimistic but pragmatic, to me at least, whether I would know what is to be known or the very knowledge to 'know' is only a hypothetical theory handed over to me by someone else, and I have no way of knowing either, since I am a bundle of all such conditions and concepts. Is there anything other than my own knowledge of 'IT'. All knowledge should end. This ending of knowledge may also be a type of knowledge, just like to desire to be desire-less is also a desire, and the thought to be thoughtless is also a thought. To know or not to know is also knowledge. Awareness of ignorance is the knowledge of ignorance. There should not be even the knowledge of ignorance. Total emptiness, total nothingness, probably, is the Reality. But one should not be aware of these two qualities also. Otherwise totality is reduced. Then would it be a total coma? It is said, in coma mind will be working and dreaming, then coma will not bring to reality. What then is the Reality? I do not know. That is what I want to know, what the Reality is?

—m—

08TH AUGUST 2007   04 00 A.M.

Somewhere along the line, everything slowly but surely falls off. I stand empty. Nothing influences me. Everything that I had held precious once, no more stays so. All values, whether you name them as positive or negative or by any other nomenclature, drop out. Valueless I become. May be that was my original nature. Or is it the helplessness of physical and to some extent mental deterioration that has created this type of thinking? I don't know. Physical deterioration is surely taking place, while it was slow earlier, now it is fast and after some time it will be very rapid. It is melting and vaporizes before long and become one with space and atmosphere, without any identity. The entity vaporizes to Entirety. What happens to my 'Real Me' in the process? There was no 'Me' earlier. It was only a hallucination created by auto-suggestions and self-hypnotism that 'I'/ 'Me' was created. There is neither. You have no way of knowing about your own self. Anything you do, any process you undertake can never give any answer because the questions seek answers, but there are no answers. When the questions evaporate no answers are needed. Question-less-ness is a state under which I am now. 'I' and 'Me' are neither born, nor exist, nor die because there is no such a thing as 'I' or 'Me' as a separate entity and yet I consider myself as an entity, otherwise this writing would not be there. Am I really writing this or is done by any other entity? There is no way of knowing. It just happens. All words, writings, religion, including the so called spirituality are only social necessities for the society to survive. Survive they do by destroying other weak social orders, weaker socially, intellectually, economically or physically, is the only consideration for survival of the society and that is natural. But at the same time, somehow I have conned myself directly to that Central Cosmic Energy from where the entire Universe derives the energy because that Energy is all pervading, omnipotent, omnipresent and omniscient. I am one with that, rather I am THAT itself, but with limited and specific expression.

—m—

01ST AUGUST 2007   04 30 AM

I become a stranger to myself, when so the entire surrounding rather the whole Universe becomes strange to me. I can never recognize myself and so the Universe. My life's journey is slowly arriving at the last step and looks very strange to me. It is beyond my comprehension, but a state I go through sometimes. At the same time I feel I am part of everything. I feel that I am the volcano; it's every bit of lava, furious floods, storms, forest fire, ice burgs, every particle of asteroids, stars, suns, black holes etc. Everything this Universe holds looks to be friendly to me. I am with them inside and outside of them. I occupy the entire space of the Universe and what the Universe holds I become that. Yet I feel that they are all strange to me yet at the same time friendly to me. There is no fear. I love everything. There is no hatred in anything. Everything is perfect and trying to become more perfect. How and why this happens? I don't know. The only answer is-'that is how they are', that is how they function naturally. But we humans qualify them. We recognize them, as furious, ferocious etc because it is beyond the powers of human control. That which could be controlled by human is neglected by him. It is the fear of physical death that makes man to fight not only against everything external (even between him-self) but also what is internal, disease of physical and mental body. Fear, however subtle it may be, encompasses all the animate objects. Survival through its own physical body to eternity is the ultimate desire of every animate object. However, I don't know for myself what it means for I am not an entity but the entirety but I don't know, at the same time, anything about anything, including my own self. In fact there is no self at all.

—m—

26TH JULY 2007   04 00 A.M.

We can do nothing and at the same time can do everything. When you try to do something you do nothing; but when you do nothing you do everything. When you understand something you have not acquired knowledge; but when you realize that you know nothing and you do not understand anything about anything, then you know everything about everything, then the real knowledge dawns. The realization is that 'you know nothing' and slowly becoming a zero. That is the true knowledge of realization. 'Self 'stands nowhere. There is no self in that state of not-knowingness, because 'You' are not really 'You are'. There is no 'You' at all in reality. The entirety is you and not the entity. That 'you' goes to sleep because it becomes empty. Emptiness creates itself. It does not require to be processed. It just arrives and leads to deep silence, the state of which can never be attained through any process because knowledge creates process and the knowledge-less-ness creates emptiness. Emptiness is the reality and not you.

—m—

28ᵀᴴ JUNE 2007   04 00 A.M.

Life moves by itself. Neither you can push it nor stop it nor make it slow. It has its own pace, gulping everything that comes along its path. It looks as if I was only a six year old child just yesterday (when probably the faculty of recollection had developed). But now I am past seventy and before I could realize what would be happening to my life, I would be engulfed by the 'Time', bringing one's book to a close. No more to read, no more to comprehend and no more to recollect, and finally, no more to do anything. Billions must have passed this way. I become a history even to my very next generation. It looks, that his race is only from the past third or fourth generation on the earth, earlier to that he feels there were no human race, though he reads history. So, to him there are no earlier generations and in turn he will not be a progeny to his great-great-grand-parents. Probably not many have seen their fifth generation. And even if any one did, it could only be a handful among the human race; and it is only for a few days, if that fifth generation child had memory to have seen his great-great-grandparents. This is the fact of life, hence none could be physically eternal and he is not eternally remembered by his own progenies who are enjoying the abundant fruits of the tree that he had planted and nurtured so that his progeny can enjoy the fruits.

—m—

24ᵀᴴ JUNE 2007   04 00 A.M.

This craze to know something which always slips away—unseen, though felt—it is not physically felt—but rather consciously aware of ? IT becomes a desirable one. I feel, it is only a built up concept to keep humans always guessing, keep hoping, keep desiring, neither the man gives IT up, nor that comes to reveal ITSELF to man finally. Who-ever got revealed had probably had a glimpse of it for a fraction of a second. Otherwise no two men's explanations are the same. Hence, may be, it has numerous and different reveal-ability. Would IT reveal by ITSELF or are there ways to get it revealed? Whatever the methods that one or any number of men may adopt for its revealing, IT may not reveal at all. But at the same time, I heard someone saying that with no efforts and with no knowledge what-so-ever about IT, one may come to be revealed by THAT. How come IT chooses one who has nothing to do with IT, while all efforts of others who are most concerned about IT are completely ignored by IT? Probably IT will never reveal ITSELF in ITS entirety lest the entire Universe may be burnt out with its entire revealing. Hence IT occupies as energy in every element of the Universe, quantitatively while qualitatively IT is one and the same without a second one. This Universal energy is eternal whether it was before or after the so called big bang. The total sum of all physical, mental and conscious elements including the element of dream is the part of this energy. Energy manifested in all its aspects. The space where gravitation does not play any part there too this energy plays its part.

—m—

20ᵀᴴ JUNE 2007   04 00 A.M.

Everything seems to be conditioned. Even your subtle thoughts, every step you take, at the back of it there is the resultant of conditioning. You were already bound and also to all your future steps. You are conditioned by the bombardment of the information and slowly they grip your mind and your way of thinking, hypnotizing you to the way of thinking of others. So, you fall in line with others; and in the process there remains no real 'You' at all. You are lost. It will be too late before you realize that you are not yourself and the same time you are 'nobody'. Along the way, while you lose your own self, you start picking up something to which you will not be lost. However, what is left of you in you is not you, but of every others. To this labyrinth you have allowed yourself to be led helplessly. But is there any other way other than being led to the way you have been treading so long? Can the way be changed? Is changing the way lead you to any non-preconceived goals? Is that goal a reality? In fact in reality there are no goals. At the same time there are no paths to tread. There is nothing that you could do nor could you 'not do'. Do, you do, but that do not value it with hypothetical and hypocritical goal measurements. The greatest activity is inactivity. Activity has neither a reference point nor the goal. Before long man goes to oblivion and no history is made of him while all the time he has been thinking of becoming someone to make a history. History is only a memory in the minds of others. You are not the history. To oneself there is no history and even history dies. But one should not die to oneself. So, where do we go from here? Is there here and there? Only when a reference point is fixed (here) then emerges a goal (there). When there is no reference point (here) which in fact is only a hypothetical goal (there) too is not there.

—◊—

18ᵀᴴ JUNE 2007   04 00 A.M.

Is it possible to stumble upon God or that Central Cosmic Energy, or does It comes to one It chooses? Is that energy has rational approach or it just hits anyone on Its way by its nature? Could I be the one who walks on its path so that one day it would hit me? How long to walk? Is there any more mileage left to me to walk? I am afraid not. Shortly, my journey may end and I do not see, as of now, that Cosmic Energy coming towards me, let alone hitting me. In this long walk of my life nothing has happened in terms of meeting that energy. But still lots of things have happened at least to keep me on the path. The path is empty. I see none like me walking alone, seeking that which is not seek-able as a separate entity. The totality which includes me has the power of that energy. Is it that energy or something in me to be aware of, that I am myself or am I not myself? Is there anything like 'I'? Sometimes my mind encompasses the whole Universe when this 'I' just simply melts out and nothing of me remains. Probably, that might be the Reality. Reality itself is hypothetical, a conditioned concept having no reference point because It is by Itself a reference point without a second one.

—◊—

5ᵀᴴ JUNE 2007   04 00 A.M.

How do you know that you know what you know? Is it the past experience of memory which is stored, retrieved and compared to know that you know? That which is experienced for the first time, though stored in memory, shall be confirmed or rejected by the second experience of the same nature. When-so, those which can never be comprehensible being depending on the various factors such as the geographical area of birth, stay, caste, creed and religion and further acquired as second hand knowledge, externally from elders, peers, history etc. So, all knowledge is conditioned. Yes, I feel, even the very concept of God is conditioned, whether by your own self or otherwise. The concept of God is a free and perpetual commodity that is used and abused to the requirement of the user which differs from place to place and individuals to individuals and also in the same individual from time to time as he advances in his age and further the influences he is subjected to. While some cannot handle this concept of God they hand it over to someone else whose cultivated business is to enhance the concept of God and create confusion and doubts, as if it is his privilege to hold God as his personal commodity to be sold to the one who is gullible. In the process, probably, that man grows to become a total ignorant person while this God man intelligently tries to shatter the ignorance of that person with sweet and convincing words about the concept of God, since there is no verifying experience in this man. This game is going on for eons, even maybe, since the man has surfaced on this planet. No answer is forthcoming still, because there are no answers to such hypothetical and conceptual questions. If the question burns it-self, then, probably, the clear answer may come out; but the questioning will not stop and should not stop, otherwise society will go haywire. For the society to be on the firm footing the concept of God, however slippery it might be, should continue. Otherwise the society also will slip away as God does. However, these peddlers of mirage, called God, should not be allowed to take the society for a ride. These peddlers are like big industrialists manufacturing God through sweet and convincing words to the gullible society. The only difference being that they pay no tax for their sale, for they have no real commodity. This commodity of God is a single man's (god-man) commodity. He will not allow other's to manufacture lest there is competition and he loses his business of God preaching. Most of them as single manufacturers are by them-selves stockiest, dealers and retail sellers at their place (Ashrams, Temples etc.,). You have to go there to buy this slippery commodity. Pay them heftily. Some of them are black marketers, by allowing filling their coffer with black money and from this black money they live such a life that, sometimes, would be envy to a billionaire.

Best way, I feel, to seek God, is to manufacture it yourself, stock it to your-self and consume it yourself. Do not distribute or sell it for it may be diluted and also it may not be to the liking others need since everyone has his own unique requirement. Slowly you stop manufacturing and ignore it. Then you come to a standstill position clearly knowing that you were manufacturing it only in your mind. Then ignorance creeps in, the real ignorance of everything firmly acknowledges the knowledge of ignorance. That becomes your realization. It hits you like a sledge hammer and you are shattered. You remain no more an entity but melts out to become a part of the entirety, the Central Cosmic Energy. In that state 'you are' not 'you are'. You do not know yourself, everything evaporates. All knowledge of realization, why the very realization itself and everything connected to realization washes completely from out of your system and there remains 'Nothing'; and at the same time everything of the Universe becomes a part of you and you become a part of them and finally you become that 'Itself'—'THE NOTHING.".

—⧟—

MAY 2007 04 00 A.M.

I feel and experience both the helplessness and hopelessness of myself not coming to know the Reality of something that I am to know, to understand and to be with. The time is running out and it may be very fast before it comes to a dead stop, all of a sudden. But when and where and how comes this dead end, I know not. Sure, it does. I know, because it had a beginning and so end should come. The beginning and end are the obverse and reverse of the same coin called life. What life is? I am totally ignorant. Ignorance brings both pleasure and pain—the pleasure is: not knowing anything about anything and the pain is: not knowing the Reality of ignorance i.e. the knowledge of ignorance. Probably, the real knowledge is total ignorance, not the knowledge of ignorance but the ignorance of ignorance, which is the totality of complete 'Nothingness'. In the very process there arises the very core and vital point, whether am I 'I am' or is there no such a thing as 'I am'. In the totality of entirety there is no 'I am' which is only a speck called entity. The entirety is the whole vast sea beach while the entity is only one grain of sand

—⧟—

MAY 2007 04 00 A.M.

The only reality, at least to me, is that I know nothing about anything. I do not know about the so called myself. Is there anything like myself? I have no idea. How do I know that' I-know' or "I do not know?' I feel that there is nothing to know. The knowledge 'to know', which rather conditions me and it is only a part of 'not-knowingness'. I have realized that this 'not-knowingness', happens only when 'I' becomes an entity by itself. Slowly but surely the realization dawns upon me as the physical age advances that however I may try I can never know anything about anything and the total ignorance is the only truth. All other things such as 'I know', 'I don't know' etc. having arisen from the ego of separateness of the entity from the entire Universe and its functions within the ambit of human intellect, that by itself creates the ego of a separate entity from that of the entirety of the oneness and inseparableness of the Universe and its functions.

However, the only thing that is left of me is 'ME'—a non-deteriorating 'ME'. There is nothing much left of me. It is slowly deteriorating. Calmness pervades and silence deepens because the ignorance encompasses the whole of me. I am the ignorance itself because there is no 'I' to know myself. To know is a process in which the knower and the knowable, the method of knowing, all evaporates into ignorance. Nothing remains, virtually nothing continues as an entity. It becomes one with the totality. In fact there is no separation between my consciousness and the Cosmic Consciousness, while the awareness of me by myself is totally absent because my entity is not separate from the entirety. There is no individual awareness because there is no individual entity which functions individually.

—m—

20ᵀᴴ APRIL 2007　　　　　　　　　　　　04 00 A.M.

It is long since I wrote or spoke to YOU. When a person gets engaged in physical activities the soul within gets to the background camouflaging as if it does not exists, while all the time it does, without which the physical activities in the world cannot function by themselves. In a way the Cosmic Energy, either grossly or subtly, functions dynamically or potentially, though some things look to be a static. In the absolute sense there is neither dynamism nor static-ism in the Universe. It is a matter of relative term for a man to comprehend the functions of this Universe with his limited intelligence.

Well, I feel, that the time is running out as far as this physical body is concerned. Is it possible to know, to understand, to realize that which is imbibed into me as to be known, understood and realized, at least within the time left over, which I know not how long? Or is it the conditioning to which I have been subjected to so far, is again subjugating me to these thoughts? This desire to know creates a gap within, of dissatisfaction, wanting, un-fulfillment etc. Most of the time, I feel that there is nothing to know, to understand or to realize. These, seems to me to be mere words which attract man towards the so called realized person and devalues the man from whatever he is. These words belittle a man. Probably it is the Brahminc (priest) culture of every religion that elevates itself on a false propaganda that their theory of God is the only ultimate truth and all other theories are low in value compared to them. They created a value based society, though a false one, to monopolize themselves in every aspects of human life, giving meaning to everything according to their own individual concepts with limited intelligence. It is to claim superiority and to subjugate the most powerful who are either economically and/or physically far ahead of them exploiting their intellectual backwardness.

Question of surrender etc. arises only when the ego pervades the man that he is a separate entity from the entirety. When he knows that he is an inevitable part of the entirety the question of separate entity of him-self does not arise; and the question of his surrendering 'to—what'? Or 'to who?' arises. All these questions have no answers. They are mere egoistic intellectual somersaults. While so somersaulting, man goes to somnambulism, creating a type of hypnotism, self-induced, with auto-suggestions about God and everything beyond him. With these, there arises a god-man who wants to introduce another theory to the society, which is already confused, so that the society gets further confused. Confused society is his (god-man's) bread. As a mirage in a desert, so is the God to the society. More the desire for God more is the intensity of the mirage. This game of running after such mirages is encouraged by a god-man while he knowing fully well that it is only a mirage and he remains still, sitting pretty where he is, posing that he, the god-man, is the possessor of the mirage. Wise sit back, neither running after nor thinking about the mirage. Mirage is a hallucinating function of the society without which the society comes to an end and decays. The society should be running and to run there should be a mirage and if there is none of them; god-man creates one for the consumption of gullible society. He is also helpless because he is a part of the society and he is bound by his own creation of this mirage and ultimately he also succumbs to it so that this mirage ultimately consumes the whole society.

—ɯ—

03ᴿᴰ Aᴘʀɪʟ 2007   **03 30 A.ᴍ.**

Is there anything like rebirth—reincarnation? I don't know. Probably, no one knows for sure, for, none has any true and authentic knowledge of previous life, if any. When so, is it possible to predict life after death? Life may be there, but may not be in the same physical form as it is now. We cannot experience that which is beyond that border while still staying physically in this side of the border.

Time is running out. Yet, I am not able to catch up with the knowledge of the Reality. What is Reality? Reality may be a hypothetical concept of 'what is beyond other than what is now'. 'What is now' is not actually comprehensible, when so, 'what is out there beyond' is something conceptualized hypothetical thought. Thought takes process in various forms and kinds, depending upon the types of conditions a person is under. Every thought has limitation. Beyond is once again a concept. Nothing could be done to go beyond, for, there is no beyond, but everything is behind. I am a sum total of all my thoughts, words and actions behind me that have taken place in my past.

Somewhere along the line, in the path of my physical existence, I started losing myself to myself, thereby zeroing on myself leading to, probably, self-annihilation. This may lead to a state of nothingness and ignorance. Complete self-annihilation may lead to complete nothingness. May be, that is self-realization, God realization.

When once we experience of crossing the border, it is very difficult to cross back to announce to others what is there beyond that border. Nor can we experience while remaining physically in this side of the border, about what is there beyond that side of the border.

To me there is neither here nor there, neither there is any border. The border is a hallucination, an illusion created by the conditioned limited concepts. It is the totality of this and that is the reality. In reality there is no duality. It is one process of function. But the phases of process of function looks to be different, for, the human reasoning always desires to know, to experience something new, something 'what-is-not'. It is once again the conditioned conceptual thought. Thought when expressed conditions man. There is limitation for expressing anything that is beyond expression. Probably, the very concept of limitlessness, timelessness, space-less-ness, infinity, eternity etc.

are mere thoughts that arise from the conditions of the philosophy that each person adopts to himself. Hence limitlessness is brought within the limits of human thought and so the Reality is brought within the limits of the human's intellect.

—◠◠◠—

02ᴺᴰ Mᴀʀᴄʜ 2007   04 00 ᴀ.ᴍ.

I have almost packed up to go when the call comes. In fact I do not know, rather nobody knows when the call comes. Always it is unannounced. But foolishly everyone plans that s / he lives to eternity. This aspect of human thought is the most mysterious. It should be so otherwise the entire society collapses, having lost the hope of the future. It is with the hope of the future one exists to-day. To-day passes on to become yesterday—a history. Even yesterday fades away. Mostly, we live in the past. We are the complete bundle of our past. Thoughts revolve around the past. Finally, we are the resultants of the past thoughts. Is it possible to be in the state of thoughtlessness? This very concept of thoughtlessness is also a thought. And yet I feel that there is nothing beyond thought. God is a concept of thought. Silence is thought. Even in sleep thought process goes on and on and may come as a dream, which may remain in memory, or may get erased. The very fact of 'Me' is a thought. When thought, whether aware or unaware (a thin line between a sane and an in-sane), is not there, 'I' is not there. Everything flows from thought. Ultimately it is the Cosmic Energy that releases these thoughts to the space from where the human brain, as antenna, draws and develops these thoughts. So, thought is both physical and meta-physical, depending upon its usage. When the Cosmic Energy produces or processes it subtly, and picked up by the brain, it once again process it and may give an expression either orally or in writing or by action or most of the time simply allows it to store itself and in the process many thoughts die away rather vaporizes away to get stored once again in the Cosmic Energy. Some thoughts, if expressed may harm the society; hence people wear masks for the good of the society and further to gain respectability to oneself. This is how everyone wants to be, so that he can become a 'somebody' while he now remains a 'nobody' and in turn some of them who are 'somebody' get back to the status of 'nobody' and slowly annihilate to nothingness.

—◠◠◠—

26ᵗʰ FEBRUARY 2007   04 00 A.M.

The functioning of the Universe is impossible to understand. Will this limited intellect projects itself to infinity whether at micro or macro level? It is at the totality and the entirety the Universe functions and at the same time every atom-protons and neutrons—must function for the Universe to function. Where the energy comes from for these functioning? Is the energy at each level self propelling or receives it from elsewhere? Is not that energy one and the same in every aspects of Universe's functioning, though at different degrees as required for that particular function? Entire energy cannot be concentrated for any one particular function. If done, it burns that part of the element. Yet, I am not able either to understand the element that functions or the energy that enables these elements to function and in unison to arrive at any predetermined result. The results being predetermined, the nature of element and utilization of that energy in quantum differs in degrees to give effect to that particular result and to function precisely, so that nothing goes hay-wire. Everything is predetermined but unknown to anyone and still search for the 'unknown' goes on and on with no end. The end may come to the searcher but not to the search. The, baton gets to the other's hand and he runs knowing fully well that his predecessor has set a non-existing goal and still runs towards such a goalless goal. It eludes like a mirage in a desert, making the runner thirstier and ultimately the person falls down exhausted and dies thirstily. Probably the only solution is to stop searching and desiring to reach the non-existing goal. When the desire dies, search comes to an end and mostly then the goal comes in search of him. But I don't know for sure, since neither do I run nor sit still. My mind wavers between these two aspects, sometimes it runs and other times it stops dead. To come to a dead stop is more soothing, more comfortable, and more blissful and yet the desire to get up and search grips my heart and search starts with hope.

—ɯɯ—

12ᴛ 07ᵗʰ FEBRUARY 2007   03 30 A.M.

I hardly find any reason to live anymore. I think that for whatever reason I came to this physical world, has been fulfilled to the satisfaction of those who are required to be satisfied with my living, especially my daughter and wife. My daughter, whom I love most and no parallel can be drawn of my love to her, has had her required level of education and married to a handsome person with the best of behaviors with higher education, who loves my daughter very much and do all the best in his reach to keep her happy. I require no more than her happiness and welfare. Sure, she will be so. Next is my wife. She has her own ways to live. She is matured enough to look after herself. My stay on this physical world would only support her socially. She has a good shelter, a good and comfortable economic condition while I no more contribute anything from my existence. When so, she will definitely be comfortable but for my physical absence. As such there is nothing more that I need to do to anyone either physically or economically.

But, to myself I have not done the most wanted one. To know and realize God, if at all He is there. Within me something still wants, to know the secrets of the Universe, the Life, the Cosmic Power, the Central Energy, and the Central Intelligence of the Universe. May be, there is nothing to know, to realize, for, may be, I am part of That. This is my last wish to be fulfilled and yet my physical attachment, the love, the pure love towards my daughter cannot be given up or parted with from my inner being. I desire to be with her. Probably, I did not spend the days with her in a valuable and adorable ways. It could have been much more pleasant and sweeter, more loving and adoring. Probably there are something more wanting in my love to my daughter. I don't know whether I have failed her to be an adoring father. I feel like meeting with her, wanting her to be with me. But she has now passed that boundary and entered a circle of no return. Let her be the happiest of all in the world. I love her the most.

—w—

08TH FEBRUARY 2007   04 00 A.M.

The day I married-off my only child and the daughter, I found myself completely empty. In a way she had occupied the whole of me. Everything I did till then, in a way, was to my daughter. When I find that there is nothing more to do for her I became a bundle of uselessness. I lost interest in everything. In a way I have become a counterfeit. Even in God I lost interest. I feel that the inner of me is fast deteriorating—fast I am growing old physically. There are lots of things to do but I have no inner urge to do anything as I was doing earlier. Why? I don't know. All meanings to do something have vanished.

Ultimate reality in life is that you are alone by yourself. My own example being that while a child I had parents, brothers, sisters other relatives, playmates etc. Now, long since my parents are dead. We were a dozen children to our parents and half of them are now dead. On the way through schools and colleges I picked up friends but now most of their whereabouts are unknown to me. So with the friends I picked-up while on different jobs and so with the neighbors at various places. Slowly everyone is leaving every other one. I got married and a wonderful daughter was born to us. My only job in the life is and has been the welfare of my daughter in all aspects, her health, her friends, her education and most importantly her marriage and above all to me, my love to her. Now, she is married and gone away to her husband's house which is half a way around the world-USA. Everyone lives with someone else and that could be for a short time, in the universal time. The only person who does not change is 'you'. You are the center to yourself around which all others rotate. This is true with everyone. Each one is a center. Around whom all others rotate-a chain reaction. I am also both the center with reference to myself and also the circle with reference to others, at the same time. Ultimately everyone goes-off by himself leaving temporarily some impression-good or bad—on others. One's life is important to one self. However, he has to be a social animal, picking up and dropping many people on the way, making friends and foes, loved and hated, cared and neglected, all such types of duality arise duly conditioned, from physical birth and to its death. That's how it is and that was how it was and that is how it shall be. No change. The only change is the garb and technological advancements in materials and in the process lots and lots of 'god-men' have cropped up from nowhere to take you for any number of spiritual rides, you being an un-intelligent, compared to them in their ways of thinking. But they too will not last long. They too are alone by themselves as you are and they too are bound by the dualities and conditions of the society. Their order/life/institutions are within the ambit of social order. Helpless 'god-men', as helpless and hopeless as you and me are. However, these 'god-men' do not accept other social order except their own, by becoming law unto them-selves, because men with economic power, political power, social, and intellectual and even with muscle power become subservient to the god-men. These god-men raid on each other with one-up man-ship, lest their God is lost and so their followers.

January 2007 03 30 A.M.

Sinner and a saint are only nomenclatures stamped by the social order. Yes, without social order nobody can survive. But it cannot be extended beyond the social necessities. Everything, to me, looks sometimes, perfect in its own order. There are no dualities. Some things are not palatable to body and mind. Mind exists and functions when physical body exists and functions. If the physical body stops entirely functioning, then mind too exits and stops functioning. So, in a way mind too is physical. However, mind being expressed through physical body it may be said that the mind is functioning in a physical manner. But none has come back to say whether the mind continues to function beyond physical body. Everyone becomes an entity only when one is functioning externally through his physical body though the mind continues to function subtly without exhibiting its existence.

I just want to go to oblivion beyond mind and physical body. I do not like to recognize myself and desire to be a non-entity which again is an expression of an entity, a contradiction in terms. This very desire to attain a non-entity status, probably, is causing me the distress, because however I may try I cannot achieve it for the reasons that somewhere in my very subtle manner some small iota of desire to be 'somebody' persists. This very fact that I cannot achieve the status of non-entity, that too at the fag end of my annihilation from this habitat of physical world, is causing me the distress and disappointment. But distress and disappointment will not bring the Central Cosmic Entirety to grip my inner being.

I most earnestly crave as if that is the only thing I need. That I should be hit and shattered by this Cosmic Central Energy and when my inner being is shattered I may come to be one with that Cosmic Being. There is nothing more to be desired than to be magnetized by this Cosmic Being.

—*⁂*—

3ᴿᴰ January 2007 04 00 A.M.

I think I will pass life's journey without experiencing the Reality of Cosmic Energy. What either this Reality is or the Cosmic Energy is, I do not know. Somehow I feel the emptiness in me is slowly encompassing my whole being. Ignorance of all this has become a definite factor. I become an empty ignorant entity, helplessly struggling within, to reach the fullness of emptiness and the knowledge of ignorance to kill the ego of self. Slowly the ego is emptying itself out of me. It is draining out from my system. While the needs of the physical body have considerably been reduced, all desires are also emptying out, but for the needs of its survival. Yet, not to make my inner self known to the outer world I attire my physical body and all that are required to be done, minimally, with the continued social activities. Nothing influences me nor makes any impact on me. Everything, every duality, seems to be natural and has no value system. And yet, somehow, one thing that has occupied at my topmost feelings and priority, which may be called as my weakness, is my daughter. I can never and never under all or any circumstances and situations, stop loving her. She is everything to me. She is weakness of all my weaknesses. And I can never give up this feeling even if God stands before me and orders. If I am to choose between God and my daughter, I would rather choose my daughter and not God; because God has everything and most powerful and does not require protection where as it is not so with my daughter. There are millions who love Him and who wants Him; but my child is loved only by a few and I am the first one of them all, although she has another who loves her, her husband. I wish even after death let me be in space protecting her, loving her always, throughout her life. Let me not be reborn elsewhere when my own loving daughter is there to become my mother, if at all I have to be reborn. Otherwise, let me stay as a soul without physical body always be nearer to her without her knowledge. I love her so much.

—∽—

23ʀᴅ October 2006   03 30 a.m.

Yes, the time is slowly but surely ticking out and sometimes it looks faster and some other times it looks slower but it is not so, it is precise to nanosecond. It will not be long before I obliterate from the memories including my own progenies, as ancestors have fazed out of my memory, to some extent my parents too, even though it is but for them I would not be here to pen this. Thereby it comes to the conclusion that we get detached from everyone and everything. It looks that I am an entity who has to live by myself and for myself. My progress, if at all it could be called so must be important to me. I should become selfish in my progress of detachment and yet the desire to live in the memory of others pulls me back due to the conditioned living. From within I am detached, completely detached, nothing influences me as it used to be earlier, and 'untouched functioning' I perform with no expectations from anybody anything. That is how I really am. Adding and forming a stronger shell day by day. To 'let go' is opposite to 'hold-it'. For me 'let-go' does not arise because, firstly, I have not held anything. I am becoming more like vegetable without any mind though functioning in the body. Even recognizing this state of being is to project the ego though subtly. Calmness and peace are slowly pervading my whole being. Sometimes I strongly get the urge to amend certain things and behavioral pattern of my life. But it is too late. What have been done can never be undone and yet I cannot predict myself as to how and what I should do next. Get detached to become a person without mind, neglect others behavior towards me, stop thinking and loose yourselves to yourselves so that you could be with the Central Cosmic Power and slowly merge and become that energy itself.

—m—

15ᵀᴴ OCTOBER 2006 03 30 A.M.

Helplessness is the name of the game of life. You are helpless to be born as you are; you are also helpless to lead the life you are leading; you are helpless to do everything you are doing now and you are helpless to be helpless. Nothing but helplessness becomes everybody's helplessness, all the time and everywhere. You are helpless but to adore the God with the hope that one day you will be free from this helplessness and in the process you are helpless to surrender to this helplessness and to seek comfort helplessly from this helplessness. Helplessness arises due to limitations; while the mind always yearns for limitlessness, to go beyond and to cross the border. When you are at the edge with only one step away to reach the beyond, your helplessness turns to 'fear-of-the-unknown' and you are hopelessly helpless but to withdraw from that one step and to come back to original limitations in which you feel secure and comfortable because of the familiarity in being helpless. Probably, even the God (if such an Entity exists) is helpless but to create 'what-is'. Accept 'what-is' than 'what-should-be', since both are hallucinated and limited and conditioned thoughts. What all I am writing now are conditioned to my limited intelligence and experience. It is the expectations to be other than 'what-is', that is causing this helplessness. To be calm, to be silent and to be untouched by this helplessness is to overcome the helplessness, which replaces one kind of helplessness with the other kind. Nothing can be done. Move on in the life to a destiny unknown. Be what you are, at least from within. Be a witness to your own self without judging anything and without being touched by anything; and that is the ultimate happiness I feel.

—ɯ—

15ᵀᴴ OCTOBER 2006   03 00 A.M.

Yes, life is both physical and mental. It is the mental function that determines the life because the mental function stops when the physical function stops. Mental functioning could be attributed to thoughts that are produced within and yet get transmission from outside, but from where? Nobody knows. At the same time mental function cannot by itself function without the media of physical which exhibits the functioning. However, man being the combination of these two cannot come to reconcile that he is any one of them exclusively, but both of them combined. He feels that he is a separate entity and these two are his possessions through which he functions, he reflects himself. But these two are 'not-him'. They are his exclusive possessions and unique by themselves, as to himself and others, because, he cannot completely transfer any of these two, whether separately or together, to any other being. When he goes, these two possessions stop functioning and the resultant of these two possessions decides his further function with different physical form and mental capacity. In abstract they are not different from each other because, the Universe within which all beings, both transient and intransient and both animate and in-animate objects, function as one without a second. All micro functions of the Universe being the only one function at one macro level and at trillions of trillions at micro cosmic level. It holds the entire Universe in

—ɯ—

6ᵀᴴ OCTOBER 2006   04 00 A.M.

I am both an entity and a non-entity. When I function at physical level, which in a way is non-existing, I am an entity. But when I function at a subtle and mental (spiritual) level I become a non-entity, because it is at the Universal level I function as a part of the entirety.

Functioning involves three basics—the functionary, the process of functioning and that which is functioned. But in reality all the three are one, since there is no functioning at all but just a Universal movement, rather its nature of its 'being'. In this 'being', I have no part as an entity but only as an entirety; the Central Cosmic Force manifesting itself as 'being' at different degrees and levels of functioning.

—⁓—

15ᵀᴴ SEPTEMBER 2006   02 00 A.M.

I am totally becoming a non-entity. I am completely away from myself. The entire Universe looks to be mine and I am in every part and function of the Universe; and still there is a deep, very deep, feeling that I am myself and at the same time I am not myself. I do neither understand nor do I feel about myself. This is a passing phenomenal thought wave or the connection through such feelings. I get to the Central Cosmic Energy. I need that Energy to act upon me shattering me completely my present position of my entity. Or is such a thought conditioned by my knowledge of Cosmic Energy which may be completely alien to the reality? What is reality? Reality is everything. The so called falsity too is reality. I feel, in the absolute sense there is neither reality nor falsity. It just is as 'it-is'. I just want to go out of my body and experience everything the Universe holds and yet be a witness to such experiences. I want not only to be an experience but also that which is experienced and be a witness to all. How come, I am unable to be so? Because of the limitations of body, mind and intellect, which, I feel, are almost physical. Physical phenomenon is conditioned and limited, while non-physical phenomenon is not conditioned by anything and has no physical limitation. So, the dimensions of time, space and causations are being conditioned and limited, have no extension to non-physical phenomenon. What is non-physical? They are the ones which we become aware of subtly, not through either mind, thought or intellect, but consciously aware of from within, without giving meaning or nomenclature by any words, without any explanations and without understanding intellectually. You are aware of it but you don't know what it is, you don't know anything about it. It is beyond understanding and beyond knowledge. When you are aware of it, you become totally ignorant of everything-for that matter you become ignorant of your own self. Ultimately, that 'you' melts away and vaporizes to join the Cosmic Energy. That is the end of 'you'—annihilation without an iota of trace of you. It is a complete annihilation of you. But you become aware of all that when you come back to your physical nature. There are no other instruments through which you can experience of being aware of 'That', but by the physical and thus limiting those awareness of 'not knowingness' to physical and this is how my experience goes through but I have no way of knowing its reality or falsity. That is how it is.

—⚓—

26ᵀᴴ AUGUST 2006   03 00 A.M.

Where do I stand as an entity before the Universe? If I am not an entity I must be one with the Universal entirety. Yet, I am no individual as such. All talks of individual come when physical form is limited to an entity. I am the totality of everything the Universe holds and still I can never, for sure, say that I am 'this' or 'that'. I am nothing, but still I am everything. Mundane desire sometimes overtakes me, grips me and I become a pawn in its hand and I am carried away. Somewhere along the line something strikes subtly and I come back to my original-calmness which percolates into me and I am engulfed into an inexpressible silence. That silence you could feel, touch, hear and even live. I become that very silence and yet I can never know what that silence is. It is a pure blissful silence, and being in that state of silence will not last long. But there is no counting of time. It has no cause and effect and it is beyond everything. It is the pure Cosmic Energy. And so when the deep silence engulfs me I become the very Cosmic Energy and to the spheres of the Universe it spreads and functions and still I would know nothing and thus I become ultimately 'NO-THING'.

—⚓—

14ᵀᴴ AUGUST 2006   03 30 A.M.

Is the death an end by itself or annihilation of life? Is there anything called death? What death is? Nobody knows for sure, for those who went through the death, it cannot be an experience since experience results in memory to recall it as an experience. But the one who goes through death cannot recall the memories. So, none, as I could understand, knows death. It is the talk of the living with conjectures and concepts on bookish knowledge. But still I feel death is not an end by itself. It is a movement, a function as natural as the setting of Sun, a hallucination created while the Sun neither rises nor sets. So also a person is neither born nor dies. It is just a process. But fear is put into the mind of a gullible person by the so called metaphysical knowledgeable person. Everyone tries to subjugate the others by any means, money, muscle, knowledge-whether material or metaphysical. Metaphysical language can be picked up by any moderately intelligent man, though he is illiterate, to subjugate the other even when this other person is materially knowledgeable, because one can always speak and write anything about this metaphysical theory for it need not be proved and cannot be compared with. So, every so called spiritual person can build his own theory and gain the confidence of others through eloquent talks and quotes of some scripts in which mostly he himself does not understand or believe.

—ﾘﾊ—

11ˢᵀ August 2006   03 30 a.m.

Is it ever possible to go beyond the limitations of the man-made conditions—physical, mental, even intellectual? Is there something beyond? Is there beyond at all? Is not everything contained in unification? Is there something attractive, something needing and something unfulfilled? Is it possible to live beyond the physical world eternally? I feel I am eternal, and at the same time, a non-existing entity. I feel as if I know the entire Universe from its pre-existence both in its present form and the one when it was formless. It is the pure energy, the Cosmic one, that had contained in itself everything that the present Universe holds and I was there then as I am now here and continue to be there in whatever the shape the Universe takes. I feel I am not confined to the physical limited body. I expand to the entire Universe and the Universe is contained in me. I hold it in my fist and I become that very energy itself. Is it a hallucination of this physical body that creates this functioning Universe? What Universe is? None knows. At least, I do not know. When that knowledge of 'not-knowingness' dawns, the reality hits the ego of knowledge and shatters it and the calmness never known, the silence never experienced, set in, and you become that very silence, the deep shattering silence itself. Silence is not physical, not mental, not emotional, but something unique, something not expressible, but something that you become yourself, where the experienced, the experiencer, the experiencing process and the experience become one without another. I know that this physical body which is conditioned by the dimensions of space, time and causation phenomenon is ebbing away so that the functioning, though superficial, should continue and my eternity is established. I am not afraid of ebbing away of this physical body. It is the nature of its function. Let that be.

But how come I am not affected by it? I am not touched or influenced by it? I know not, for I feel I do not ebb away, I do not wither. I open one phase to another. I stand aside from the entire functioning of the Universe. I smile at it. I enjoy the bliss of the Universe and its function, the energy it draws, from where I do not know. But I do know that I am a part of that energy and I am the very energy itself with all its powers and intelligence it holds but to a small degree; and still I am not that. But, I do not know what that 'I-am' is and I can never know anything about 'I

God, if at all such a being exists, and maybe in the concept of human being or maybe invented by one to exploit another person, can never solve the manmade problems. Though it is not beyond HIM-the God, because the man being what he is, the problem remains with the man eternally while the man passes on, because there are no solutions to the problems. Any problem which has no solution will not remain as a problem. So there would be neither problem nor a solution. On the contrary God himself becomes a problem to many and so was to me long time back. Since God cannot be found through any method, the solution dissolves and thereby the problem of God also dissolves. And God is not a problem anymore to me. All such concepts have run out of my system. I have not replaced one God with another as I did earlier. I am now neither an atheist nor theist nor spiritualist nor the seeker. I am just I am. But I don't know what that 'I am' is. For, there is no 'I' there. 'I' is just a function and also a part of the function of the Universe, though very insignificant. When 'I' is lost it does not remain as an entity. However, there is neither completeness nor incompleteness in the Universe. It just is. There are no dualisms in any function of the Universe. It is the man who creates dualism because of his ego, to show that he is always correct, always superior by creating dualism, or otherwise man decays and human race comes to a naught.

09ᵀᴴ August 2006   03 30 a.m.

Someone may think that my astral travel is a hallucination, an auto-suggestion or an auto-brainwashing, call it by anything and but while on travel when I look down on this earth I could feel the paper thin culture of the human race. The culture of saving himself from his own created onslaughts, let alone from the fury of the nature, which again is very thin. Compared to the entire functions of the Universe the human function is only a speck. When

I am on astral travel, I occupy the entire Universe without any limitations of time and space and without to the subjugation of Karma (The result of cause). Nothing stands and nothing matters at that level. Everything becomes un-understandable rather unperceivable. I expand my conscience to the entirety of the Universe. When I am in that state I will not be in the knowledge of being in that state. That knowledge of being in that state comes to me as memory only when I come back to this limited physical body. I would not know whether the real 'I' was in that state or now is in this state. I am not 'I am' or there is no 'I am' at all. Mostly I am not 'I am'. It melts and expands. And in the process 'I' is completely lost. To be in that state is the desire created when I am in this limited state. This very writing may be while in that limited state. Writing has limitation, depending upon the limitation of knowledge and experiences. To me, un-knowledgeable experience being the reality, this knowledgeable experience is unreal and is not known while in that state. It is an after effect resulting as a memory with limitations. I become limited when I am in physical state, so too in mental. Knowledge, in a way, is physical being limited. Knowledge is not self-generated but received from the Universal Cosmic Knowledge and Its Intelligence, when released is picked up by a human according to his/her limited capacity to comprehend, to understand and wisdom to live accordingly. Even when this intelligence functions differently in different people and also in the same person differently at different times, the totality of its function is that of Cosmic Energy and thus every animate object functions with the intelligence of the Cosmic intelligence energized by the Cosmic Energy and I am a part of that Cosmic Intelligence and Cosmic Energy itself.

—ɯ—

06TH AUGUST 2006   03 00 A.M.

Sometimes I fly high beyond the entire galaxy to some other unknown sphere incomprehensible where there is nothing, and yet everything exists there, where I have no body or mind and yet perceive and experience everything not knowing that I am experiencing, because at that stage the object experienced, the process of experiencing and also the experiencer are not different but one and the same whole. These experiences reveal, only subsequently, in the form of memories, being imprints upon my soul or my personality of inner core, or whatever it may be called. When experiencing 'I am' not 'I am'.

And at other times, which are long, I get down to earthly business or physical life, tramping, maybe, someone's foot, though not deliberately. However, the bell may toll any time and I know it will not be long before it tolls and I stand ready to go when called. This readiness will not make that toll a surprise. And I also feel that there is nothing more for me to do in this life. Things have come to a definite shape and stage and, they would take care of themselves. My readiness is not painful to me physically while waiting for the 'D' day. Everyday is one day nearer to that 'D' day though when that 'D' day comes is unknown. But nothing can be done either to advance or to postpone that 'D' day even by a fraction of a second. Everything goes on as if the 'D' day never comes. 'D' day is only a movement, a displacement or a replacement of the physical life. It is also one of the Universe's functions. This function is only infinitesimal part of the functions without which also the Universe's function cannot be complete. It is a part of the Cosmic function to which I am also subjected to as everything else and still I am not touched by this function while I am a part of the Cosmic function.

Almost the evening is coming to a close and the dusk is setting to go into the night and then the darkness encompasses to say the day is done and further waiting for the next day to dawn. The wheel of life completes its one round passing through many, both treaded and unthreaded paths. Some wheels have bigger diameter and some small. But the journey has to go on having come within the framework of the wheel, rather riding the wheel. Both are part of each other, the wheel and the journey of life. There is no individuality and no separate entity. It just functions and you are just a part of that function. You have no right to ask any questions and even if you ask one, there is no answer, for nothing can be an answer since nothing is understood, even the question cannot be understood. The question is only of un-perceivable words. Words by themselves have no meanings but for hypothetical meanings given by man to comprehend what others say. They are mutual understandings, for mutual physical benefits. Imagine if the human had no 'Power-to-speak', but a dumb one like any other animate object. Then would God have existed? Would have this Universe existed to man? May be, but that which does not come within the ambit of awareness (understanding) does not exist to that being, although it does exist to others to perceive it. It is the 'power-to-speak' that has created the whole Universe including this very writing. That is why, may be, it is said in a Holy book that 'the word was with God and the word was God'.

—ɯ—

21ST JUNE 2006 03 00 A.M.

I think, I will not come to suffer physically before this body falls finally. Slowly it is working inside my body. It looks as if some micro-organisms are multiplying and traveling all over my body, sometimes crawling, sometimes jumping and some other times in groups. It looks it is happening on the surface of my skin and that is how I feel their movements, silky movements, but it might be happening inside the body too, which I am not aware of. When I try to catch the movements with my hands they are not there. What these movements are? I don't know. I don't want to know also, because I can never know.

There is some sort of wanting other than what they are. This crazy thing, unfulfilled and dissatisfactory requirement, to experience what is not experience-able, to attain what is not attainable, to reach what is not reachable, to bring down, that power of what cannot be brought down, is slowly eating my vitals. I want something, I do not know what, other than what all are there. That 'something' must be a mirage, something different and something never known or heard. That something might be unique, different and never known. Whatever I do 'to know' that, it can never be known. It is my craziness, it is really happening, which, in fact, is the reality. I am just crazy about it. To me there is neither real nor unreal. Whether it is visible or not, I do not know. It is a physical phenomenon with reference to physical body. That which is stronger prevails over the physicality of me. Would this be so on the other side too? May be, the stronger the inner personality, the better are the chances of standing in that long queue to reach out. Sometimes nothing matters even that Central Cosmic Energy does not matter to me. If it is there let it be there and 'what if' attitude generates in me. Let me dive deep into the ocean of ignorance even not being aware of that ignorance. Knowledge of ignorance is not ignorance. Ignorance of ignorance is the true knowledge and it is total. Losing one's awareness is real awareness so losing once ignorance to ignorance is real knowledge.

—m—

03RD JUNE 2006 03 00 A.M

Slowly the physical functions are ebbing away, so the mental too. When these two completely stop functioning somehow some energy starts functioning. Was not that the same energy that had already been functioning through the physical and mental functions of a person as such? It was functioning but at a different degree. However, the entire potentiality of that energy cannot come to function as it had limitations because of physical and mental obstructions with their own limitations.

Coming to the knowledge of anything, the only thing I know for sure is that 'I know nothing about anything'. This ignorance has become true knowledge to me. The fact is, the approaching of an end to this physical body. This is neither pessimism nor optimism but pragmatism. In spite of me and despite of all my efforts, the entire Universe and its functions are strange phenomenon to my concept. I am like feather, a dry insignificant leaf fallen from a small tree in a huge forest though I was once equally a significant part of that tree adding green luster to the individual tree though insignificant to the entire forest. Slowly I started loosing colors, as did that small leaf and finally fallen from out of my own incapacity to hold on, as did that small dry leaf. But is not that a natural function of that leaf? So I am too. This is a definite process. While that leaf had not had the knowledge of process of involving its life, I am possessed with the so called knowledge, but without understanding it. The only understanding I know about myself is, that I am not understandable to myself. I can never understand anything of myself because I am not myself; not an entity in the process of understanding the entirety.

—⚊—

05ᵀᴴ JUNE 2006   03 15 A.M.

I dreamt a dream last night wherein I had become everybody and everything of the entire Universe and yet I was a separate entity dreaming a dream. In fact I was myself that dream when 'I' was not there.

—⚊—

03ᴿᴰ JUNE 2006   03 00 A.M.

One way ticket is not sold by God. He wants you to have two way tickets to reach Him and come back to this world, though to a different destination. It is always a journey, going, living and coming back. Station to reach may be different but the journey has to be performed. It can never be stopped, as the earth is on a repetitive journey in the same path, which it has to perform or otherwise the entire earth with all its possessions comes to a naught. So, each individual person has to inevitably perform his journey according to his own Karmas. Even a small tiny thought wave adds to the account of his Karma, and leads to a particular path tangentially, proportionate to the Karma. Even living (existing) in a particular physical form is a journey, from one movement to another. All cells in a physical body have to perform their own journey as the totality of Karma of that human being. God alone sits in the single control room controlling the entire Universe with all small details of every individual; whether animate or inanimate objects that He has created. That is how the things are. One can never escape the eternal journey in the vehicle of physical body, whether of human or otherwise, taking everything in its stride, some in a bullock cart on a bumpy country road, some in an automobile on the smooth surface of the bitumen road and some others flying in the sky. But everyone is born to perform his journey and that is life.

—◯◯◯—

15TH MAY 2006 03 00 A.M.

When man becomes helpless either he surrenders to the unknown or becomes a rebel since he sits at the edge and anger will be boiling in his stomach. He will be jumping and restless. Sometimes he curses everything and everybody including God. He slowly looses faith in the society, in the God and ultimately in himself. This is reality. In spite of showing that he has surrendered, right within him he has not done so. Though he continues externally to be calm, internally he is a volcano. It is the calmness, in such situations, from within, that will be important. After some time things from within settles down to calmness, everything evaporates, stillness pervades inner space of man. If he tries to cultivate it, it is possible to reach it, touch it, experience it, with this inner calmness, if had he developed inner calmness previously. I am now in full control of it and I become the very calmness itself and if somewhere one iota of anger is left dormant, it may become a volcano. One has to take care of this dormant spark hidden and camouflaged within oneself. There are no methods to completely eliminate it. Everything, anger, hate-racy, jealousy, selfishness, cruelty, enmity etc. are natural phenomenon of a man due to his egoistic desire to be 'somebody'. If someone tries to see you as 'no-body', then he wants to prove and establish that he is 'somebody' and in the process he not only destroys himself but also others.

Is there anything beyond thought to human beings? It is the thought process that creates everything. If the thought process stops probably that would be the end of human life. Is human or any other species superior to human exists on any other regions of the Universe? May be or may not be. However, the ego of the man's intellect is not prepared to accept that proves to be superior to his intellect. Everything, even God is subordinated and subjected to human thought. I think I am what my thoughts are. Is it possible to separate oneself from ones thoughts? Rather one is the very thought itself. Thought and I are not separate two entities. I am the thought and the thought is from the Cosmic, so I become cosmos through my thoughts. The totality of everything is one Cosmos. What Cosmos is? I do not know, as what sugar is cannot be known to the sugar itself since it is that itself. So I am the Cosmos itself. In reality all these writings too have no sense or meanings. These are conditioned thoughts. Thoughts too are conditioned according to the individual's life. Man is helpless because he cannot be other than what he is, a thought conditioned individual. There is no independent man. Man is both a master and slave of his own thoughts. He is both the jailer and the prisoner of his own thoughts. He cannot be beyond his own thoughts because there is no beyond. Anything that is said to be beyond is his conditioned concept. That is how he lives, a master and the slave of his own thoughts. There is neither mastery nor slavery in any of his thoughts. Thoughts having been produced by the Cosmic Energy, it has no dualities in itself. Best is to let everything go—'let go', rather 'let go' of oneself, because at no point of time a man understands himself let alone the so called God, who is his own creation. Man has created God and not the other way, with a view to keep the society in order, otherwise the society would kill him.

—⅏—

03ʳᵈ May 2006   03 30 a.m.

I have nothing to blame anything of outside. Slowly, but surely calmness is decidedly setting in, as if I am in space with no sound at all. External calmness can be achieved but the internal one is differing and defeating. The desire to be what I am not is probably the main reason for disturbance. I have not attained my potentiality, might also be the reason, which, in fact, are the reflections of the Cosmic Energy. Where I end up I do not know. Every thought is transmitted by the cosmic energy. I think, the thoughts are the real transmitters of everything including the so called me, the God and the entire Universe. Suppose I become thoughtless (even the awareness of the state of thoughtlessness is also a thought), then everything vanishes including the self. But where to?. To no—where. Ultimately I have come to the definite conclusion that nothing can be understood. Understanding arises when there is an entity to understand and that entity should have the urge and capacity to understand and there should be a subject matter to understand and the interaction between these three as a process should take place. If any one of these three is absent, understanding never comes. Most important one is the entity and the subject matter and still understanding will not come because of the limited intelligence of man than the intelligence that created the subject matter. So, a lower intelligence (human intelligence) cannot understand the higher intelligence which has created the entire Universe and controls it's functioning in entirety.

—⁂—

6TH APRIL 2006   03 00 A.M.

There is neither birth nor life nor death. All the three are one that is functioning from one level to another as a continuous process of the entire Cosmic Universe. It is the duality of thought that illusions the different levels, of birth, life and death. They can never be understood in their individual perspectives. These can never be understood either in individual stage or the collective stage. They are just 'as-they-are'. And any interpretation of these will have only mere words and is only an intellectual exhibition without the real understanding. What the real understanding is, can never be understood. It is like an ant at the tip of an heir in the tail of an elephant trying to understand the entirety of the elephant and also its biological and chemical functions in entirety, though the tail is a part of the elephant, and the biological and chemical functions of the tail are almost the same of that of the entire elephant.

Religion is a word coined by man to meet his selfish ends for creating boundaries and to rule the subdued followers and to stamp them as Hindus, Christians, Buddhists and Muslims etc. There is, in fact, no religion in the functions of the Universe. A child functions as she/he has to. The child has no name, no religion etc. per-se. It is the adult who conditions the child to his (adult's) own limitations which he acquired or rather forced upon him by his elders and his society. This is a chain reaction binding one link to another although each link desires to be on its own without conditioned bondage of other links. Mystery is always created by an intellect to control the ignorant.

But on the contrary for the ignorant person he is a mystery to himself because he will have no knowledge about himself and that is the true knowledge. But those who say that they are knowledgeable are really not so. The one who says that he is ignorant is really knowledgeable of which he is not aware of. Awareness is not the truth to be arrived at. Not knowing either the awareness or not being aware is the true awareness. When once the knowledge of awareness comes, it becomes false awareness; because, awareness of awareness too must die and that is the state of not being in duality. To die to everything is to live in everything is reality. Ignorance of everything is true life.

Every breath brings all the three into one, the birth, the life and the death. As breathing too is a continuous process so also all the functions of the Universe too. No one can answer as to why a man is in the manner he is and why not the other way and why this Universe is functioning in the manner it is doing. The only answer is: 'That is how the man is and that is how the Universe is'. There cannot be any other way and even if there is one, it cannot be adopted, because there is no duality in the functioning of the man or the Universe. So trying to find any duality in these functioning is false and illusory. In the abstract sense there is no duality or non-duality. Everything is just as 'it is'. Then where from these conditioned knowledge comes? It is the freedom of these conditioning from everything including from oneself that brings the true knowledge and the true knowledge is the total ignorance which includes the ignorance of ignorance.

The worst bondage that a man imposes upon himself is the religious spiritualism. It is the slavery of the mind to subjugate to some conceptual definitions of God. The real spiritualism or realization is to free oneself from the shackles of spiritualism and God. Freedom from dogmas, from the so called divine ones or otherwise, is the real. The true Freedom is to become free from God Himself. That is the reality.

—◆—

9ᵀᴴ APRIL 2006   03 30 A.M.

I am really tired of being a human. I do not want to be any being anywhere in any part of the Universe. Somewhere deep inside me a feeble voice says that I just want to be 'a nothing'. Is it possible that 'I' becoming 'a nothing'? Where do this 'I' vanishes to become one with the Universal Cosmic force completely losing its identity as an entity? Am I an entity? I am both an entity and nonentity and at the same time I am neither. When does this 'I' comes to an end? I don't know. Since there is no beginning to this 'I' there cannot be an end also. What is the ultimate position of this 'I'? There is no ultimate at all, since in reality there is no 'I' at all and yet the mind, a subtle part of this physical instrument, plays havoc in the human's life. Tired physically, emotionally even in the so called spiritually, I crave for some sort of permanent and deep slumber to eternity, losing everything including this 'ME' into that Cosmic Energy, as a drop of rain losing everything it possess when it drops into an ocean. Can this 'ME', a drop of this human life, loose itself completely its identity, its entity, its individuality in the ocean of Cosmic force? I wish it could. Does a mere wish, a part of the same cosmic energy takes me to that ocean? I don't know. I wish 'I' comes to an end. Once again a hypothetical wish for this 'I' to come to an end. The end pre-supposes a beginning with two dimensions the time and space and to a great extent 'cause-effect'(karma) dimension also, while the eternity is beyond all these three conceptual dimensions, conditioned to human race due to his supposed intellectual superiority over other animate beings, in which the hypothetical and the hypocritical spirituality too becomes a part.

—w—

21ST APRIL 2006   03 00 A.M.

Today also I feel the same. The same tiredness, exhausted mentally and physically but spiritually wanting something; unfulfilled crave for something unknown. What is it I want? I just want to be away from everything even away from my own self which is intolerable to me. In this search I fail to myself. I need nothing other than the permanent peace, permanent tranquility that comes with the permanent rest in the cradle of the Cosmic Being. All these arises from 'to-do' or 'no-to-do' certain things and in the process indecisiveness sets in. I want to end the time just now, it should not be extended. I hate to do something which I never like and yet had to do, some social obligations. Can I not be freed from everything including from my thinking? Can I stop thinking? Ending thoughts is ending me, because I am the totality of all my thoughts that are already dead but coming back as memories. These memories are the projections of the dead thoughts conditioned by many factors and also individual conditioned concepts. The thought is already dead and gone back to the universal 'thought-stores', to be drawn as and when wished.

—w—

06ᵀᴴ MARCH 2006   03 30 A.M.

Whether you love God or not He always loves you and guides you, without making His presence recognized by you. May be, you think that since you are not getting what you desire, or things go against your wish that God is against you. Neither is God against you nor is in favor of you. Everything happens just as they have to. It is you who give value to the result of your actions based on your intention and desire. Simplicity of living is to loose to multiplicity. Spirituality has become a fad, a social necessity to fool oneself and the society at large. Publicity of oneself as the crusader of God is becoming a sophisticated façade which ultimately leaves the person far, far away from the God, because that person not only worships himself but also desires deeply and secretly that others too worship him, thus occupying the place of God to himself and to others, But God would run away since He is being treated as secondary. In fact God can never be secondary anywhere. He stays and watches subtly and smiles and still helps this self-proclaimed god-man. If at all a man is a true seeker, he shall confine only to himself and the God without bringing any type of intervention by any means of publicity, economic profitability, rituality, with any type of assumption of mission etc. God would get the things done from only such persons who do not claim that they are messengers of God and who would not hood-wink the gullible public and take them on a spiritual ride on a journey to acquire material abundance to himself.

03ᴿᴰ MARCH 2006   03 30 A.M.

God is my entire and exclusive person, whom I will not share with others. He stands by me always. I am aware of Him at my side, smiling, encouraging and holding my hand (all in subtle manner) and guiding me through the crises which I have created by myself against His directions. His directions come to me as my sixth sense which prohibits me in certain things and permits me certain things. Nothing, nothing even the entire Universe and its wealth matters to me when the entire and exclusive Owner of the entire Universe stands by me and is with me. It is enough for me to be with Him. How peaceful and blissful though there are some tremors sometimes, both mental and physical, but deep within I am myself with Him, because we are of the same nature while I hold a physical body he does not, while the entire Universe which functions under his control unlike mine. He is the entirety and I am a small entity trying to merge in His entirety.

—◊—

01ˢᵗ MARCH 2006   03 30 A.M.

Today is said to be a New-year day for Hindus that too for some in South India, but not to all Indians. How come, I wonder, it is only for a few and I do not understand what the new-year is meant for those who feel eternity of life, which also I understand, is the philosophy and spiritualism of Hindus. Deep down in me I also feel my eternity. There is an identity and at the same time there is no entity to identify that identity. Is not the entire Universe the Cosmic function reflecting through different mediums with different degrees while the Cosmic Energy being qualitatively the same everywhere and in every sphere of the entire Universe? Slowly, but surely I am loosing this identification of a separate entity as myself. There is no myself and yet, while functioning, through the physical body, with its entire natural phenomenon, I separate myself from myself. It looks as if I am waiting for the arrival of my own self on the eternal sea shore where the cosmic waves create the hallucination of functioning. There is neither functioning nor dis-functioning. It 'just is there' and at the same time 'is not there'. Everything from eons looks to be the same, though on the thin surface, that human's historical and scientific life has changed.

Happening is within the ambit of time and space. Happening is the effect of 'cause and effect', they being the obverse and reverse of the same coin. There is neither cause nor effect, for there is no coin at all. When happening is not there, there is neither time nor space. The eternity having no space and no time dimension and as such it has no influence of cause and effect. These are the man-made dimensions for his conceptual, intellectual and physical necessities. Otherwise, they have no existence by themselves and do not act by themselves as they do not exist except in the human mind. However, the 'I' in the human exists to eternity. And from eternity to eternity do I pass through these functions of cosmic effects. And yet I am myself for myself, an entity with a spark of light and energy of that Cosmic Being with whom, deep within, I always stay. I walk with that Being, pervading me all round. I cannot cross over, or there is nothing beyond that Cosmic Being. Even beyond there is that very Cosmic Being. There is neither beyond nor behind. It just 'is'. But it can never be understood. To understand is to separate oneself from that Being, which is impossible. Here, the object to be understood, the process of understanding and the subject that understands are not separate. The object, the subject and the process are the same with different facets. Man's nature being what it is, he always feels superior to everything, even amongst his own race. Some men feel that they are more superior even to the Cosmic Energy, forgetting that they are an individual spark of that Cosmic Energy.

1ˢᵀ FEBRUARY 2006   03 00 A.M.

I feel that I am totally blank. Yet I am aware that slowly but surely something irresistible is eating into my vitals and making my physical body fragile and taking me by inches towards the 'D' day which I cannot predict when and how it comes. I hope the end comes unaware and before I could realize, it should be over. No one can save any one. Even the God is bound by this game, though He has created it and laid down the rules and regulations of the play. I am also prepared, but a deep silence has occupied from within and the calmness has overtaken me. Nothing matters to me now. May be, things were different earlier in the life but now as age advances, probably because of the physical incapacity, it is slowly ebbing away and also due to certain setbacks, the life also becomes sober and all relationships slowly also wither away and dropout by and by. Yes, the laws of nature to birth and life extend to death too. It is inevitable that everything that has a beginning should come to an end. The only matter is whether we are fit to face it, irrespective of its coming with or without physical sufferings. If it comes with physical sufferings, have we got the capacity to endure it? Most of us are not having that capacity; as such, the intensity of physical suffering would still be more than what actually it would be. If we have that capacity, probably, the intensity will be least. All these are inferences when one is in good health and comfortable in life—a sort of 'arm-chair philosophy'. Well, now as for me, I don't know how I would act and ultimately go through it. Only time will tell, not to me, but by to those who survive me and who witness my last moments.

30ᵀᴴ JANUARY 2006   03 00 A.M.

Of late, I feel, I am losing grip on the relationship of almost on everything and everyone and thus this, in a way, dragging me to some unknown force which I call as the Central Cosmic Force. I am getting into this whirlpool of Cosmic Force, to where, once entered, one cannot escape from. I tried everything in the life to realize if there is God. Neither did I do nor do I need anyone who did. Even if that person had realized I had no way of knowing and he would not help me to realize. Here, maybe, my approach was wrong. Realization has to come from the efforts of oneself and for oneself. All my efforts went in vain. Maybe, as for me, God may not be there; because God himself, with all my efforts to go towards Him, must have closed His doors, at least to me, I think. Otherwise as claimed by others that 'if one takes one step towards God, He will take hundred steps towards you', has to have been proved to me too. But it did not. Why? I don't know. Ask God, if you can, why He did this to me? Nothing seems to be alright. Everything seems to be going against. Well, maybe, my desires are misplaced or my desires are too many or very high for my status. I want to break from this. I want the God to be with me always. Will He stand by me? I am trying, beseeching Him to be with me always for eons to come. Come stand by me O God. Let me see whether YOU can.

—⁓—

25ᵀᴴ JANUARY 2006   03 30 A.M.

Slowly but surely I am inclining towards that D-Day of this physical end. What next? I don't know. The world goes on, making no difference whether you are alive or dead. May be, for a few days some people may feel my absence. But time being the best healer; they will take my absence in their life as natural. My only prayer to God is that I am ready to go with Him after my daughter settles well in her life, so that the entire burden of searching a groom and marrying Megha should not fall on Sharada alone while she will not get any help from anybody in as much as I could do with all love and responsibility of a father. So, God, keep me alive till Megha gets married and settled well, then I will be ready. Hope this prayer will be granted to me. I feel strongly that Megha will be taken care of by that Cosmic Being whom I pray while I am in direct contact with Him. My relationship with that Being is one-to-one basis. We are friends-pure friendship without any bargain (except the above request) between us or without any barter. Let me see how that Being reacts to my simple desire to keep me here till Megha marries and settles down well in her life. I am sure I will not be failed.

—m—

24ᵀᴴ JANUARY 2006   03 00 A.M.

Nobody helps anybody exclusively. Everybody helps themselves by so called helping others. It is a misnomer to say that somebody helps somebody. No, everybody help themselves. Today, somehow, I have overcome the entire fear of everything—of myself and the world. Let me face even the death. What is the worst that could possibly happen to me, if I kick the concept of God, from out of my system? I might be subjected to, by God Himself, for my physical ailment leading to some extent mental disturbance. Well, I have decided to face it. I want to keep, somehow, everyone out of me. God may punish me physically if I keep Him out of my system. I have come to the conclusion that I can be without God, whom, neither have I seen nor aware of, but only a mentally projected one, as a concept. Why should I be afraid of keeping out of my system the concept of which I have nothing to do? I am mentally restless today because I want to be out of myself and I want everyone from out of my system, but in the process, may be, I may come out of myself. This concept of coming out from out of oneself is only a conjecture. Only when you feel that you are an entity separate from one and the only cosmic function of the Universe, the hallucination begins. Maybe, this hallucination too is a reality. But, for 'reality' there should be something 'unreality'. What is reality is a relative term. It is a part of duality. In the process of duality, the hallucination of birth, life and death occurs. There are no man made processes or procedures for the functioning of the Universe. The Universe functions beyond the reach of human rationale, intelligence, for the human rationale and intelligence are short lived with limitations while the Cosmic Intelligence is all pervading eternally, from which the entire human race has drawn so far, only a handful of water from the ocean.

—m—

23ᴿᴰ JANUARY 2006   04 00 A.M

Is God inevitable in the life of human being? How come only to human beings the God is necessary? Just because he has the intelligence to manipulate the less privileged persons of his own race, either intellectually or economically or socially? Is not one person exploits another in the name of God? Has God really served human beings? I am afraid not. God on the contrary has dis-served the human race by encouraging division in the name of religion, war etc. All ills of the world can directly be attributed as 'because of God". The more you try to go nearer to Him mentally, the more He runs away from you, psychologically, because God is a psychological concept of man. He never comes to your help during the days of your difficult situations. The more you depend on Him, the more He makes you a mean slave of His. You go down and down day by day in His name. He watches, and maybe laughs at you to His full content at your degradation brought upon you by yourself on yourself, in His name. Forget Him, then, He runs after you, begging you to remember Him through many media's which are his selling shops where there is no bargain. He puts his hand into your pocket and empties it, so that you should go after him begging to forgive and to give back your money in other forms. Each is a beggar to each other. God begs you to remember Him and in turn you beg Him to give health, wealth, love, peace et.; both are being barters, which are dualities in nature by themselves, while you are taught through these mediums other than to be so. While these so called agents are His slaves and they snatch your money wrongly calling it as your voluntary contribution for their luxurious living. You go slugging in the hot Sun, barefooted on hot tar burning holes in your soles with torn shirt, while these so called god-men with or without any formal education and without lifting a little finger sit and roll down in Rolls Royce air-conditioned cars, living in palatial buildings from the money that was snatched from you. The moment you are empty in your pocket they kick you out. Their love and regards to you is directly proportional to the thickness of your pocket. In the process you not only become bankrupt economically but also intellectually, for you would have mortgaged completely yourself, thus permanently becoming a slave to their way of thinking and by then you would have reached a point of no return. Now, you have become a hallow person, mentally sick, losing your capacity to think independently and you are already a simple walking dead person subjecting yourself to such god-men slavery and thus the word God becomes an inevitable end of man's life.

5ᵀᴴ January 2006   03 00 a.m.

So much has been said and written and so much is being done about God and spirituality. Small and big organizations build monuments, temples, churches, mosques and *gurudwaras* in the name of God and religion. Religion should only be a way of life but not a cult. Cult leads to bigotry and fundamentalism and ultimately divides the entire human world bringing hate-racy leading to war and loss of human life, which further nurtures hate-racy. Who is responsible for all these? Is it not God? My God and your God are fighting each other through you and me in the name of respective Gods. Well, somehow I should get rid of this personal God provided there should be a Universal God-because God being a concept of a hallucinated mind with hypothetical theory can never be held responsible. The God is like a mirage. God exists to a thirsty man and slips away when he goes nearer to it, not realizing that the heat of the desert has created the waves of water. But in reality there was false lake, non-existing one and yet play havoc in the mind of a thirsty person. Once failed, he seeks another lake, another mirage at another distance and once again runs after it and becomes still more thirsty not getting water and in the end dies for want of water-which he never finds but in a mirage for the simple reason there was no lake in a dry desert. Thus the God also remains a mirage to such a seeker and that is life.

Some men always take gullible persons for a ride assuming a lake and showing one from a distance-through a mirage in the dry desert of human life, knowing fully well that it is only a mirage.

So, having failed in every search in every book, in every temple, in every theory and also from a person who claims to have had some hallucinated experiences due to his own aberrations of mind, called a self-realized man, comes to his own conclusion that there is no God. When this happens he becomes fearless, faces death squarely and the so called life, smilingly without any result of influence by the life around him. Probably, the ultimate reality is that the search comes to a definite and final end and he will not have any opinion about anything. He stops discussing about God, let alone arguing either rationally or emotionally about God. God makes no difference to him, as to whether God exists or not. He leaves it to those on their journey to agree or disagree about the existence of God between themselves. And the debate goes on and on as long as there is a hypothetical God. For some people, the desire and the hope that somehow one day they will see God, keep them going. It is always hope in tomorrow that keeps man searching for God. This desire whether for material or metaphysical benefits, assumes God. Man goes to God for the fulfillment of all his desires. As he does not get any help, or there is no one to help, he seeks some other way to get help. He is caught in the whirlpool of quick sand and if he is mentally weak he can never get out of it and ultimately it sucks him to his death without a trace. It is his own making to step into the quick sand. The quick sand is there, it would not gulp him unless he steps into its orbit. This very writing may also be in a way of stepping into the quick sand and it may be an otherwise argument of non-existence of God. I should stop writing and keep my mind blank-blank with ignorance. I am arriving to be ignorant; rather it is arriving at me. In fact ignorance is me. This knowledge that I am ignorant is the real self realization. I am the totality of all ignorance. And I am in fact the ignorance itself and so is God. And God is totally ignorant of everything. Ignorance of ignorance is the ultimate truth

20ᵀᴴ December 2005   04 00 a.m.

Man, when living, may create certain impacts especially on those of his family and that too, probably, for their economic and emotional security. But when he is dead and gone, the impact of his absence slowly dies down and after some time he is completely forgotten. So, nothing matters on his death. Life gets adjusted to the present living conditions. It is the dead man, who is the loser in the end, for having contributed his complete life to someone else's material comfort. Is such a living, a living? It is simply an existence. But take it that he did make some impact for a long time after his death, may be, not only on his family but also on the society and nation or the world at large, even then slowly he becomes a history. Nothing will matter to anyone. But, however, that is how it should be. So, what is the way out? There are no ways to escape, except for him to think for himself about his escape from everything including from himself. Is it possible for anyone to escape from himself? Yes, provided he does not try to escape from himself. Escaping from what and where to? There is neither going out of nor coming into life. Life is just as 'It is'. Nothing could be known about anything of life. Just because a person is dead physically it cannot be said he is dead. Death is something mysterious to those who think it as an end. No, death is a function of the Universe. Man and all other animate objects, why even inanimate objects, in the long run, being within the Universal function is part of this cycle. When this is understood, though it looks to be un-understandable, man frees himself from this cycle. However, whatever may be the understanding it goes with the ideosynchronised concept of death that leads to complete ignorance. The true ignorance brings calm, deep silence in the inner conditions of oneself though the physical body is a matter that had the beginning, growth and decay and that is the natural phenomenon of all. This is all I understand. But why I cannot understand the other side. Because there are no answers of the other side and the question burns itself. Any answer to such question is not an answer. All answers are hypothetical based on certain convictions apart from the individual concepts of some information. All information are second hand. They are not acquired information from self and original experiences. Even many self-experiences are not original. There are no original experiences. Someone must have already experienced that experience. All thoughts, all dreams, all experiences are drawn from the Cosmic World which is the storehouse of the Universal Energy though subtle. Subconsciously thoughts of individuals can be drawn by any amount depending on the capacity of a person to draw. How that capacity is created in an individual, can never be known. He just has. Why he has only so much while the other has much more or much less than him? No answers are available. He just has that capacity that's all. Any answer to any of these things would be false and it cannot be the answer, because there are no answers. For example to say why the earth should rotate in the way it does but not the other way round? That is the natural law and that is how it is. To ask why a man does not have an eye at the back of his head? But, that is how he is, is the answer. Some questions do not have answers at all. All answers are derived from the Cosmic Energy. So it is the same Cosmic Energy that is manifesting in the different objects at different times in different ways and also in different capacities with different degrees, while the nature of Cosmic Energy being the same. What is Cosmic Energy? It is the totality of all the energies the Universe holds to function itself in unison. Is it possible for a person to go beyond the Cosmic Energy? No, for the reason no object whether animate or inanimate can get separated from the Universe and its functions and as such he cannot separate himself from the Cosmic Energy even in his death. Birth, life and death come within the circle of Universal function fed by the Cosmic Energy. However, these may be my own concepts, but still, I feel, the total ignorance. When the ignorance dawns and comes to stay permanently, it may be called as God realization/self-realization. Ignorance is the God, is the Reality. Ignorance is the bliss, it is divine, and all powerful while the knowledge is subjective and objective, but ignorance is neither subjective nor objective. It just 'is'. That is the Reality that is the Truth, the one without a second, the one beyond any attributions. It is all pervading, omnipresent, omnipotent and omniscient. That is the only Truth. Truth is always only one. That is me, the entire and the whole ignorance.

—〰—

18ᵀᴴ DECEMBER 2005   03 30 A.M.

Honestly, nothing interests me other than to be to with the Central Cosmic Energy eternally. Will it happen? May happen. 'May' is a term of hope for the future. Now, here and at this moment will it happen? Will I be there being here at the same time? Possible. I want to be there more than here. My wanting, a desire, may be the obstruction to be there. I do not find interest even in God. Sometimes I challenge this so called God, by asking 'what-if'? He might be the only one to have all the qualities, qualifications and attributions that none have. I feel that these are all man made, because man does not have any of these, but desire to attain, by projecting his own concepts of achieving. I don't like to be other than what I am, irrespective of whether He is there or not. He being with me is fine, but He makes no difference to me for I don't want anything from Him. What all I aspire personally, like peace, tranquility, bliss etc., are all status of mind created by myself from the transmission of such waves to my mind by the Cosmic Energy naturally when I so desire. I don't have to be grateful to anyone including God, even if He is said to be not only the creator of all things of the Universe including me. The only thing I am concerned about, to some extent is, that He may give me some physical inconvenience, He having powers to cause such things. He can do nothing other than that. He stands there always, stating that 'in case you forget Me, I will remind you that I am there by creating inconveniences to you either physical or mental'. This game He plays with all ordinary mortals, but not with me. Even in this game He plays 'I am not interested' while He makes me a pawn in His hand as He does with others, but I will not allow Him to hold me. This is not an ego but the reality to me. Since I don't know whether He is there or not, since I am completely ignorant about Him, the knowledge about Him and the power He possess.

What is the worst that He could possibly do to me? He may curse for the worst diseases to this physical as well as mental body and ultimately kill me. That's all He can do. I am prepared to die physically. Let Him play His game and I am ready to meet Him squarely at His level.

—〰—

15ᵀᴴ DECEMBER 2005   04 00 A.M.

Is it possible to reach the edge of the Universe and step on to the other side of the sphere and to the other level of life? Can I go beyond the life? It did happen many a times but never did I understand while I was there. Only after the event took place did I realize that I was there. While experiencing of my being there, I would not be aware of it, but only through the imprinted memory that dawns subsequently about this experience. But the memory itself is not the experience. Memory is the present thought process of the past events. Is it possible to reach the other side every time a person desires to step out? I don't think I could do that. Some word, some scent, some unknown force drags me to that region. It does not take place on my desiring it. Desire is, wanting to be there often, again and again. But whatever I may do, however I may try, I cannot on my own volition, reach there. It just happens by itself without any preparation from my side and when I least expect it to happen. But it happens on its own; but not with my desiring it. Why should this happen to me? I know not. It may be happening to others as well. I am completely ignorant of that sphere, of that level, of that experience which is beyond this mundane life. There I am, blissfully at the very core of the Central Cosmic Energy emanating by itself perpetually, spreading gracefully and divinely all through the Universe, for the Universe to function. At that level, there are no thought processes because there are no physical beings, no desires, no wanting, just being there, non-physically, is beyond the words of expression which of course is physical. Even desire to experience it again and again, is becoming mundane. Link by link I am breaking this chain of desire since desire is physical and psychological but not spiritual. Desire is physical but that experience is spiritual. Whether it happens for a fraction of a second or for hours, I have no way of knowing; because at that level time stops, it is beyond time space and causation. There are no effects because there are no causes. Time, space and causation are physical and hypothetical man made measurements. Honestly, I desire to detach myself from these experiences also. I should not give much importance to them. They may be happening to scores of people. Nothing is big about it. It just happens. That's it. And 'what-if, if-it-happens?' attitude comes to me. May be, I recognize myself at that level of being, that I eternally belong to that region and also to every region including this one of the Universe. There is neither coming nor going. It is just 'being'. And I have no control over it and at the same time there is no necessity to control. It is a blissful happening, but I have to go beyond this blissfulness, beyond divinity, beyond all the qualifications and attributions man makes to that un-known. 'It-just-is there' without any qualification or description. All qualifications, attributions and descriptions of that Cosmic Energy are only mundane but in reality there are no divisions as mundane (physical) and spiritual (metaphysical). The entire Universe is one totality of just being there, functioning in Unison while I am completely ignorant of any of these things. I can never understand and I shall not contemplate to understand them and if I did, I will miss it, I don't want to miss its core and my blissful ignorance of any of these things, which is the reality to me.

—⁂—

13ᵗʰ DECEMBER 2005   04 00 A.M.

When I look back upon the path I walked through, it looks as if it was only yesterday that I was in the middle school, escaping through the open windows and running to mango groove which was then existing just where the present *Manasagangothri* (campus of *Mysore* University) is. I was the most mischievous boy, a rebellion of the day in the family, having had no interest in the school as it looked silly to study any bygone history or for that matter hypothetical mathematics, except for the literature, especially English. When I came to High School I was more fascinated by the dramas of Shakespeare; the characters of Mark Anthony, Lady Macbeth etc. This led me to libraries. I was mad, mad to read and read. I would sit for 48 hours without sleep and read a book in one-go. Books, especially, of Victorian Era, have fascinated me. Probably because, I feel strongly that I was one of those persons in England in those days. There were classical books of those days. Lots and lots of books were purchased by me and I treasured them, ultimately and recently gave them up to a library, free. Books have created a mesmeric field and probably contributed to my ego of knowledge-a false pride. Slowly I gave-up books for deep contemplation. *Sri. Ramakrishna Ashrama's* books in the beginning and later Dr. *S.Radhakrishnan's* books; and further *J.Krishnamurthy* (JK) and *U.G.Krishnamurthy* (UG) have influenced me a lot. However, slowly but surely it was drawing upon me this ephemeral, transitory phases leading to the eternal knowledge of ignorance. Ignorance is the knowledge of all knowledge-mother of all knowledge—and I was lead into this vastness of knowledge of ignorance. This ignorance has created deep silence within me and the true light of knowledge of ignorance was realized. With the knowledge of ignorance, all dualities have shattered. One Universal Cosmic Energy came to function and I was sucked into the Whirlpool of light of ignorance and I became a part of it ultimately, rather I became that itself, without 'ME' as a separate entity. I have realized that I as an entity had no individual identity. When-so, there was no individual 'me'; there was no 'you' or 'he'. It became one Universe. I loved the whole Universe and felt that I possessed the entire Universe to myself. I hugged it with both arms. There was implied understanding between the Universal Cosmic Being and myself, that we two were inseparable to eternity. Whatever may be the sub-sub function at any level, even of a speck of dust on grain of sand, we two were in it at the same time and also at the highest level of functioning. There was pure love and we two held hands of each other, jumped and laughed like children, looking at the entire Universe, understanding, respecting each other between myself and that Cosmic Being. It looked as if we are the only two staying at the center of the Universe wherefrom the Cosmic energy was emanating and spreading to the entire Universe. There was bliss, happiness and understanding as if we were the only two eternal lovers, inseparable souls, with me taking into various physical forms and yet holding the hands of that Cosmic Being to eternity. This was a peculiar knowledge, maybe a concept to others, but to me, it was the reality, that I was always with that Cosmic Being, merged deeply, blissfully in that ocean of love and yet it stayed and functioned at my level as if that Cosmic Being was a person and had no one else other than me and I also had no one else other than that Cosmic Being. It looked as if we were the only two occupying the entire Universe and loving the whole Universe. It was a peculiar relationship between me and that Cosmic Being. When I had to function through this physical body, I did so as of a son, a brother, a father, a husband, a friend etc. and sometimes as a tough person, without these functions touching my inner core. Sometimes, a pre-monition would take place as to the coming events and sometimes I would see the whole past. When I came across certain events I felt that I had undergone and experienced these events and they were not new to me and yet some other time some events though have had taken place could never be understood by me in spite of their physical appearances. And now slowly this part of physical function is ebbing away to give place to the new functions at different levels. I myself was aware of it. Sometimes when I looked forward to, for I knew, at the end I would meet a new personality of me to function in different physical form and yet eternally staying with an incomparable Love of that Cosmic Being and be merged in that without recognition of me. It was the most joyful living from eternity to eternity.

11ᵀᴴ December 2005   04 00 a.m.

Man being what he is, he wants to experience the same thing again and again, but differently every day, if it brings pleasure to him. He desires that these experiences should benefit him physically and economically which, he feels, automatically bring social advancement to him. He wants to make a history to himself, but when he becomes a history, alas he will not be there to enjoy his history-hood. His history is that which remains in the minds of others about him. And he craves that people should always keep him in their mind even when he is dead and gone, let alone when he is alive. But human nature being what it is, which includes himself also, everyone occupies their own mind by themselves rather of others, most of the time, always trying to elevate themselves while lowering others, thus unaware of themselves going down day by day.

Time slips away and this physical body wears out and one day its functions come to a grinding halt to be burnt out. Anything one desires to attain, if at all there is any such thing to attain, has to be when one is in physical body only and that too if that physical body is in sound health. Otherwise nothing can be attained, except to spend all the remaining energy to re-attain the physical health of the body. Hence a healthy physical body is the most important one for the attainment of the unknown.

—ɯ—

9ᵀᴴ December 2005   04 00 a.m.

Are there any forces functioning at some level, each trying to hold the sway and annihilate the other? Or, is one force-The Universal Cosmic Force—displaying itself in such dual functions? As for me, I do not know that an evil-spirit exists. May be, to those who are selfish, base, spiteful and having desire to hold the humanity in their grip and the power to subjugate others to their desires, such evil spirits exist and they try to misuse them. Or maybe, they convert the pure spiritual energy to arrive at their own goals. But to the one who is living with the pure spiritual energy, these evil spirits can do nothing; and they get destroyed in the presence of such a pure state with just one glance. The weak in mind succumbs to these evil spirits. Some evil spirits may project themselves in the garb of pure spirits and misguide the others. The person who is involved with such spirits should try to convert that energy in him to the advancement of spiritualism to attain the pure Cosmic Energy; while all such material benefits derived from such evil spirits should first be neglected. One should not stop at that level. These powers, to produce materials, heal some sick persons at a touch etc.; come naturally while on the way to reach the Inner Core of the Universe's Cosmic Being; and such power should not be allowed to destroy a person halfway in the path. If a person is strong spiritually and determined to reach his goal, he will not succumb and allows himself helplessly to be used by these spirits, conning and hallucinating himself that he has a mission to perform. These hallucinations are created by these evil spirits in the person whom they use. That person should be cautious of these evil spirits. Man being already thirsty, is made more thirsty to the material benefits with excuses and convincing reasons and logic and that he is being used for a mission and what that mission is, he knows not. A certain type of environment is created by these spirits which hold that person and convince him that he is on the path to spiritualism while actually he is on the road not only of his own destruction but also of the destruction of those surrounding him—he drags them-to his path and they follow him, because, they somehow succumb to his way of thinking, being weak spiritually by themselves. I have come across many persons of such nature and they could not touch me. Maybe, there were some shallow threats. Realizing it, I moved on, they could never touch a hair of me, let alone my spirit in 'ME'. If they try to reach my spirit, in the process, they get completely burnt out and may convert themselves to pure spiritual beings. I don't have to be aware of my pure spiritual being, because I am that itself. All my requirements such as food, shelter and clothing may be met with as to for others, externally, but from within I am one with that Cosmic Energy which does not display Itself in the form of miracles etc. Maybe, when I come in contact with these instruments of evil spirits, I will not have even a very insignificant set-back, but on the contrary for these evil spirits there will be a great forward path. It is good that in these paths there is likelihood of these evil spirits becoming pure spiritual beings. Beware, Oh you instruments of evil spirits, that, here I am whom you can never touch however close you may try to come but never so close spiritually, unless you shun to act as agents of such evils. Come with me; let us take journey together in the path leading to the Pure Cosmic Energy, if you dare, as I do.

20ᵀᴴ NOVEMBER 2005 04 00 A.M.

As the age advances, somewhere along the line, I have lost myself and slowly but surely the knowledge of ignorance has crept into me and what all I had thought that I knew were only superficial and of ego factors; empty knowledge, probably to assure myself as a literate and knowledgeable person. But this knowledge of ignorance has struck me with a sledge hammer and everything was smashed and shattered into pieces, unrecognizable. I have become a stranger to myself, because I know not 'Myself'; since 'ME' is not existing as an entity separate from the entirety of the Universal function. I live, rather function in ignorance. However I may try, I can never, ever understand the ways of the Universal function and the Cosmic Energy thereto behind this function. Is not 'ME' a part of this Cosmic Energy, functioning in the way it has to? Is it possible to function in any other way than it does as 'ME'? In the process of function, birth, life and death are just phases, while may be from eternity I am functioning and to eternity I continue to function under different physical facets. Neither the birth, nor the life, nor the death could be understood. Understanding is only an imprisoned ego, memory projected as thought. Past is dead but lives in memory and there is no such a thing as present time. Future is only a hope, conceived from the past memory—a projected concept of the dead past. One can never hold one second of time to make it a living present; nor could it be extended to future. Every second of time is independent by itself, neither connected with the past nor having connections to the future. It is the memory of the past that creates a hallucination of present and future, a hypothetical projection of the dead past—rather memory of that dead thought. Time just slips away between the fingers and can never be held to show that that second is the time as present. Life is a bundle of past thoughts and conditioned ones. Thought conditions me to this concept of Cosmic Energy and Universal function, while I do not know whether there is such a thing as Cosmic Energy and its functions and whether it is functioning. These are my conceptual thoughts conditioned by myself to myself. Everything is conditioned to function in the way they are. The entire function is one big function in totality of the entire Universe. It is from the astronomers and astrophysicists did man conceived the knowledge of the Universe in unison, the galaxies, its milky ways, black holes, planetary systems etc. It is said that space has no limitations but the man being what he is, with all his supposed knowledge and intelligence restricted himself to dimension like time, linear measurement etc. though hypothetical ones, but accepted by the entire human world for the convenience of his functioning, in different fields, have been a great player of twelve dimensions, the human being has so far coined. However, I feel, the thought is the mother of all dimensions. It is the thought that creates everything including me. It is my thought that has not only created me but also has created others and the entire Universe with reference to me. I am the thought itself. Thoughtlessness is also a thought; as desirelessness is also a desire. Desire is, rather, a thought. When thought ends desire ends and when thought ends, life ends and a thoughtless man is a dead man. A dead body will have no more thoughts. As long as life is there, even when in coma, probably, subtle thought process goes on; which is the symbol of life. Death of thought is the physical death. So thought in a way is physical. However, without these subtle thoughts, physical world does not exist by itself, but has no meaning of its function without the human thought at least to oneself. The energy of thought creates Universe and the individual, who in turn conceives the Universe. Behind all these forces the Cosmic Energy functions. It is this One Energy which is functioning at different degrees and facets according to the capacity of each of those facets to function. These are, once again, may be, my own conceptual thoughts. In reality I am One Big Bundle of Ignorance. I am happy I am ignorant and I would be still happy if I become ignorant of my own ignorance and become the very ignorance itself.

—⟋⟍—

19ᵗʰ NOVEMBER 2005   04 00 A.M.

There is a very strong urge to understand the life, but for sure it would be a vain urge; since nothing can be understood in the sense of their reality. First of all, is there anything called life? I don't know. Is there me in me? I don't know even that. What is all this, why creation. There are no authentic answers, because there are no 'why', 'how', 'what' etc. in the order of Universal function. It just functions as it is. 'Why', 'how', 'what' is only human ego that arises because of his power to speak. I, since decades, wonder at the power, the energy, and the most wonder of the wonders of the Universe of the man endowed with the words-ability to speak. Yesterday I was speaking about the power of man to speak. It is impossible to imagine the human race without the ability to speak. Probably the only difference between the other animate objects and the man is that the man can speak. And probably, this absence in the other species is made up by intelligence in them to protect themselves from the onslaught of the superior species and each member of one species has the same intelligence as that of another member of the same species, i.e. equal intelligence, unlike the human species between themselves. Nothing could be known. Yet, I know that I am a one small tiny wave of Universal function expressed for a fraction of a second which creates the hallucination of being a separate entity of the Universe, as is the wave created by the sea. Waves cannot be separated from the sea and the wave cannot be other than water. This tiny wave of human race cannot be other than the Universe's function and the Universe's function cannot be other than the Cosmic Energy, as can be compared to a tree consisting of roots, trunk, stems, branches, leaves, buds of flowers, raw and ripe fruits, with seed within, which, ultimately has within itself all the potentialities of a tree that may be separately grown and yet part of that tree itself with conditioned continuity of that tree. When fruits are ripened the function of the tree is fulfilled and it passes on all its physical and cosmic potentiality to every tiny seed equally within the fruit. This is how the whole Universe functions in cycle, passing on all the potentialities, one like itself to the next repetition of functions, as it is the order of the things of the Universal function, while here the time cycle may vary, but the repetition of function is common. So the Cosmic Energy is common but its expression may vary. I am that small and tiny dust particle of the eternal repetition of the function of this Universe.

—ɯ—

11ᵀᴴ NOVEMBER 2005   04 00 A.M.

It is long since I have been instructed, by some force unknown to me, to hold pen and start writing what it dictates. I don't know which power expresses itself through me—an instrument in its hand.

Yesterday, I read about 'mind'. What mind is? No-one knows for sure. Is not the mind a thought? It is the thought that creates everything. Through thought process we recognize the entire Universe and God is only conceptual projection of thought. Thoughtlessness is also a thought, as desire-less-ness is also a desire expressed through thought. Desire is a dual concept created by the conditions. I am conditioned to have been born to a particular parentage, caste, sub-caste, creed, religion, country etc. However, slowly I am freeing myself from these bondages. Yet I am bound by the society. I am helpless. I have only freedom to think. Even, probably, this very thinking is conditioned, because thoughts are not independent. They come from the Cosmic Energy. Rather, the entire Universe is the expression of that Cosmic Energy. These expressions, though, create hallucinations in the mind of man that he, as a man, is a separate entity. But in reality, I feel, the entire human race is just a fraction of one of the facets of expression of the Cosmic Energy—because man is not outside the Universe—he is a part of it. The expression of Cosmic Energy change as the power of expression change, accordingly the waves of energy change and create an illusion of phases like birth, life and death. However, they are one expression at different wave-length, the basic energy being the same in all the three expressions. The chemical expression of physical body has the same energy expressed differently according to the needs of the cells of a particular organ and also collectively for the entire physical body. It is the cosmic energy that energizes each cell in different organs of the body, each organ as one individual though look different, but in totality their functions being the expression of the entire physical body. So, Cosmic Energy functions as One Being though expressing differently for different functions of the Universe. I am one of these expressions and at the same time I am also the same. Hence I am not I am. I am part of the Universe expressed differently for different functions but I am that Cosmic Energy itself to eternity.

—m—

30ᵀᴴ OCTOBER 2005 03 30 A.M.

My inner being takes me beyond to other spheres or rather to some other level of existence. There, I feel, everything is perfect. However, perfection becomes too dry without any feelings, to arrive at, to struggle for, to look forward to, to have hope, everything a man desires to live for, vanishes with perfection. Perfection may be a concept but expecting to reach, the way to reach, the feelings to reach is something more desirable than to have reached. At this very moment I feel the presence of *Sri. Ramana Maharashi* and Sri. *Ramakrishna Paramahamsa*, the two great beings, India has ever produced. These two great beings have not only influenced my life but have occupied every cell of my body. They are the only two to whom I could go to, rather who stay with me always, unparallel and yet they never knew how they have completely changed the lives of millions while they were in their mortal body and even now changing millions of lives. Mostly they are working now more than what they did while in their mortal body. I feel, today they are going to visit me in their subtle and causal bodies. I want them very badly as I have never wanted anyone else. Will they really visit me and stay with me? Will they leave behind a small spark to engulf me? Will it happen? I wish it does. Lo! it happened and I lost myself completely. I am totally confused, I pray for strength to withstand this. I surrender completely to them. I pray God to come and stay with me at this moment.

One early morning, in 1961,*Shri Rama Krishna Paramahansa* stood before me. I bowed-down to prostate and touch his feet, but he immediately vanished blessing. I learnt later that a physical person cannot touch a person in subtle body.

—m—

24TH OCTOBER 2005   04 00 A.M.

I strongly feel that I am an eternal being in spite of the limitations of my physical body; and to some extent the eternity also goes with the physical body, but only with different chemical and biological combinations, perhaps. In reality there is no such a thing as combination. Everything is vibrating by the same force but at different degrees, which creates illusion to human understanding. Man thinks he is the only specie capable of understanding. To understand what?, himself?, or the functioning of the Universe in all its expressions of nature, animate and inanimate? To me there is no 'ME' at all. The whole Universe is one complete function and every entity is a part of it, rather that itself. This is only a way of expression, for I do not know anything about anything. A mirror cannot see by itself but through another mirror and when done there will be infinite reflections of each other-an illusion created—while in actuality there are two objective mirrors. However, the Cosmic Energy is only one, but its expressions are many according to the physical nature of things as in case of electrical energy energizing the physical objects like fan, bulb, oven, refrigerator etc.; according to the nature and capacity of each physical form; while a refrigerator needs energy for cooling, the same energy is needed for an oven to heat up. However, the quantity of the energy may vary but not the quality. Quality of energy cannot be adulterated. Energy is pure and perfect unlike physical objects of nature like air, water etc. which can be adulterated and polluted and so, the so called life can also be adulterated and polluted physically, mentally and to some extent spiritually too. In the real terms there is no such a thing as adulteration for there is no such a thing as pure. These are dualities created by mind according to the physical body's requirements and mentally created projections, subjected to each other, as reference points.

—m—

18ᵀᴴ OCTOBER 2005   05 00 A.M.

Nothing makes anything. We, as individuals or as a race cannot but be in the Universe as helpless beings, because there may not be any other way than how and what it is. Everything has to function explicitly, accurately with no questions asked and no answers forthcoming and with no hesitation or over zealousness. Acting, just like unintelligent vegetable without expression what-so-ever. There is no intelligence in the nature. Nature is like a preprogrammed robot and it functions accordingly without any intelligence of its own whether in its weather, tsunamis, earthquakes, volcanoes, forest fires etc. There is no intelligence in any of these nature's functions. It is the man who interprets the nature according to his physical constitution-cold and hot etc., which is bodily phenomenon, so also things like hunger, sleep etc. which contain certain tolerances depending on the individuals. Probably, the entire nature and the Universe must have already been programmed to function and to die—to annihilate—during the course of time, it must have already been started. Everything happens the way it should because there are no other ways to happen. But in the process of functioning certain phenomenal 'by-functions' take place which man interprets them as 'life'. What life is, in reality, yet to be known to man. Who that 'I' is? I do not know. Even as to whether 'I know' or 'I do not know', even that I do not know. There is no way to say 'I know' or 'I do not know'. May be, there is nothing to know and may be, the so called intellectual ego of man teases him by stating that 'I know'. **But does he really?**

—ɯ—

17ᵀᴴ OCTOBER 2005   04 00 A.M.

Slowly but surely a person in his advanced age starts believing lot many things especially if it is said to affect his children, which he would have laughed at and ridiculed at if it was said when he was young. He would not believe those things that would affect him, but would rather be cautious if it affects those he loves. Everything would have washed-off from him, because he would have completely wiped off and made everything blank at an advanced age and nothing more can be written and nothing more can influence him in either way. He neither challenges nor agrees to anything that any person would either try to prove or disprove, but he knows that it would make no difference either way. For sure, he would have arrived at by himself and on his own that he understands nothing and what all he thought he had been claiming to have understood, were merely due to his conceptual intellectual ego that he had conditionally cultivated. Now, from the very root he pulls out of his system all that he had believed earlier and he stands empty and naked to himself as the most ignorant person.

All his spiritual experiences, his astral travels, out of body experiences, unique experiences of the Light, his seeing the future, forecasting of other's life, and happenings, and everything that he gathered, are now to be of no use to him. He becomes a speck of dust, maybe that were all hypothetical hallucinations, for sure he knows not whether they were simply his conceptual, hypnotic auto-suggestions or just happenings at other level and at different degree of his existence. He knows not whether he is 'he—himself' who is existing or something else exists as 'he' and ultimately knows not whether there is existence at all. Nothing, nothing could be known to him. He cannot recognize himself as an entity while all the time he had been conning himself and hallucinating himself that he was an entity, unknown to himself. But this concept of him of himself has slowly changed. Now he knows for sure he is not an entity he thought he was, but a grain of sand functioning as such on the vast shore of the eternal Universe and before long that grain of sand will turn to be dust of many particles and spread out losing even that shape of dust and would merge with the entire Universe with no earlier identity either of sand or dust. Probably in the atoms of this dust the Universe reflects itself and exists equally because that atom of dust cannot cross-over the Universe and say 'I am a separate entity from the Universe' and at the same time the Universe cannot say that it is the WHOLE and complete without even that one atom of dust. Even that one atom of dust contributes to the wholeness or the completeness of the Universe. Thus, that atom of dust, though in different form, is eternal as the Universe is. Neither there is 'coming' nor 'going', but just being is 'what is'. And that 'what is' is the sum total of what I, you and everything is and 'what is' can never be thought to be other than 'what is'. And I can never know what this what-is' is. Probably this very ignorance itself maybe 'what-is'. Ultimately there is neither intelligence nor awareness but only ignorance. Ignorance produces fullness, its sooths, it sings lullaby, creating stupor and even that awareness of ignorance will go to coma—and probably that is the goal—to go to coma, to become vegetable without being aware of anything and yet be functioning in the material world of existence. It just is happening. Coma is slowly encompassing and engulfing fullness before long. That is 'what-is'. These are not mere words but happenings-real happenings, at least to me and also to that atom of dust.

—m—

06ᵀᴴ OCTOBER 2005   03 00 A.M.

'My prayers have no meaning whatsoever, for whatever will be done, will be done according to THY wish', is what one always says in the end and surrenders to the unknown God. It is the man's crazy idea to pray God for all the material comforts for himself—maybe at times at the cost of others—on the tiny earth of this Universe, that the Cosmic Energy of the entire Universe has very little consequences and attention. HE—that energy (for the present let this energy be called as HE) knows very well that man is getting competitive with others of his own species on the insignificant surface of this earth which is almost like a grain of sand on the vast sea shore of the Universe, that man is trying to make a permanent home holding on to all types of securities that man thinks it would help him to eternity. Probably, even the concept of God, created by man, to help himself, is helpless or does not have any interest, as man has towards a tiny ant. Surviving permanently at any cost is the man's goal, that too on this earth, while so much is available unknown to man. Had man known all the unknowns, he would have killed himself to attain it. There would have been a competition between man and man and to die to go to such places or spheres, millions of light years away from here. Man would have built a machine to attain the speed overriding the light years. However it becoming impossible the best for a man is to give up what he cannot attain even a very tiny one and to allow himself to 'Let go' and to 'Let go' of everything and himself too; and then probably he would attain.

—⚏—

3ᴿᴰ OCTOBER 2005   04 30 A.M.

May be only a few pages or even only one page is left over before this life's book is going to be closed. I know that it is coming to a close, but when and how, I don't know. How soon God reads this book, so soon it gets closed. If He leaves the last page unread for some-time and for some reasons best known to Him, He would definitely takes it up and completes it before I could realize what is happening and it will not be long. Is there anything I could do to stop Him from reading the last page of my book? NO. I can only be passed on to another binding and may be, with repetition of the same story with different sets and scenes. It, the book, may be a thin, or a thick, or middle sized one, I don't know. I will go on be shifted from one binding to another eternally with no stop unless the reader gets tired and forgets me, which may be very seldom. As he reads I go through the hearing while I do not know what comes in the next line or in the next page or in the next chapter and in what forms it comes to be read. It is already there, written and printed by Him un-erasable, according to my own karmas written one page at a time, one paragraph at a time and sometimes one sentence at a time and even one word at a time, not missing even one letter, they will be read as they are, perfectly, precisely, aptly, timely, pausing where it should be paused, with all signs, such as commas, exclamatory, semicolons, colons, full-stops etc. as they are. No interpretation, no interruption, no hurrying, no slowing, no fault in pronunciation, no skipping, all perfect according to the script and the story it will be read from the first to the last word in the book of the humans life. Maybe there would be a pause when one chapter is closed before going to the next chapter. All chapters are interconnected. There will be no dis-joints but perfect links and continuous one chain. Yet, no-one can predict how it goes, what lies in the next line, next word, and next letter. The future is unknown, unpredictable and the past is forgotten, otherwise the present reading will be disturbed. Everybody is a book, to open and to close, but none knows what it contains. Some may have one line, some may be pamphlets line, some thin books, some moderate, some may be large ones with many pages and many chapters, and some may contain a blank page also and the next binding may be a book of many pages written.

—∽∽—

1st October 2005   05 00 a.m.

The greatest human desire is 'Not to Die', even after losing all the limbs one by one and also being insane. In the process of existence everyone desires to become 'some-body'. No-body desires to remain as 'No-body'. Though everybody desires to be 'some-body' some others desires to be a 'special-some-body'. Attaining the 'some-body-hood' may not be difficult but to maintain that status is really the toughest one. To become 'some-body' in any field—whether materially or metaphysically; or socially or spiritually—is the goal of human nature. To become 'some-body' in the field of 'god-men' and to behave one like, takes a great strain. A slip in the process of maintaining this 'some-body-status' always creates fear of losing all the qualities that go with that status and takes that person to a vertical drop in the event of even a small slip, for he stands at the pinnacle of the social order. All these positions and status are simply sociological. A god-man's status is all the more difficult to maintain because only when he becomes 'no-body' with complete surrender, which causes him to be in extreme humility and simplicity, would really lead to god-head, otherwise in reality he can never be a god-man. Such a man does not desire to be 'some-body' and automatically becomes from 'no-body' to 'some-body', that will be in the nature of that god-man. He will not be aware that he is 'some-body' or either 'no-body'

No one needs to struggle to be a 'no-body'. However, society will not progress if everybody remains to be 'no-body'. Society's progress depends on this desire to be 'some-body'. Every person however in-significant he may be, desires within his own narrow circle, to be 'some-body' at least in that circle. This striving hard to become some-body creates ego by stampeding on other's ego at all costs. 'One-up-man-ship' in any field is the goal of human nature. However, hardly anybody can leave any foot print on the timeless sea shore of the eternal functions of the Universe with its waves consuming every foot-print. This 'some-body-ship' as is not only what one thinks of oneself but also what one expects others to think of him in the way he conceptualizes himself as 'some-body'. So, this 'some-body-ship' is to live beyond the functions of the Universe. Everything will be wiped off. Even the Universe itself will be wiped-off one day. It is crazy to live in others mind, while, in fact, no one allows anyone to occupy his mind however great that person maybe because man's mind always occupies about himself. And occasionally allows others to peep in but not alone to occupy his mind. He always replaces one person with the other in his mind while constantly without allowing any space to others. This some-body-ship is his own creation, is his own projection giving status to that some-body-ship of his. He ultimately becomes a beggar, begging alms of recognition from others. The moment they refuse to contribute to his alms of recognition, he turns violent to destroy the other person either physically or mentally and purposely putting on the show of negligence (udaaseen) and slowly starts dismantling the other person and in the process ends up destroying himself with self-pity or bragging of one-self, and in the end' completely destroys himself. This is the history of man-the man who was 'some body' during his life, while may be proved in the future that he was not the real some-body but he was falsely claiming to be a some-body, to be thrown-out of that status. People will not hesitate to dismantle and destroy that status of his some-body-hood even after his death which he had attained during his lifetime. This is the real function of the human race, always to be some-body in any field whether the field is of a dacoit or a god-man. They have become some-body in their own fields and try to remain for a long time in the minds of others lest they may lose the status. However, when they really try to leave that status in their own mind the nakedness of their own self reflects which may force them to escape themselves from themselves and try to reach to occupy others mind permanently which can never be done. The reality is to face one-self but not to run from oneself and thereby remain to be no-body. No-body-ship is the reality. Not being aware of oneself of this status is the reality. But to some-body either as a saint or as a sinner is falsity. In reality there is neither a saint nor a sinner. God too, I feel, is selfish because He wants to live constantly in the minds of others lest He be lost. He too becomes a beggar for recognition; otherwise He will be dead to others. Therefore for Him to be alive, be begs, directs, and even threatens day in and day out that His subjects be in constant remembrance of Him. Thus God becomes a beggar to of His own creation because He craves, instructs and even warns His creation to remember Him always as their Master. But in fact, He becomes a slave to His own creation and in the end both the created and creator become beggars to each other.

—ᴍ—

10ᵀᴴ SEPTEMBER 2005   04 00 A.M.

What is happiness? Is it not the other face of worry or sorrow etc.? In the absolute sense there is neither happiness nor unhappiness. Both seem to be mental status, sometimes projected and expressed through physical acts. Deep within due to some physical and external influences, the internal creates either happiness or unhappiness according to the degree of physical and external influences. In fact both are one. Mental or the internal cannot exist by itself without the physical existence. However, life being an eternity with physical change these things too change from phase to phase of physical existence. I could feel these things happening in the so called coming and going and my own happiness in the form of bliss expands to the universal limitless dimension. I feel, I am every—where and at the same time nowhere. During the Astral travel, I am not physical yet I feel I am with everything that is happening in the Universe. Scientists say that the Universe is expanding and growing but on the other hand, I feel, that their knowledge is expanding and growing while the Universe, as it were, is completely unknown to the scientists and maybe the Universe is contracting and diminishing with packets of concentrated Cosmic Energy, what the scientists say as 'black-holes'

However, somewhere in a tiny corner of my own inner self there is a very tiny expectancy, a tinge of un-fulfillment, a tinge of dissatisfaction of not arriving at, of the incompleteness, of not knowing the Reality, of not achieving self-satisfaction, of something still wanting etc. Desperation, sometimes, grips me from within. Wanting something, desiring something, other than 'what-is' is holding me up. Somehow I want to kick off everything and get out from everything including my own self; escaping from one-self. I want to be out of myself. This desire to escape from myself is very intense, squeezing my very core—to attain the unattainable, to reach the unreachable, to be merged with the non-merger and to lose myself completely without any trace of my individual being, is all the time gripping my heart to breathlessness. May be this by itself is the Attainment.

—m—

03ʳᵈ September 2005   04 00 a.m.

Everyday rather every moment is a step towards the 'D'-day. While the D-day, though fixed to the point of a second, it is unknown to the walker. Is there a journey? Journey presupposes a starting point and also an end point. To me, there is no journey at all. It is just functioning of phases. It may not even be functioning, since I do not know deep within me what all these functions are and why these functions are. Of course, the questions are not there because answers too are not there. The simple answer is '**I, FOR SURE, DO NOT KNOW ANYTHING ABOUT ANYTHING**. I am completely ignorant of everything. Since there is no 'I', in reality, there is neither intelligence nor ignorance. It just 'is'-even to some extent it is impossible to know what that 'is' is. Even God is a hallucination to an intellectual and to an atheist. It is an auto-suggestion, day in and day out, with all the inevitable conditioning of the mind from day-one to D-day. Sometimes the word 'God' challenges me as to understand it, or may be, that concept of God challenges my conditioning. I do not like to succumb to this external challenge, for it is a desire of different degree, though of the same kind. Any desire, even the desire to be desire-less, is also being a desire and is more a physiological and sociological phenomenon. For there is no such a thing as mental or physiological without there being the physical phenomenon while both are supplementary and complementary to each other, in a way they are one and the same at different level of degrees, but kind being the same, the desire to be, to become, to achieve to arrive at something other than what 'is'. While 'what—is' is unknown, what would be other than 'what—is' also becomes unknown; but desire persists till last.

The whole mischief of the human race is, that man is not only an animate object but also has the unique power of expression through words. If this power to speak had not been there, probably, man had to live in nature, like other species, without knowing anything other than basic and natural physical needs but with no responsibility to the progenies and the opposite gender of the same human species. There would not have been the Society and other developments as have been now. Man has made these developments for his survival and in the process he is destroying the whole human race by dividing it into religion, caste creed etc. and also by inventing science and technology which should have been subservient to man but on the contrary man has become subservient to these technological inventions. Now, man having been accustomed to these technological advancements, which are his creations, cannot for a moment live or even exists without them, independently. Man is now riding a ferocious Technology Tiger. We are conditioned, through a figure of speech-communicating by many means such as writing, speaking, visualizing etc. To think the absence of power to speak is disastrously unimaginable, beyond the human mind. Thought processes are projected through words for the existence of human race in the way it does now.

So, God is the creation of the man through his words. Thus, God becomes a subservient to the words of man. All flatteries are made to God, so the contempt is also expressed in the same language whether spoken or written. However, even the power to speak is conditioned and limited to fulfill the individual's aspirations. Knowledge is conditioned while the ignorance is vast, limitless and is not conditioned by any other person's sayings or opinions but of individual and it is of individuality unlike knowledge. Knowledge is mostly borrowed and is a second hand information, not self-acquired experience which is unique to oneself. Hence, I feel, the ultimate reality is ignorance-this very definition may be a borrowed one. These very thoughts are vibrations from the Cosmic reaching me through its waves which might have already been there in the cosmos left by someone else's thoughts. So Cosmic storage of thoughts too are conditioned and limited while the ignorance is beyond

—ɯ—

02ND SEPTEMBER 2005   03 30 A.M.

Somewhere along the line, maybe at the fag-end, one comes to realize that the search made so far, the so called knowledge acquired, rather the entire living was not the reality. However, what reality is-becomes un-realizable, inexplicable, inexpressible, inexperience-able, un-knowable etc. is the reality; the only other surety becomes strongly realizable is that 'I know nothing about anything'. Not knowingness is the realization, is the affirmation and awakening to oneself and the end result is real ignorance which dawns upon me and shatters all my expectations and hopes. I do not understand what others say. I have gone through all such egoistical saying that 'I know everything', having not known even a fraction of any fraction of a thing. Everything is just as 'it is'. I do not know even what they are in reality. For the purpose of communicating we name certain things for universal acceptance and identification of things. Otherwise, by themselves, they cannot be known even if one lives the life of that very thing. Man can never know about himself and his functioning. He just functions in spite of himself. He also stops functioning in spite of himself. Nothing he can do other than what is required for his existence materially, sociologically and economically, that he does all these hypothetically and hypnotically to auto suggestions and self-brainwashing and most of the time hypocritically also. Slowly, the world is moving to prove that 'the fittest will be the survivor' whether spiritually, metaphysically or materially. Helplessness is all the more proving, of late, especially when I try to propose certain things, the things turn out otherwise so what this otherwise will be most unpredictable and may be wise too. In all the matters, ignorance is the only truth and the ignorance of ignorance becomes the reality and maybe called as self-realization. I do not know even that.

—m—

25TH AUGUST 2005   04 00 A.M.

There, within me I become aware of the expansion of myself to the entire Universe. Somehow, I become the very Universe itself. I find myself in every atom of the Universe. The entity 'ME' becomes the entirety 'WHOLE'. Time, space and causations come to a dead stop. Nothing moves. It looks that 'I' is there in all the atoms since time immemorial-eternally. Somehow, it looks that everything is in me and me in everything. Nothing looks strange or older or new. No theory of God, rather no God, occupies my mind. There is no duality in me. I become the Universe and Universe becomes me. If this body dies, still I am in every atom of my body. However, the chemical combination may change. I feel that from the pinnacle of the Universe, rather from the center of the Universe, I can encompass, hold, merge in every activity of the Universe and yet at the same time, I am not any of these activities of this Universe. Nothing touches me. I am immovable, an eternal being not influenced by any of the functions of the Universe. Sometimes, as I have been saying, when I witness some scenes of history or even the present events on TV, I feel that I am very much familiar with most of them. I feel that I was a part of that history and also presently I am there. I feel as if I was not only the witness but also the participant of every event of those histories (past), and the present and future events. Yet, nothing disturbs me. The fear of self being lost is no more there. The fear of death has vanished, because to me there is neither birth, nor life, nor death. These are simply functional events of the Universe-they are the eternal functions and I am the main personality in all these events untouched and uninfluenced by any of these events. These are really happening to me. If I allow this to take over me I do not know where it all leads to and ends. Somehow I withdraw myself from these experiences to the present physical body existence. Some word, some sound, some writing, some thought or even some smell triggers me to take off tangentially to that expansion of my consciousness to the entire Universe. I am the whole and also the part of the Universe at the same time. That is 'ME'.

—⚡—

08ᵀᴴ AUGUST 2005   03 30 A.M.

God, if such an entity is there, whether He or It, maybe sleeping in deep slumber, otherwise He would have visited me by now for all the efforts I have put forth inviting Him. Maybe, my invitation and efforts have fallen half way through and might not have reached Him or even He might have ignored me as a worthless to be visited; though I really, honestly, fervently want Him to visit and leave a permanent mark on my soul of his visit. Will He, or will He not?, is the predominant thought in me. Before long I have to vacate the place and having the knowledge that I am not here, He may cancel His visit. So, any meaning, any purpose would be attributable only when He visits me before I leave the place. When once He visits, my hanging on to this place makes no difference either to me or to Him. Hence His visit is all the more important now when I desire most for His presence and when I am here. I am hanging on to this place hoping against hopes that it will not be long before He visits me. However, He knows best as to when He has to visit or not to visit at all. How does that make difference whether He visits or not? I think, my mind and desires being conditioned to His existence and His visiting at a time, though at different places, makes an elation of His visit. As I said earlier, this desire is a hope against hope. Or did He already visit me? But, was I in deep slumber? If not, did I not recognize Him? May be, any. Sometimes when He visits, persons having been conditioned with the so called knowledge, cannot recognize Him. The very so called knowledge of Him might become an impediment to recognize Him and I might be one of them. Or is He only a hypothetical existence? I don't know. I am ignorant about Him while He is not about me, because He is said to be omnipotent, omnipresent and omniscient.

—ɷ—

04ᵀᴴ August 2005   04 00 a.m.

Why one should seek the so called God? Is not seeking God a condition dumped on us by those who have never reached God? Is God a rare commodity hidden from the entire human race from time in memorial, eternally slipping away? Is there, in the first instance, such a thing as God? Is it not a conditioned and conceptual hypothetical idea handed over from generation to generation to make the human society hypnotized so as to fall in line, so that every individual could live and let live in harmony and peace? Is not this a social law's necessity? Whatever may be the arguments from any side, as for me, I know for sure that I don't know anything about anything, let alone God. But some claim that they do know God and I do not understand them. And I have no claims on either side. I just exist with calm and peace within me, though sometimes the outer disturbances do influence me momentarily and externally only. I just 'am'. I am neither 'I am' nor 'I am not'; for I don't know either. I am a stranger to myself sometimes and I am not aware of my own self. Within I am almost in coma stage about which I am aware of externally and intellectually. Even if God is there, why do I need Him unless I want something from Him either in this present physical world or in the so called next world, if at all it is there. Always, I assume a part of a beggar at the other end, always seeking something from Him, begging Him something or the other? It is the desire that makes man a slave to God, always with stretched hand at least for his companionship. Why should I need his companionship? Why should I stand always at the receiving end? If He is there eternally, so I am, may be at different footings. He may have the entire Universal power to do and undo things. Let Him have it. The worst He could do to me is to punish me physically with pain and diseases, economically, socially and mentally, if I ignore him. Neither I would praise Him nor condemn Him, for I do not know anything of Him and even about His existence. Let Him be there and I here. Let me pass through my life of existence with all the conditions imposed upon me by the society, the religion, the caste etc. as I am born choice-less, so do I lead my life choice-less and die choice-less and these will not touch my inner core. I am already conditioned, I am the totality of all these conditions and there is no freedom from any of these conditions to anybody whether he is a saint or a sinner. The very thought of freedom is a conditioned one. Freedom from what and to where? One condition replaces the other condition. If I am freed by myself from the physical, I shall be conditioned metaphysically, both physical and metaphysical being conditioned concepts of human race. There is neither rationality nor irrationality in these conditions. It 'just-is,' so I am just 'I am' and nothing else.

—◊◊—

4TH JULY 2005   05 30 A.M.

Somehow, I feel that I am left alone, uncared and unwanted all round even by the so called God. I feel that He is not interested in me, in fact at no point was He. I thought, let the whole world shun me, let everybody become strangers to me but let not He leave me. He too, I think, seems to have gone away from me, for the reasons best known to Him. Probably, I need Him all the more now because I feel that I am betrayed, that my faith in people is getting lost, I feel I am cheated. I feel that people are telling lies in the guise of good behavior externally, and I am completely disheartened and maybe He knows it best. He may be having different plans for me. Yet, I being an ordinary human being with all desires, hopes, expectations, I feel I need the correct and honest guide and a friend in Him; but He seems to be elusive, a mirage, or are all my imaginations running riot and that there is no such a thing though He, I imagine, stands by me at every point of time in my life? Is He not there when I most need Him and turn towards Him for guidance and blessings? Is not He my imagination, my foolish concept and my own auto suggestions of His existence? Is it possible for me to see Him physically as I see somebody else? But He seems to be elusive, an imagination and vaporizes Himself before anybody could glance at Him. At least I can see and feel that vapor of nothingness. He is not there. I feel He seems to think that I am not fit to be His companion. Well, maybe, I shall be further hurt for abandoning me. Why He wants to be away from me. I want Him to be with me permanently always and at all times. I hope He hears me and comes back to me.

—◊◊—

2ᴺᴰ JULY 2005   **03 00 A.M.**

I have read a lot on many subjects especially those which are supposed to guide me to the ultimate truth but nothing has taken me there. My experiences and lots of thoughts and deliberations at every stage of life were in search of that ultimate truth which is beyond the human perception in spite of all types of intellectual somersaulting. Finally it has dawned upon me for sure that 'I can know nothing about anything' and 'nothing can be known about anything'. The only thing that I have come to the definite knowledge is: 'I know nothing' and I can never know anything and what all I had thought that I knew were my ignorance and egoistical reactions to the world. This is the definite revelation that has come upon me, not through external sources but from within. Everything is just as 'it is'. There are no dualities. The qualification of dualities is only a hypothetical measurement of social life of human being to survive, lest, the strongphysically, intellectually and economically subjugate the weak and yet the weak is neglected not only by strong ones but also by themselves. The weak subjugate themselves to others because deep within them there is a hidden desire that they should become the strongest—that is to rule and subjugate the so called strong. Even amongst the strong, there is always competition for 'one-up-man-ship'. In the end the time is the leveler of everything. And yet, time is only a relative and a subjective dimension hypothetically created by man for his own physical and social necessities and survival. The Universe in its function is not bound by anything not even by time, other than its own function. How anyone would know that the Universe is functioning? It may be through his perception of mind. The Cosmic energy which is the central pivotal force from which the entire Universe draws that energy for its function, does not have any qualifications the human beings utter. But it just is there without any qualifications or attributions. And if a person has the capacity and urge, he can draw more energy from the central force thereby though the quality or the quantity of this energy does not diminishes in any way or gets polluted, He can recognize that it is the same energy that he has with the other beings. This energy is all pervading, eternal, and perennial and as such it neither gets diminished nor loses its purity, in whatever quantity one draws it to one's capacity.

I do not know anything about the center of cosmic energy which is eternally self-generating. I do not know anything about It. It could only be a conjecture of thought process, maybe an aberration of mind, conditioned by every means from my birth to death and even after death, in spite of my desire to be independent from all these conditions, though there being no such a thing as absolutism from these conditions. The very concept of God is conditioned under which I am not an individual and I am not a separate entity independent of these conditions. I am a bundle of all types of conditions. Even rationalism is a condition. This mind, somehow the entire of me, is conditioned. I am by myself is not intelligent but I am the projection of the Cosmic intelligence hence 'I am not I am'. I am just a process of function of the Universe and though I am of a micro second function in the eternity of the Universal function, without me, why for that matter even without a speck of dust on a grain of sand, the Universe is not complete. I am a part of this completeness of this Universe and at the same time I am not 'I am' and therefore I and Universe are one. I and the Universe are ONE

—m—

27ᵀᴴ MAY 2005   03 00 A.M.

Why this creation? What does it, in any way, creates and to what purpose? I am questioning this creation because I am a part of this creation and have a faculty of intelligence to question. I am really tired of everything even the so called God, who, if at all He is there, is slippery and can never come to man to give company in man's agonies and troubles. You create and offer them to man and ask the man not to take it. Then why do make it in the first place if man is not supposed to touch it. Why this? I am crazy to find you out and know who you are and why you are so elusive and I want you so badly, so that I could find a solution which I presume you have, as I am conditioned to an understanding that you have final solution to everything, because everything is your own creation. I am really tired physically, mentally and spiritually in finding you out and maybe I remain tired, for I may never, ever find you. But yet my craziness never goes out of me to find you. Is it possible to find you? Or you are not there at all and it is my hallucinated, imaginary conditioned mind that creates you and at the same time the mind wants to find you out? Is not you my creator and in turn are not you my creation? I am really tired and pray you to reveal yourself to me. I want you more than anybody else who wants you. All talks, all flatteries, all slogans and all hypocritical attributions of your qualities, I have heard enough. I am not interested in any of the qualities you possess or theories about you, but in actuality I want to find you out. Come on, reveal yourself to me in the physical form at least for my sight to have witnessed you. Would it be possible for you to do this? I think, you will not and may be though you are capable of doing it you would rather desist lest you are exposed to the human vagaries and desires thereby limiting yourself to the physical form. I am really crazy and no appeal, no prayers, no sincere cry would help me to find you out, probably because, 'YOU-ARE-NOT-THERE' in the way my conditioned perception says. But however, I do not know what other perceptions I should have about you for you to reveal to me as in Reality, you are.

—⁓—

20ᵀᴴ MAY 2005 03 30 A.M.

What is self-realization? Is there a Self as an entity in the order of the Cosmic functioning in the entire Universe, in totality? The only realization that has come to me, after a long time of searching, is, that I am a completely ignorant person of these aspects and I can never ever understand anything about anything and that there is 'Nothing' to realize. I am a part of the cosmic function, its energy, its intelligence, all in a limited framework according to my capacity which I know not myself, but that cosmic intelligence probably knows. Even I don't know what this Universe is, how it functions and whether it is to be called as Cosmic energy. Somehow being a part of the Universe I feel that I am also functioning as a part of the Universe with the same cosmic energy energizing my functioning and as such I feel I have the same qualities it has at the central functioning point, but what those qualities are I know not. Any nomenclature or attributions of those qualities are only conceptual conjectures conditioned since my birth on which I had no control or independence to decide. Even any independent decision will have to be within the same framework of universal functions replacing one with the other and there are no other choices at all. However I may struggle, however my intense desires are, even if I cross to go to the edge of the life, I can never be other than what I am—an ignorant person knowing nothing about anything. I also know that this physical body is slowing down and one day stops functioning and I who is functioning through this body has to quit this physical body to another one erasing all the memories of functions through this physical body though the resultants of functioning through this physical body do results in my further functioning in another physical body (*Karma*), which is a continuous process without an end, eternally, as this Universe functions, though under different facets with different capacities at different level and degree of function, but of the same kind. I somehow feel that I being a part of the Cosmic Universe, I am eternal and my end does never come since there was no beginning of me though I know nothing of my own self let alone the other aspects of the Universe.

—⚏—

15ᵀᴴ MAY 2005   03 30 A.M.

If God is everywhere, where is the question of either we going to God or God coming to us? If every function of the entire Universe, in its totality, is the function of that Cosmic energy, the question of good or bad karmas will not arise. The Universe functions in the way it does and there are no other ways. If there is one, that also is within the framework of Cosmic function. Here, I feel, there is no individual function or even individuality. It is the entirety of one function. It is a continuous function without break or without slowing down, or speeding up, although it gives different concepts to different human beings. God exists because human intellectual concepts exist through the power of words (oral and writing). If only this, power to speak, a very infinitesimal part of infinitesimal human being, had not been there, there would not have been the world as it exists today in material, social, economic and geographical forms and the Universe would not have existed to the man as it does now. So it is the concept of the strength of words that creates Universe and God. That is why it is said in the holy books-'the word was with God and the word was God'. But for the capacity to utter words, the human too would have been like any other animated species. So, what an enormous strength, power and energy that words hold, which in fact completely metamorphosed the face of the entire Universe. Expression, through words with Universal understanding, through communication, has been the foundation of human existence today. However, having no authority to question as to why only to human beings this power of speech is bestowed upon and not to any other species and to coin the conceptual word God, about which nobody knows for certain and even if known and experienced it would have been distributed as any other physiological commodity, that the man is doing now. Every individual, groups, institution, societies, religions are still to catch hold of this God. They are only in the process of doing so since the human spicy has surfaced on this earth, but have not arrived yet. He, the God is slipping away from everyone and everything. To me, God is simply the energy element in the function of the entire Universe in totality while any individual function is being within this totality cannot be separated as an individual function having individual character, though unique, is the reflection of the totality of function at one particular facet at certain degree and at certain time. It is a continuous process without the beginning or an end and as such is eternal, whether before or after the effective birth of the Universe (big bang). Yet nothing can be understood. Hence, God, if one can call so, is the expression of Central Cosmic Energy at various degrees through different facets at different times and at different places, but still it is the ONE EXPRESSION only without a second one. Where the degree of expression is more in a facet, we see God in that and pray for the elimination of our weaknesses and shortcomings and we pray for guidance and bliss which we think is its basic nature. And if possible we also pray that a part of that Cosmic energy be part of us, so that the society can behold us as holy men, the so called realized saints, god-men etc; not for God's own sake but for the egos sake of such individuals to capture and control the society. This is how the human society functions.

—ɯ—

01ST APRIL 2005   03 00 A.M.

What is Reality? Is it not a concept? Real, unreal etc. are mere concepts of dualities and one can never know what the reality is. Time, space and causation and five elements and other dimensions etc. are only concepts because this body too is a concept. In reality everything exists in the observer. Not outside. And yet they are not known to the observer. He does not know himself as the observer, let alone the observed and the act of observation. In fact none of the three are there, the observer, the observed and the observing. But there is nothing concrete in any of these three. For nothing can be known about anything, all the three being one. Not-knowingness is the state of my being. I do not know whether I am an 'I am', an entity, whether the Universe is there or whether I am there within the Universe. What the Universe is, I do not know. What 'I am', I do not know. But I know for sure 'I don't know'. In this state of being of not knowingness I lose my self-identity and the idiosyncrasy of fear slowly gets in and I want to come back to the original physical position. I struggle to hold on to the mundane physical existence but sometimes I escape not by adopting any method or by wishing, but without my helping myself to escape. I have no part in this escape but it happens by itself with no fore-warning, neither in the process of escape nor going to the other spheres, I have no part. I go to the eternal no-existence of self. I am neither away of this or that sphere. Even some spheres are material. Hence I feel that I am beyond that sphere too. In fact that also does not exist. Nothing exists to me. I do not exist to myself. Everything comes to a dead stop. Nothingness engulfs me and I am out. I desire intensely to go to that state when I am in this physical state. But when I am there I do not know I am there. I would know that I was in that state only when I return to this physical state of existence because there is no 'I' as an entity when I am there. Whatever any person may say I have no arguments with anyone, because I do not know anything about this physical world or of the other world or my state of being in any of these two. Every function of every individual, whether animate or inanimate objects, are the functions in totality of the whole Universe reflected in different facets with a different degrees and at different levels. I am at a particular level with different degree of function. Every function is universal function and I am within this function, and still I can never know how and why it functions in the way it does, without 'how' and 'whys' of human concepts. It just functions in the way it has to function. Not knowingness is the state I am in. It is the reality, at least to me. I know that 'I don't know' that is the reality. Even that very 'I don't know' is the reality or not, I do not know

—◁〢▷—

28ᵀᴴ MARCH, 2005   04 00 A.M.

Time is running out, slipping between the fingers, for the time cannot be held to show that this is time. Time is a hypothetical measurement by man, relatively and physically too, while it is only a concept with reference to many hypothetical matters especially his physical body which undergoes changes every other second—change towards deterioration, change to meet the end, having had the beginning. Time as a measurement is accepted universally for the benefit of mankind. There is no escape from the Time to anyone, whether a saint or a sinner, whether a rich or a pauper, whether intelligent or ignorant, whether animate or inanimate. However, everyone is ignorant as to when the time meets the end.

In a way time is timeless, it is eternal. Eternity is the reality with different facets of physical formation. Concept of time is both physical and metaphysical. Thus, time becomes spiritual too. When a person goes beyond time, there remains neither physical nor metaphysical concepts and there remains nothing. 'Nothingness' becomes the reality because nothingness lies in ignorance. Ignorance is the ultimate reality and that is the status of real knowledge—the knowledge of 'Not-Knowingness'. That is the knowledge—not knowing anything about anything. That is self-realization, as I feel and also may be God realization, for God is only a concept of conditioned mind. We are all conditioned. Man, due to his so called intelligence conditions himself creating a barrier around him, making himself a prisoner of his own concepts of God, spirituality, religion, nation, region, caste, creed etc. including all rituals, sociological, economical etc. with self-hypnotized auto-suggestions to reach the so called goal, which he has hypothetically set for himself and start walking on that pathless path; while in reality there is neither anything to reach, nor a path, nor any other process of reaching. The fact is there is neither coming, nor going, nor reaching. The whole process is hypothetical—a show, a process for others consumption, the process is to take the gullible people for a ride and snatch their valet. Money is the ultimate goal of most of the so called spiritualists, to grab the money of others but not to earn it. This is not a pessimistic view, but the reality. We fall into the trap of the so called spiritualists, the trap of sweet and moral words, trap of false assurance of taking us to God, while as I said before, there is neither the process of reaching nor the reachable. Everything is here and now. Reaching is in future. Reached is the past. So, if I am to be called as a reached person, it is in the dead past. While reaching being in the future, it is a hypothetical concept, which in fact does not exist; and present exists either in the dead past memories or in the hypothetical non existing future. Future is a conceptual projection of the similar dead past. Concept is not reality. So, the future is not reality. The reality is-the dead past remain in the present memory. Memory can be wiped out with a slight alteration in the brain matrix which is physical. So, memory in a way is physical. But the reality is—there is neither physical nor the metaphysical world. They exist in the brain matrix of an individual. The reality is, as for me, the total ignorance of everything and I am the totality of all ignorance. That is real me.

—ɯ—

27ᵀʰ MARCH 2005   03 30 A.M.

All reaching, all writing, all knowledge, whether material or metaphysical, all behaviors whether acquired or inherited, make no difference whatsoever to the Reality. The reality being, in spite of all intellectual explanations, all types of interpretations of Vedas, Upanishads, Bible, and any such other holy books, in the end leads to ignorance. As it slowly dawns upon this realization of truth—ignorance becomes, at least to me, the ultimate truth. Any claim of knowledge is merely a conditioned concept by self and thrust upon the individual externally. One can never be sure whether he is a person himself as an individual entity or one of the many billions of animate objects and trillions of functions of the Universe, which are beyond the human definitions of Time, Space and Causations. All causations are the functions of the Universe vibrating at different degrees and at different levels. And these functions are beyond the human intellectual concepts. There are no dualities in the function of the Universe. It just functions. It is a futile exercise of human ego to give meanings, definitions and nomenclatures to any or all such functions of the Universe. It is beyond the human intelligence to know what the Universe is, let alone its functions. It is the ego of the man that says he knows God. God is a concept given by the very primitive man and extended to the modern present day so as to run and reach that goalless goal through the pathless path, while there is nothing to reach. It is a mirage escaping at every forward step of a man who is thirsty, creating a hallucination as if it exists at a distance and yet always non-existing while keeping a pace between the man who runs and the mirage itself. While the running is real but reaching is false, because it is a conceptual and never ending one. Man has been running after it and still has not reached and I am afraid that he will never reach and at the same time he will never stop running. However he may try, he cannot reach, for in reality there is nothing to reach though that mirage bacons the man with temptations to fulfill his thirst which is self-imposed and there is no water to quench his thirst, because his thirst is not real thirst, but a self-hypnotized auto suggestion of hypothetically and hypocritically created by the surrounding conditions from outside, percolating hopelessly and helplessly into the inner being of man, creating thirst in him to which man succumbs and ultimately dies disappointedly. Non recognition of mirage and to stop running and to close the eyes to such mirages is to reach the reality.

There is neither a door nor any knocking on it nor any person on the other side to open the door. All these phrases are mere words copied from old text and conditioned to that way of thinking. However, since I do not know anything about anything; I have no arguments either with the so called spiritualists, or moralists, or sociologists, or even theists, or atheists or materialists or any one or all of these, by any name.

I am just, 'I am'—a total ignorant person in all matters including of self. This ignorance has created a deep silence in me though I do not participate in anything that goes on around me, though I am required to participate and exhibit all such emotions as a normal person does.

In the end of the physical body, the mind, the occupier of the body, too annihilates and the totality of the personality comes to an end and yet the resultants of all that is secured to form the coming personality of the self.

—⁂—

26ᵀᴴ MARCH 2005   03 30 A.M.

I still fail to understand why one should go through certain rituals, as some do, to know God. The word God is coined, probably, by those who were strong intellectually but weak economically and physically. It is the intellectuals who always desire to be ahead of others that necessitate the creation of God so that they can subjugate others who are otherwise strong. Further these people claim that God can be reached only through them and provided their orders are followed in total.

To me, the relationship between oneself and God is direct irrespective of the quality of oneself economically, sociologically or religiously.

Probably, there have been more killings of mankind on this earth in the name of God and religion than in all wars and disease put together.

However, an individual continues to seek God based on his conditioned concept of living from birth to death. Individual contributes for the search of God through self-hypnotism and auto suggestions extended to mass hypnotism through a particular institution following certain rituals and dogmas. Man becomes helpless and surrenders to such institutional setups. Man is totally a helpless individual so far as the God is concerned. Helplessness is the only inevitable path that he has to tread and in the end only helplessness, disappointment, dejection set in. So, the expectations of reaching turns to be a false one, promised by hallow and shallow words, though sweet and convincing in which the very same persons who preach may not believe themselves. When I too walked on such paths, somewhere along the line I stopped and came to a definite conclusion that however I may try and whatever I may do I can never ever know the path to reach the unknown and the unknowable. All paths are unknowable or there are no paths at all since there is no goal to reach the Unknown and Unknowable. Unknown remain to be unknown. Slowly and surely the ignorance started firmly setting in and I became completely convinced in the firm knowledge that I have reached a point of reality of my ignorance and I can never understand anything about anything and at any time neither did I understand during the earlier days. What all I had the knowledge about my knowing was only a sham, a shallow and a hallow one and was ego-centric. This self-ego, an entity called me, should die for the entirety and the totality of the Universal function. Even the entire Universal function is unknown and not understood. Nobody can say as to why it functions in the way it does. Every individual with some conditioned theory can come to his own conclusion and he has that right to himself. Earlier I used to feel that if the unknown is not known life had no living. I then thought that even if the entirety of oneself is completely destroyed on the way to know the unknown, it was worth it. And yet ignorance cannot be overcome and it becomes reality, at least to me. In place of 'Me' ignorance occupies, rather 'Me' becomes the very ignorance itself. Let me not pass on my ignorance to others. Let them be comfortable in their self induced comfort of their own created opium like knowledge. Let me be in my comfort zone of ignorance.

—m—

25TH MARCH 2005   03 30 A.M.

What life is? I don't know. The entire function of the entire Universe is one totality of life. Everything seems to be dynamic for it contains in itself the same energy with which the Universe functions. This energy is dynamic, throbbing, palpitating, breathing, and functioning beyond the human perception. Man is an infinitesimal part of the entire human race which is almost of a one-millionth second in the vast timelessness of the eternity. There is an urge to know, to understand, to experience the entire function of the entire Universe. I want to know the beyond, the desire and the urge is very strong and real,—to know what it is after the physical end? To conquer the beyond? Only when the mental attachment with this physical body-though it is natural for the body to desire eternity-vanishes, then probably, the fear of death vanishes too and there occupies the real urge to know and to behold the experience of after death. That urge to know is beyond my control. Somehow, my definiteness is becoming stronger, I feel, the eternity of myself and I do not fear the death for there is no death to me, while there had not been any birth at all. The process of life is beginning-less and endless. I feel the strong surety of my deathlessness yet I have no knowledge either of the past, or of the future and equally about the present. From eternity to eternity I am there, I feel. Somehow it looks that I belong to that 'out-there' and not to 'in-here'. It looks I am in constant move from galaxy to galaxy from one part of the eternal Universe to the other part while the one I have visited last must have moved out to another sphere far away. The one I visited last looks new on my next visit. Each time my visit to each sphere looks new. Nothing old stays back. Change is a constant phenomenon of the Universe in its functions while 'I' remain the same old eternal being without any change, without any birth or death. I am just 'I am', witnessing myself as one constant source of that Central Cosmic energy and yet functioning in a separate manner altogether different from any of the functions of the Universe. I feel 'I am' both constancy and consistency too. My visits are 'out there' does not require any medium unlike my visits to different places on the surface of this earth. My visits 'out there' are devoid of any wants and desires. Wants and desires arise due to physical requirements through which my visits on the earth are fulfilled. While 'out there' being non-physical there are no wants and desires. No such things are known there. The visit 'out there' is ethereal and by the soul unlike the physical here. As wants and desires are physical, so the fear also is physical. Absence of physical fear will surely be in the absence of wants and desires. However, man exists through his physical body and is bound by one of the most important dimensions-time. All physical, whether animate or inanimate objects, are bound by this dimension of time inevitably. None can escape time physically. Having realized my-self the reality of my physical existence, there comes a moment as to whether this physical existence was/is worth its existence. Though the physical body is intricately woven to each other part but holding the whole as one and still some parts of the body deteriorating more rapidly than others. And when more parts deteriorate more rapidly, then the whole deteriorates rapidly too and as a person realizes this rapid deterioration of his physical body, he does realizes of his unworthiness of his physical existence. Then all his knowledge converts itself into nothingness. Nothingness arises out of ignorance. Nothingness has no desires or wants or has no known or unknown fears. Nothingness is really the bliss and the life itself.

01ˢᵀ MARCH 2005   03 30 A.M.

All wishes are just dreams, since nothing seems to bring any contentment. If one wish is fulfilled another crops up very fast. In the process lot many falls-out and in these fall-outs man sees himself as a failure without counting those which are fulfilled. Man's life moves round and round to achieve something which he feels it cannot be achieved. When achieved he is disappointed and unsatisfied. One after another desire queues-up with no end. His life is full of disappointment and he lives to achieve his desires which are almost like mirage in a desert.

—ɯɯ—

02ᴺᴰ FEBRUARY 2005   04 00 A.M

Somehow there is discontentment, some agitation of mind, something wanting, something vacant within me and I am short of it. I want something beyond reading, beyond any rituals, beyond attending Ashrams etc. even on an auspicious day like the one of yesterday—Sri. *Swami Vivekananda's* 142ⁿᵈ birthday celebrated at RK Ashram. While this happens, I don't know why nothing interests me. Nothing brings either happiness or sorrow and yet something is wanted. What that something is I don't know. Not money, not physical, not mental pleasures, but something beyond this world. I want to touch the entire Universe with my inner being. I want to hold the whole Universe within me. Contain myself in the Universe. I feel that the entire Universe is mine, selfishly may be. Is it possible to contain the eternal Cosmic Energy within me and me within that energy? Why not this Cosmic Energy touch my soul and metamorphosis it?. I want this to happen at the earliest. I am restless for this to happen to me. I want that Cosmic Energy to assure me that when once it touches my inner being it becomes a part of me and I a part of that. Is it possible for this to happen? I don't know. However, I want this to happen to me. I long for it and crave for it to happen. I am restless. I want that lightning to strike my very inner core and transform me completely. This restlessness of me has no meaning to others. But to me it is important that it should happen. Will it happen? It is a matter of its own decision. Many in the past and may be many in the present might be craving much more than me and still it might not have touched them at all. I am not worried about others but about my own self and I am sure before long it happens to me. I want it to happen to me, as desperately as I want a breath of air when my mouth and nose are sealed. So badly, so urgently I need it. Will I get it? Sure, it has to.

03ʳᵈ FEBRUARY 2005   02 30 A.M

What truth is? Is it not the other face of the false—a duality? So, truth can be brought within the limited understanding of falsity, or is it different? Truth by itself has no nomenclature. It is the human tendency to give nomenclature to anything and everything that which is palatable to him, whether physically or mentally or emotionally; and that which goes against any of these as a lie, morbid, and immoral etc. In the absolute sense there is neither truth nor untruth. 'It just is' and nobody knows, at least I do not know, what 'it' is. If somebody claims that he knows 'it', he, to me at least, may know only one facet of 'it' out of billions of facets 'it' has since it is dynamic and always in movement, changing with its inbuilt unpredictable qualities, for the limited human mind and intelligence to capture. If a bolt is capable of having certain intelligence, it is like that bolt trying to understand the entire, huge complicated and dynamic machine, claiming itself as all knowledgeable, though without that small and insignificant bolt the entire machine is not complete and sometimes the function of the entire huge machine may come to a stop for want of this insignificant bolt. To me knowledge dawns when I know that 'I can never know'; when I realize that 'I can never realize'; when I know that 'nothing can ever be known about anything'. All talks of God are conceptual and limited, however and in whatever the manner I may project myself. Slowly but surely and truthfully I have realized that I can never ever know anything about anything and what I claim to know is only my ignorance. Ignorance is truth and reality. It is of after long years of contemplation, meditation that I came to a definite conclusion that I 'can never know anything about anything'; and what all I claimed till now that I was knowing was only my ego-projection of knowledge and it was purely for the consumption of others when I either opened my mouth or my pen; but deep within, I know that I know nothing about the Cosmic functioning of that Universal energy. What I claim today, I myself may disclaim it tomorrow; because it is beyond the human perception, ever changing unpredictable; and that might be its nature, who knows. The result of this ignorance is, that I am subdued, I became calm, silent and smiling at myself because I am incapable of any opinion and stand still with awe and aghast feelings at the Cosmic functioning of the Univers

29ᵀᴴ January 2005   03 30 a.m.

Everything from God downwards to a dog is subject to human fancy. God can be twisted, stretched, condensed, wetted, dried and burnt to any shape by anybody to his / her fancy while the dog can never be done so. The commodity of God is available in plenty and perennially in whatever form and content a man needs and always at any place and without reservations for all purposes from a pauper to a prince, from a sinner to a saint. From birth to death and even after death the name of God is taken. And yet the mystery and the most wonderful part of God is, that He is not seen by or known by anyone. He is elusive, slippery, unfound, unrecognized but ove-r valued and placed at a very high pedestal, for the very reason of his unavailability. God is not a consumer but He is consumed by one and all in all shades and shapes and quantity and quality; yet everyone, at least I am, is ignorant about Him. Thus God is the total ignorance of man.

—ɯ—

27ᵀᴴ January 2005   03 30 a.m.

There is a rat-race on the pathless path to reach the goal-less goal—the God. God is a hyped word for the mad to run after. Some people let loose the race for their material benefits. Everything they do will be, mostly, in the name of God. God being only a conceptual word, irrational, without authentically tested to prove his presence of existence, they always create the race. This race has commenced, probably, when human beings came into existence on the surface of the earth and will continue till the entire existence is wiped out. As long as man exists, God too exists; but only in the mind of man, which is continuously implanted by the successive generation so that the man can be controlled and made to fall in line of these concepts, lest he becomes a rebel in finding this conceptual God by himself without any external help. It is more than five decades since I have been running this race to ultimately realize that I have never understood either the race or the path or the goal itself. I think, in reality, none have understood any of these; though some claim through many examples of their arriving at the goal. May be they have arrived at to one of the billions of facets of this Cosmic Energy's function and they had the light touch of it for a fraction of a second and afterwards claiming that they had the experience of arriving at the entirety of the central point of Cosmic Energy. I know that I cannot go nearer even to a fraction of one facet, let alone entirety of it. When-so, how could I claim that 'I know'? I know that I know nothing about anything. It is sure and it is also a reality that I have finally arrived at by myself to the greatness of complete ignorance and nothingness. With this arriving at the conclusiveness of ignorance and nothingness, I am loosing myself, for what all I thought I knew were only shams, were only egoistic projections of the so called knowledge but in reality I now know that I knew neither then nor do I know now. I know nothing and nothing could be known in the future in spite of every type of somersaulting of my intellect or knowledge. They were only my egos on the thin surface of the ocean depth of knowledge. But now deep down in me, I know that I knew nothing though it looked that I knew everything. Slowly and surely this physical body is deteriorating and one day it will come to a final halt. Then what? Nothingness will be the finality. Then what happens to me; if at all there is a separate entity called 'ME'? Is it possible to separate 'ME' from my physical body? Is 'ME' to be known only when the physical body is existing? Is not this physical body the one and the only instrument through which 'ME' is reflected? Is this 'ME' perpetuates without this physical body? These are hypothetical questions, which in fact, have no answers. Whether these questions have any base for the answers to follow? I can't say. I am ignorant of everything as such. I am a movement from one moment to another in this vast eternal function of the entire Universe. The Universe functions under its own Cosmic Laws with different degrees under different levels and at different times. Whether time acts as an agent for the Universal function or is it once again a conceptual hypothetical dimension created by man for its own functioning? Man functions within the ambit of Universe's function. So he created time, space and causations, while the Cosmic functions may be beyond these three dimensions, rather devoid of all dimensions created by man.

In the process of advancement both in age and knowledge it has dawned upon me that one can never understand anything of anything. Ignorance as knowledge comes to a man at the fag end of his physical existence and he becomes a ZERO in all aspects of his life so far led by him. Finally arriving at this knowledge of his ignorance, he surrenders himself to the unknown who might be the ultimate knowledge; and further moves on to further destiny of his physical body stops functioning. Man is just a happening in the order of the Universal function, though a part of it, without whom the Universe is incomplete.

—⚏—

26ᵀᴴ JANUARY 2005   04 00 A.M.

Is God an aberration of human race? From the moment the human race began, probably, the word God too must have been implanted in men, but it is only a concept surrounded with mystery, elusive, unknown, inexplicable, un-understandable and yet most desirable, most wanted above everything else. Under different names of God, men have inflicted most treacherous acts of killing other men. Killing of men by men in the name of God has far exceeded all other killings under wars and diseases, yet God never came either to save those who were killed or to punish those killers who killed in the name of God. What a dangerous concept it is—the word God. Is not God a social problem? So that the society being made to follow certain morals for the peaceful existence of the entire animate and inanimate objects. I feel the unknown always causes fear. So the God being unknown is the most feared of all fears, for it is said He may cause and inflict physical injury and mental agony even to the strong in order that the weak too can survive peacefully within their limitations, especially when the word God is kept in the forefront of the man's functions. Man having not known himself, can never know or understand God. For, God is only the human coinage. Man has brain-washed himself which brought certain chemical changes in his brain matrix and a type of stupor and it is said that such a stupor can be arrived at immediately if one takes drugs like LSD, Brown sugar etc. Maybe, I don't know.

—ɯ—

22ᴺᴰ JANUARY 2005   03 30 A.M.

Somewhere along the line of living, rather existing, man drops many things and equally picks up a lot many things. Probably, at the evening of his life he wants the night to arrive quickly and wants to be done away with his existence. He is tired, wasted and desires for the quick end so as to lead a new and fresh life, if at all such a thing has to come to him. Though he knows nothing about 'after', he still needs the hastening of his evenings. It is not pessimism of the present or the optimism of the future. Future is only a projection of the past. Future exists only hypothetically in the concept of time. Sleep he needs. A peaceful, deep, silent sleep to get rid of everything he wasted in his so called life. Life, without knowing that and which he intensely desired to know, he feels, is wasted. But, for sure, he will never come to know for there may not be anything to know at all. It is the conditioned conceptual mind from the primitive human race that creates the wanting to know the eternal. Eternity too is a dual concept of time. Time being a hypothetical one, eternity too is a hypothetical one. There is deep dissatisfaction, deep wanting, intense requirements to know something than what all have been known and what all that can be known. To be in the old physical form, which is deteriorating day by day, is a heavy burden to one-self. The self is an entity. That entity being he, he somehow desires to discard his physical form though without which he can never come into existence. The physical form is only a media, an instrument through which the entity of self is expressed. However, this instrument is not the self-entity. Both are separate, yet, both are supplementary and complementary to each other as both require each other to express the functions of each other in totality. One cannot function without the other independently.

—⁓—

20ᵀᴴ JANUARY 2005   04 00 A.M.

Nothing satisfies me. Something is wanted. I feel empty and wasted. Something is still to be fulfilled. What that something is? I don't know. Time is slipping away. I need to know to realize, to be permanently with that point of Central Cosmic energy—the so called God. Is there a God? I don't know. Even if He is there, is it necessary to know Him to be with Him? Some type of lethargy grips me from within and finally I 'let-go' the things. Nothing seems to be important, even God sometimes seems to be of no importance. Do I need any external help to reach God? I feel nobody can help me; rather they would help themselves if I go to them. Slowly, but surely my life is ebbing away, going down listlessly without any mark left behind, like writing on the surface of water I become and go to oblivion of the Universe. Universe functions in-spite of my not being there rather anybody not being there. Even without the entire human race. In the functioning of the Universe I am a grain of sand on the vast shore of the Universe's sea; and yet it does make difference of the absence of that one small grain of sand, for the Universe is not complete without it. Probably, I have given too much importance to myself. But now I have to 'let-go' of everything. What is it that I want ultimately? I am a non-realized person. Is there anything to realize? Nothing seems to me to be so; because ignorance is coming to settle permanently with me. I am aware of that ignorance. Not knowingness is the state of my being. Whatever I may do, however I may try, whatever method I may adopt, nothing matters. Nothing happens. Ignorance prevails strongly from within. As the Universe is functioning so this body too, according to the laws of each, which I am ignorant of. I can never understand anything either of this Universe or of my own physical body. My physical body is slowing down in its function which is also a part of the entire function. Is there anything beyond, yonder? I don't know. With the end of this physical body do this 'I' too come to an end? I don't know. I don't know what is in store for this physical body to go through to reach its end. Let me close this for now, since I am an ignorant man not knowing anything about anything but still crazy to know something but what that something is? I don't know. I feel that I am completely empty from within. However this emptiness satisfies me in a way I feel complete with this emptiness. Emptiness and nothingness, probably, are the ultimate. In nothingness I see the eternal silence and in nothingness I feel everything. To me nothingness is the reality.

—⧓—

18ᵀᴴ JANUARY 2005   05 00 A.M.

The miracles of all miracles is the word—God. God, to me is a mystery, elusive, unseen, and un-known. Even feeling about God from within requires some sort of mental status. Is that mental status created through some subtle thought that would pave the way to the pathless path towards goalless goal—the God? Is there a God of human concept? Is the human concept of God derived from the scriptures, holy texts and from the words of the so called god-men? Is such a God, a reality? What reality is? I can't say. Yet, I strive to know because I am conditioned to aspire for the Reality. I have been, without my knowledge, drawn to this dual thought of two entities, myself and the God. Is not the entire Universe, known and un-known to the man, is the functioning of the Cosmic Energy? Energy, irrespective of through which medium it functions, is nothing but the Cosmic Energy itself and it is very dynamic and eternally functioning at different degrees and at different levels according to the capacity of the medium of its function. Physical body of a man has its own limitations and the Cosmic Energy has to function in that limitation or otherwise either the body will not function or it may be burnt out. It is the same Cosmic Energy that functions in all animate and inanimate objects of the entire Universe, both seen and unseen. As such that which is beyond human intelligence is stamped as a mystery. God becomes a mystery, because He is elusive and beyond the limited intelligence of man. God cannot be a personal property of any individual or of any institution. God cannot be individualized or institutionalized but at the same time God is the personal property of every individual, though not of every institution. In spite of conditioned hypothetical and hypocritical claims that only a certain type of following leads to God, which is a tall claim, while every individual can directly commune, in his own way, with that point of central Cosmic Energy. If a man tries to seek help from outside then the trouble starts, for he will be lead to the path of that person and in the end this individual looses his path. But, irrespective of what path he lays to himself, if at all any, man can travel in his own path and seek his destiny. For that matter there is no ultimate destiny at all. It is an eternal process of creation. There is no individual entity functioning apart from the totality of the entire cosmic function. It is foolhardy to struggle to be an individual entity. 'Just be', is all that I feel, is the reality of the function of the individual entity. Externally, socially, culturally, economically I might be functioning in the eyes of others, but internally I am just 'just be' without being a separate entity. When the realization of ignorance and 'just be' are authentically realized, nothing matters. All fears of every kind evaporate, including the fear of death, which is fear of all fears. What is this 'just being'? It is the original pure status of man without any external influences. Like a child surrendering to all the happenings, be a witness to your own self's happenings and then the ignorance and nothingness pervades your whole being

And that is the ultimate Reality

—m—

15ᵀᴴ JANUARY 2005   04 00 A.M.

The entire human race accepts the elusive God by whatever name or form one may contemplate. Even the so called rationalist and atheist will somewhere in the corner of his being, is afraid of God, who he thinks may bring bad things in his life if he condemns God. God is eternal in the minds of human race, for God is elusive, cannot authentically be proved, nor can be shown, nor can be held to say that 'this is God'. God is a concept conditioned by the social and religious beliefs. And yet, the entire cosmic force having, may be, a central controlling point, controlling the entire Universe and its functions according to the Cosmic Laws which man can never understand. The more deep a man goes in these aspects, the more realization of his ignorance dawns upon him. While ignorance is the ultimate truth he can never arrive at the reality of the Cosmic Energy. The reality is his helpless ignorance. Not knowing anything about anything in-spite of his tall claims of the so called God realization. Maybe, he sees only a fraction of a small facet of the God while there may be billions of different facets. No one facet can resemble other. When-so, how can a man claim that he knows God in totality? Can a man understand the entirety and the totality of the Universal function from the speck of dust on a sand grain to a black-hole, which, it is said, gulps more than three hundred suns, (as reported by NASA in January 2005) and billions of light years away? God must be much more powerful than such incidents, for it is only another facet of the Universe's function, from a small wave of breeze on the face of a man, which are of different degrees while the function of the Universe at different level of variations in degrees, but maybe of the same kind. So, a person who says that he has realized God may have experienced a fraction of a small facet of the central Universal Cosmic Energy and maybe such different persons might have had the experience of different degrees, though it may look to vary from each person, for that energy being dynamic varying at every movement and moment and as such no two persons experiences would be the same and for that matter the experiences of the same person at different times would not be the same. When emptiness prevails the Cosmic Energy rushes in, because the energy of the physical thoughts and the Cosmic Pure Energy cannot be together. The thoughtless state is a state of being in emptiness which only comes back as a memory subsequently, but when one is in that state of thoughtlessness one cannot be aware of it. If he becomes aware of it, it could only be through subtle thought and irrespective of whether that thought is subtle or gross, the Cosmic Energy passes out.

Ultimately nothing could be understood. All methods, to understand, go in vain, for it has no path. It strikes a person who may be chosen randomly by it with no background or preconceived qualification to strike. But every human being craves for that glimpse of Cosmic Energy and holds that energy to him-self, though he may not know the purpose as such. His desire to hold that energy is created by those who claim that they have it and that to have it one has to follow him and go through the path laid down by him. Each institution sells only the word of God (but not God himself) because God cannot be sold, as He is not a limited commodity mandating that particular institution to sell Him. He is not to be bartered. He is always available freely and in abundance to anyone and everyone who has the capacity to receive Him. No words, no holy texts, no rituals, or any institution can sell God, as some institutions do. God requires no raw materials to manufacture but these institutions through mass hypnotization with sweet and emotional talks pushes these persons to almost insanity. Slowly God becomes a costly commodity while in the beginning he was given a little taste of Him only through words, only as a complementary one, to hold and control in sway the entire mass of followers. Selling God does not require any investment. Only if the skill of words and control over the language, interpreting, quoting (mostly ends in misinterpreting and misquoting) without understanding and experiencing themselves, in reality, of God. The reality to me is my arriving before the eternal wall of IGNORANCE.

If I am to be taken as an entity, it is a mystery as to why should I be born with the type of the physical body I have, with the type of the mental dispositions I possess, both acquired and inherited, and also the inclinations towards the conditioned concepts I have, though I know nothing of these things. First of all, I don't know whether I am an entity or a part of the whole. If I am a part, then I have no body, mind or spirit of my own, but I am only a process of function along with the function of the Universe and as such everything, every action and every thought is not separate to me but a part of the Universal function. Then, there is no 'I' at all. I, material, metaphysical, past, present and future etc including God becomes illusory. Then 'Nothingness' comes to prevail. Nothingness is the real knowledge. When this knowledge of nothingness strikes you, you become calm, silent and in a way enter into a stage of coma and yet always aware of the physical world. This probably is the ultimate stage of reality. In spite of this realization and arriving at with full conviction, man's mind craves for something different, things that something must still to be attained, for the mind can never stop at anything. It is this mind that has to be taken to nothingness and once the mind becomes nothingness itself, then the entire Universal knowledge enlightens.

—⟋𝔪⟍—

04TH DECEMBER 2004   04 00 A.M.

Ageing is a natural phenomenon for the physical body to, slowly but surely, deteriorate and also pick up diseases on its way to the final day. I feel the same about this body, but still I feel the permanency of 'ME' and shun the fear of death. It looks that I am eternally going to live although I know nothing whether I had any past life—the life I came through to this life. What is it that gives self-confidence to my eternal living? In spite of everything, 'I' from within says that I should live this present life eternally, which is impossible, as I know. But at the same time what holds me in the 'life-after' and is there any? I do not know.

Of late nothing interests me even books which I had read with so much of such intensity, no more interests me. To some extent even the God does not interest me. All institutions, all god-men, all other persons, all materials, everything, have no sway in my life, as they did earlier. Even the death has no influence on me. I have become calm within and nothing moves me and yet a feeble voice, somewhere in the remote corner, within me, says that I need to know more about the mystery of the Universe, the Cosmic Energy and their functions and I desire with all intensity at my command to know, to understand and to become a part of the Cosmic Energy and the functioning of this Universe. I want to contain, hold to myself the entire Universe in my fist. I want to become the very force itself. And yet, they stand as mysterious entities to me. I know that force may not strike me but I want that to strike me and destroy my present being and convert me to be a separate entity for all times to come. It could only be a wishful thinking. Everything is a wishful thinking. Only a wishful thinking makes a man to pull on, is a sort of intoxicating substance and a subsisting factor for a man to anchor on. Some hope, even in the last minute, that somehow somebody, some force would bring back him to his original life is the fundamental force in a man to survive the vagaries of the human race. He desires the power to hold the entire Universe in his fists, is one of the basic instinct of every human being. I would, on the contrary, want to merge with that central Cosmic Energy which holds the whole Universe in balance. I desire to be that energy itself without being a separate entity of myself. I want that energy to strike me with all its force and in the process this body may be burnt to ashes. It is fine with me as long as that Cosmic Energy is going to be with me and I become that energy to eternity.

—ɯ—

13ᵀᴴ NOVEMBER 2004   03 00 A.M.

Is there a way out from all questions of God which are raised from the time immemorial? I am afraid not. The simple way out would be to eliminate the concept of God itself. The concept exists, but not the God; for sure no one knows whether such an entity like God exists or not. Even if exists, how does that matter to any individual? Has then God failed? I am afraid not. But the approach, that is, the concept of God has failed. Man, as far as I am concerned, never, with all his intellectual capacity at his command, can perceive God as He is. For sure, to me, I can never understand anything about anything. I am incapable of understanding or perceiving my own self, when so how can I perceive anything beyond me? Somewhere along the line of this physical life, even when thinking is becoming physical, slowly but surely the concept of understanding, intellectual capacity, the mental vibration etc. start falling; and in their places the strong and authentic knowledge of 'Not knowingness' establishes itself firmly. With this, all acquired knowledge become useless, even of God; and in the end there remains a blank ignorant mind. And then the whole of me becomes empty. This state of emptiness is the Reality. I am a bundle of emptiness. This very 'I' is emptiness. Not knowingness is me. This is my state, the state of being in emptiness. Being in that state, I am not in existence at all. There is no 'I'. 'I' is dead along with the knowledge and so I am already dead and yet I live eternally along with the Central Cosmic Energy.

—m—

26TH OCTOBER 2004   03 30 A.M.

The Universe exists to me because I exist to the Universe. The Universe cannot be a separate entity from me, though I am a very insignificant part of the entire Universe. All my aspirations, desires, want, greed, anger, peace, surrendering attitude, everything, is one bundle of me. And also it is all the projection of Universal Cosmic Energy, which is pure and divine and cannot be measured in the scale of human intelligence. What happens to the Universe when I shed this body? Nothing? But something does happen and yet the Universe functions as if nothing has happened. To me at least, it is the greatest and the most significant happening, the aftermath of this body's annihilation.

Will all the knowledge both material and metaphysical, all experiences acquired, also annihilate along with this physical body? Sure they will, for the simple reason, that these knowledge are physical. However the Cosmic Energy and its vibrations being eternal, they do exist as a part of me. I become, rather I am the very Cosmic Energy though in a way, very insignificant, as a spark of fire is the same as the fire itself with all its qualities and kind, but of different degrees. So I am the same Cosmic Energy in all its qualities and kind but of a different degree. But the mind that is physical is the storehouse of all those experiences I acquired which I go on referring to when I succumb to such desires to refer to and not when I need not refer to. All these references are stored as memories in me, though they seem to be dead, but potentially active kicking me all round and always. I am the sum total of all my experiences stored in my minds memories. So, these memories are the thought waves and I am these memories. As such I live in the dead past. I exist in these memories which are past and dead. My existence is not of myself but of the dead past memories in me. The dead thought of me that I may hypothetically project and call it as future which is nothing but based on the past memories of experiences which are dead and still project as reflections in my own mind. As such, I am the totality of all these experiences of which some are completely erased, some are partially erased and some are fully alive and kicking me from within. So, I live neither in the present nor in the unknown future, but in the dead past. In a way I am already dead, while I have not taken birth but for this physical body since I have neither birth nor death while I am the eternal being along with the Central Cosmic Being.

—ɯ—

03ʳᵈ October 2004   03 30 a.m.

There is no path to go as there is no place to go. Coming and going are just phases and phrases. In reality, at least to me, while the whole Universe is one place beyond time and causations, it is a constant one functioning under its own laws. I really wonder whether I am, 'I am' or 'I am not I am'. What this 'I am' is not comprehensible to myself. In these concepts, fear of death vanishes, calmness and silence engulfs me to my inner most self. Somewhere deep within me a feeble voice says that I am with the entire Cosmic Energy which is one with every function of the Universe. There is no separation between the Universal function and the Cosmic Energy that energizes its function. A type of recluse strongly holds me. I am convinced that I am not what I am externally, but I am that which I am internally. That internal 'I' can never be explained or shown to prove its existence but only felt and become aware of and be one with. A type of 'let-go' occupies me. Deep silence and deep calmness engulfs me. I become the very silence and calmness which has some sort of unique way of bliss and divinity within themselves and happiness with strong homeliness and oneness with the entire Universe comes in. I feel that I am with that One who was always there with me since eons eternally—I as the inner personality and not the external one.

While there is no path whether physical or mental, why not Cosmic path, why not me act as a wireless set to communicate directly with the point of central Cosmic energy with millions of channels connecting to each of the creations, whether animate or inanimate, having only one-way from that Central Cosmic force as regards to all the objects, except human beings who will have two way lane so that man can reach that central point and the energy emanating from there can reach the human being. Only with the two way communication, understanding develops and the recognition is made and slowly the rapport develops and each become one with each other. Thus oneness is established. The switch board, for this two way communication, is human's mind. The channel is the intellect and the energy for the communication comes from the soul, which, in fact, is energized by the Central Cosmic Energy. Thus the soul energy of the human being and the Cosmic Energy become one. This happens when both the paths are open. Then, the identity of each other is established. But how to open it? Take the help of that energy to open the path from your side by switching on your mind then naturally the channel gets opened to reach the destination of the cosmic central force. Sometimes, there is some sort of wave in the mind which just wants to go to deep sleep, even not wanting anything including God. It is just deep sleep without involving the physical body. Something wanting, but not capable of achieving it, makes the mind to go to a deep sleep. Physical body, I feel, is the greatest impediment to this type of deep sleep. It is the physical body that creates all types of wants and desires while deep within one may not desire anything but just be in silent sleep. It just wants to escape from everything including from oneself to reach and be with that 'ultimate nothingness'.

15ᵀᴴ OCTOBER 2004   03 30 A.M.

I bow my inner head with all humiliation at some great divine souls who were on this earth for the good of everything. Who they were, is unknown to me and also there might be some living beings even now without exhibiting their presence while in constant connection with that central Cosmic Energy point, which is the guiding stock, engulfing in very deep silence and calmness which is also timeless, causation-less and space-less but eternal self propelling energy both at micro and macro level of the entire Universe. Into that silence I drown and become that very silence itself. There is no knowledge of self or recognition or self awareness in the realm, but still holding myself to myself lest I cross the border to a point of no return, though it looks to be controversial. At that stage, I am there and also I am not there. How could this be? Because I am a micro Cosmic Energy while that is macro Cosmic Energy. I am with it and I am that itself

21ST SEPTEMBER 2004   04 30 AM

Nobody can run away from death, nor resist it nor fight it to win. Birth is the future death and vice versa—birth of death and death of birth. Birth and death are the obverse and reverse of the same coin—the life. With any one surface defacing makes the coin counterfeit rather valueless. It just remains metal so with the death. The body has no value. Any value of the body can be ascertained only when the 'life is' and not when the life is not when the 'life is not'. To make body more valuable it should have lived valuably too. What this value means? And how it is measured? All measurements are hypothetical and social ones. Even God, spiritualism, philosophy etc—everything is social nothing beyond social values. Social values are conditioned values varying from country to country, state to state, religion to religion, caste to caste, family to family and lastly individual to individual. But at the same time some rigid ones prevail all over the world in some aspects. So conditioning of a human being to a set of values makes him to act within certain frameworks but even the subtle social values condition the same frame of mind—brainwashing of man, which is imbibed in him which he cannot escape till last. At the same time he picks up some of the values as he grows up in the society which the society offers to him, some social values are compulsorily conditioned and some are optionally conditioned. So the values are basically conditioned whether they are compulsory or optional ones. There is no escape from these conditioned values. In these conditions probably man finds the values of his own life—rather hallucinates himself, conns himself by auto suggestions of these conditioned values. Even the dead body has the conditioned values imposed by the living. Even the memory of the dead are conditioned. And to achieve these values man succumbs himself and in the process he looses his individual values as an entity. In the abstract sense there is no such a thing as individual entity. He is born, lives and dies, in the process of Universal function which he never comprehends or understands that he is the part of the entire Universal function. Ultimately, to me at least, there is neither birth, nor life, nor death in the process of Universal function. It is just a movement from moment to moment to eternity. In everything, in every moment the Universe functions to eternity and also to infinity though they are once again concepts of conditioned mind which in fact are not understood. They are simply projections of universally accepted concepts—hypothetical ones and some are hypocritical too. So values remain concept of the society, to aspire for anything beyond is like a blind man searching for a grain of black pepper in a vast and darkest midnight of a new moon day who, in fact, is ME.

Any person can sell God to gullible public. God being an immeasurable commodity which also slips away and at the same time needed by everyone, snubbing the egoists, making a man humble and docile. It is invisible yet can be attributed to all kinds of flattery, perennial and nonexpendable but expandable. Only thing a person needs is the capacity to conn people, take people for a ride, brain wash them all through with sweet and mesmeric words showing calmness and control and in the process build the so called spiritual empire and run it as an industry without raw materials, without machinery, without labor and without capital investment. It is a one way road to richness. It has no set of rules or subtle way to put forth, irrational, illogical for there is nothing to prove God's existence and still go on saying God is there. Words about God can make people fall in line. People become almost slaves to a person who holds talk of God, as if he is the possessor of God.

—m—

13TH SEPTEMBER 2004   05 00 A.M.

There is no 'you'. When once 'I', 'you', 'he' is expressed, then separation comes in, while the entire Universe is one containing from a microbe, a speck of dust on a grain of sand to vastness of the entire Universe and seems to me to be the one that is functioning at different levels proportionate to each to its capacity. What it looks to be a dysfunction is also a function so with the destruction according to the laws of the Universe; which we mundane human beings with conditioned concepts and limited intelligence cannot comprehend, cannot understand, cannot experience. Universe functions on the self-propelled eternal Cosmic Energy. Every thought, subtle feelings in me come from the waves of Cosmic Energy. I am the expression of the same Cosmic Energy as a grain of sand is, which I cannot understand but has the audacity, the hypocritical superiority to look down on every, so called, inferior functioning, though the human functioning is not, in any way, superior to the functioning of an insect. Everything functions as it is created with the expression of the same Cosmic Energy as I or any great saint is, but at different levels of expression.

When I think on these lines, I love the whole Universe, my conscious expands to the whole of Universe and I become one with the Universe as if I am with the Universe in its eternity. I hold in my bosom the entire Universe with all love at my command. Then I submerge into the ocean of Cosmic Energy and lose my individuality, which in fact, there is no such a thing as individual at that level of function and yet I do not understand anything of this Universe. It looks as if it was only yesterday that I was a five years old boy in first standard, but now nearing to the evening hours of life of this physical body. The value we conceive, we perceive, we conceptualize, we imagine are quite different from the value the Universe measures. Everything is equally important in the function of the Universe. When realized a deep humiliation occupies the whole of me and my personality just melts away, evaporates and merges with the ether of the Universe. How come do I feel the intimation with all the different spheres of the entire Universe from eternity where, time, space and causations no more exist? Conversation by a deep silence and understanding, a deep loving and respecting feelings are exchanged between me and all these spheres of the Universe. Silence, a blissful silence, is the divine talk at this level of these spheres. I feel, I know them and they know me from eternity. We accept each other with love and regards. This is something unique, something inexpressible, something deeply committed with no iota of doubt between us. There is that mutual love, mutual understanding, mutual respect to each other between me and every part of the entire Universe, unknown to others. There is no knowledge of birth, life and death at this level. I stay above all the dualities for I am eternal going through phases of functions of the Universe from eternity to eternity. Timelessness is eternity, space-less-ness is eternity and causation-less-ness is eternity and in this eternity 'I' has no separate entity but is the very Universal Cosmic function itself in its totality and entirety. In this function though 'I' is lost, but there remains certain consciousness of this Cosmic Universe including its own self and that is 'ME' and also that is IT.

12TH SEPTEMBER 2004   03 30 A.M.

What is this living' ME'? I am dynamic and active not static. Where from this living energy comes? How come I am not aware of it? Which is that 'instrument' through which I am aware of myself?. Is it possible for myself to be aware of myself? He who is aware has the knowledge of his own awareness. So, the awaree, the one who is aware, and the awareness are the same. There is no separate instrument through which this awareness is aware. It is self propelling knowledge that comes from 'with-in' while the 'with-out' too has the same potential energy. It is the same Cosmic Energy that is one in both from 'with-in' and 'with-out'. But still it becomes a mystery, an aghast wonder to me because with this limited 'ME' is it possible to know and understand the 'INFINITE THAT'. Is there 'THAT' which has separate qualities than this 'ME'? I don't know. I can only project the conditioned comprehension of 'THAT, while 'THAT' may be different or may not be different in existence as separate entity, as this 'ME' imagines. Yet, somehow deep within some gut feelings whispers to me, that this 'ME' is as eternal as 'THAT' and the physical body of 'ME' is a kind of function of 'ME' at a different level in as much as a tree or a rock functions. Everything is dynamic though some seems to be static. That which looks externally static is in fact internally dynamic since the atoms of that object are held together and bonded to each other to have the shape and form. In a way I feel that I am a part of this whole and the whole is the totality of all functions of every part and it is the Cosmic Energy that runs through every part of it to make it dynamic and at the same time a make-believe static.

I fly (astral travel) to different regions, beyond our Solar systems, of the Universe and I feel that I know all these regions from yore and eons. They feel one with me and so do I. I am not a stranger to any of these regions or any of the functions of the Universe, but yet sometimes I become a stranger to 'myself'. Sometimes, I feel that friendliness or oneness even with volcanoes, the lava, the strange silence at the tip of the Everest, I dive into the very center of the Sun and come out in seconds to another sphere and after traveling through many spheres at different levels I come back to this physical body to assume the same old self. I look different to myself which has no meaning to others. I am a strange person from within to myself though externally I am the same as others.

—⁂—

07ᵀᴴ September 2004   04 00 AM

Nothing, nothing explains as to why should I be born at all; and born to a particular parentage, in a particular country, particular caste, religion and above all as a male; thereby conditioned in every aspect. Is there any freedom from birth and thus freedom from death too? What is birth? To some extent one can know what it is after birth, but no-one knows what it is after death. This unknowingness creates fear. Fear creates God, once again an unknown. In spite of long years of existence, hearing a lot of different opinions from many sources, from different religions about God, still there is no way of knowing God. Everything that states about God is only a hear-say, theoretical, conceptual talk, bookish, beyond understanding and experiencing. Somehow, all that one holds while in youth-full days with madness to find the reality of God just evaporates as the days pass on to old age. Is God a storekeeper in stock of every desired fulfillment as goodies? Would I step out of life without experiencing what God is? Maybe, for a very few-infinitesimally-few in the whole of human history, probably, an iota of God might have been revealed. But, maybe, it was their mental aberration, a hallucination or self-hypnotism that they felt they had crossed the border of sanity to find God. But no one can know how they were in their inner mental attitudes and how they function internally at that point of time after crossing the border. Expression by words of their experience is only for the consumption of gullibly person like me in the end. I end up not knowing anything about anything. Probably, to me, the reality is that I know nothing about anything. I feel in spite of this nothingness, that I do belong to the entire Universe and I am the owner in enjoyment of the entire Universe, though it is beyond the understanding for some others, and to some extent even to me. This feeling arise within me for a few moments, that I belong to the whole Universe and the whole Universe belongs to me. We are not strangers to each other rather I become the entire Universe itself as if I am holding the entire Universe within my very core of bosom. When such an experience is experienced, fear of death runs away from me, for, I feel, that there is neither birth nor death but only eternal existence beyond the fear of mundane span of physical existence. The entire Universe, I feel, is only a handful of physical functions of its own. I grow within, far, far bigger than the Universe itself. All conditions melt away and nothing binds me. There is an awareness of me growing the biggest within me, and that power, that energy flows both from within and without. It runs into me, manifests itself and goes out to the Universe. All desires dry up, look meaningless, for they are unworthy. There remains neither the fear of God nor the fear of devil-the fear itself being the devil. My consciousness awakes to the Universal consciousness within me and I am the very Universe itself which functions on its own without any influence on me and I let allow the Universe to function according to its natural laws. I do not question its functions. Rather I see that its functions are in friendliness with me, for I see my own reflection, of my awareness, of my own self in those functions. I feel the perfect understanding between me and the functions of the Universe. We love, respect and understand each other. I feel that I am more important as, rather more important than the function of the Universe, since I occupy the entire Universe and the Universe is held by me within and at the same time it is also functioning outside me. We look to be the only two entities and of the two I feel I am more powerful, but with respects and regards to each other. Neither do I do anything nor does the universe do anything adversely. We go hand in hand and nothing separates us, for there is nothing other than we two in eternal existence, for I am the Universe and the Universe is me. We are always there eternally together inseparably.

—⟋⟍—

10ᵀᴴ AUGUST 2004   04 00 A.M.

Somehow, it is slowly but surely crawling into me that I am not an individual but a part of the entire Universe and my 'self' is not a separate entity but a part of the 'whole'—which, in fact, is beyond my knowledge to know what that 'whole' is? 'I', if it is be so called, is being destroyed and zeroing on to 'nothingness' and to 'knowledge-less-ness'. I am becoming blank except to know about the knowledge of physical needs of hunger, thirst, sleep and sometimes anger too-which is only a momentary one. Why this is happening? I know not. There is no 'I'. It is some sort of 'let-go' emotion or is this 'I' ebbing away to 'nothingness'? Emotions are drying up and yet I work, give legal consultations with no desire what-so-ever.

There is neither fear of death nor desire to continue with this physical body, and still when physical pain comes I take action to correct it. In spite of all this, a deep silence, deep calmness within is engulfing me, and to those readers of this it looks to be false because I do look normal with emotions of anger, laughter, sadness etc. which, in fact, are not making any influence on me as they were doing earlier. I am loosing myself to no-where. Probably, prayers, meditation, calling upon God etc.; are evaporating. All emotions are, to a great extent, running out of my system, though not completely. It is impossible to understand the functions of myself let alone the functions of the Universe. There is neither dynamism nor static-ism. They function in unison. From where this energy for function of the Universe comes or generates, it is impossible to know. How this brain and body work? I do not know. It just functions or so I feel and so I comprehend. Yet, the very function is completely devoid of emotions. Universe functions precisely on its own without any influence or emotions. Emotions are from the human beings against the Universe's natural function

Time, to me, makes no meaning. It is a hypothetical measurement of movement from one point to another in a given space. In abstract there is neither time, nor space, nor cause, nor effect. The entire movement is just a function. Even the function is not, in actuality, the function, but it just 'is'—and what this function is? I do not know. In the end I do not know whether I am functioning or not functioning, whether I am 'is' or 'is not', whether I am aware or in slumber, whether there is anything like 'I' or not. Sometimes I am my own witness to this 'non-existing-I'. When the 'I' is not-existing the witness too is not-existing. And all these thoughts are non-comprehensible, leading to nothingness, because of 'my-own-nothingness'. Neither 'I' is existing nor non-existing. What existing is? I do not know. Existence is a movement from moment to moment. Movement is time and function is time. When time is non-existing, then, movement and functions too are non-existing. In a way everything is 'non-existing'.

—ɷ—

23ʳᵈ July 2004   03 30 a.m.

It becomes difficult to address God who, to me, is still a dream. God is more a word than reality. It is always easy to address an unknown, slippery person, who is only a concept, for He may not read this, let alone giving a reply. When so, one can write anything one wants to. It is more a writing to oneself than to anyone outside. It is a self-hypnotism, an auto suggestion and lastly it is something beyond comprehension of either within my intellectual concept or awareness of consciousness about God. In spite of all such knowledge, I do, somehow, may-be due to have been conditioned from the day of birth by the society, by the culture, by the religion, caste etc; I feel, there is something beyond me which I know not what. And that something is not only beyond but at the same time is a part of me too. I am a part of the entire cosmos and that cosmos too is a part of me. When so, how could I be a separate entity from the entirety, the cosmic energy? I am also energy from the same source, rather the same part of that source, but of lesser degree while the quality being the same. But to make God and me as two separate entities is something not understandable at all to me. This happens because human beings with a little intellectual capacity and ego of knowledge, though limited, go to measure the immeasurable, the eternity, binding all the events to the dimensions of time, space and causations. Intellect creates problems and mind craves for solutions; and when it becomes helpless, because of its limitedness, it ultimately surrenders to the unknown source. Problem Vs solution, pain Vs pressure and all such dualities are just movements of that moment, and that is the universal function. In fact, there are no dualities at all. It is not possible to understand what function 'IS', of this Universe. There is neither the dimension of time, nor space, nor causations of actions, but only functions, which the human measure according to his scale, though a hypothetical one, he derived for his own benefits. Everything is a happening of the Universe and ultimately everything is nothing, and nothing is everything; because none understands anything about anything. And that is the reality for me too.

—⟋⟍—

14ᵀᴴ JUNE 2004   03 00 A.M.

Surrender is the after effect of helplessness. Yes, we are helpless from birth to death; we are helpless to be born, and when born, helpless not to choose our parents, caste, religion, country, social status of the family etc. We are helpless in our conditioned bringing-up. We are helpless to be in the society which has its own system. We are helpless in our education because that is what is offered. Either we have to go through the mill of the offered education or be out of it. There are no other choices. We are helpless to choose a job and also in the valuation of money and ultimately we are helpless to live as others do. We are helpless to be caught by the diseases like heart diseases, cancer, diabetes etc in spite of our not contributing to such diseases. We are helpless in every aspect of life and even choosing God for that matter. Some organizations-some systems of religion (including atheism) are thrust upon us. Our thinking is already conditioned from day one to D day. So what does this helplessness leads to? Surrender; but whom to? To nothing but to the reality of helplessness itself and to loose oneself in body, mind and soul, completely to an unknown and unexplainable situation, that is all that can be done and that is the reality.

—⟋⟍—

03ᴿᴰ MAY 2004   03 30 A.M.

There is nothing more depressing than to know yourself that the D-day is not too far. But you don't know what that path is and how to go through it. It looks to be very painful and disturbing to all those who stand by and watch a person going out of his physical body. Nothing can be done than to accept the fact. Is it so easy to accept the fact and put up with it? I am afraid not. Now, I know that it is very easy to solace others in their pain but not so to oneself when one is the victim of such a pain. Well, what is to be done then? Make up your inner courage to catch hold of you with full grip and believe in some force unknown and unseen and yet existing beyond you, to help you to pass through the passage of time. May be, some help may come from that unknown source so that you could assure yourself and go back to your normalcy. To this assurance, give up yourself. And in this self-assurance lies the self-courage, which, to a great extent, un-burdens your thoughts. Well, the only way is to completely surrender yourself without questioning that Cosmic Being and move on to the D-day as and when it comes, though you know not when, but you are aware that it is lurking somewhere in a corner. Having known it, I am growing from within. Calmness completely engulfs me, peace is catching me and the mind is turning towards Cosmic Force. Nothing matters now. The only probability is to improve the situation, if possible. Even that improvement would be limited and also within the function of the Universe.

—— ⁂ ——

5ᵀᴴ January 2004   03 00 a.m.

Am I not a part of the Cosmic Energy which is all pervading, omnipotent, omniscient and omnipresent? Is not my thought a wave of the very Cosmic Energy? Is there anything like 'I' in this phenomenon? Is it possible to separate the entity 'I' from the entirety of the Cosmic Energy? 'I' is a hypothetical delusion. Maybe that delusion too is a part of the Cosmic Energy. When everything, which includes thoughts, words and deeds of a man, even in a most microscopic way, too, are, I feel, nothing but the waves of the Cosmic Energy. Hence, ultimately there is neither 'I' nor 'That'. It is one sum total of Cosmic Energy. When 'I' is there, 'That' will not be there. When there is no 'I', then 'That' will be there. However, to understand, to realize, to experience 'That', 'I' should be there. But this 'I' is only a projection of 'That', which is the cosmic consciousness. 'I' is a facet of million-eth of a small reflection of that One Cosmic Energy, as a ray from the Sun is also the Sun. A ray cannot separately exist from the Sun. A ray is a microscopic projection of the Sun and Sun's energy. How could it be possible to separate a ray from the Sun? The 'Sun is', so the 'Ray is'. If the sun-is-not there' so the ray is also not there too. So, 'Ray-I' is only a fraction of a facet of the reflection of 'Sun-That'. When 'I' and 'That' are one, neither of them exist as separate entities, but simply they together function as only ONE Cosmic Energy. And yet, I become restless because I deeply, with all my being, with utmost urge and with all forces at my command, want to know, to realize, and to experience that Cosmic Being, in all completeness. Somehow, there is complete emptiness in me. I am a vacuum. I want to fill this emptiness, this vacuum with that very Cosmic Energy. I want to experience, to be always with that very ultimate Cosmic Energy, Cosmic

Intelligence and Cosmic silence. But how to? I do not know. Nothing for sure would quench me. Slowly but surely, of late, as my physical age advances, shattering all the egoistical knowledge so far acquired brings me to the fact of realization that it is impossible to understand, to know anything about anything. And yet the urge, the restlessness, keep haunting me, to know, to experience, that Cosmic Energy in its fullness. In the process the only way, I feel, is to keep completely surrendered to this knowledge, which is not real to me, of its impossibility of knowing and the impossibility of experiencing; for I being a particle of Cosmic dust on a grain of sand on the eternal shore of infinite Ocean, how can I understand and know the Cosmic in its entirety, in its fullness?

Man being what he is, he struggles with all his energy, being completely helpless, to know that which challenges him. In the process he arrives at something which he has not expected to arrive at and yet this arrival will not satisfy him. It is a game he plays by himself and with himself and upon himself. And in the end it dawns upon him with all its force, with all its reality, that he can never, ever understand and that is beyond him to know, to understand anything about anything and what all he thought he knew were only his ego of having known, while he had known nothing and he would never know anything. May be, there is nothing to know also. Even if there is something to know, it just is there and he can never know what it is. So, everything functions in its own natural way. There is neither 'to know' nor 'not to know'.

At the end having known, having realized that I can never know anything about anything, I completely relax, silence pervades me, calmness descends on me and ignorance becomes the true knowledge.

Ignorance is the reality and truth to me, from which I can never escape, however I may try. That is 'the Truth'; not 'a Truth', but 'The Truth' at least to me.

—∞—

04ᵀᴴ JANUARY 2004   03 30 A.M.

God is eating away the human time. It is God you hear wherever you go. God has occupied the whole human race. In every action, word and thought God comes first. It is to the satisfaction and appreciation of God that man behaves in a particular way, though man is not aware of it. Every work, every second of time, every thought wave whether known to man or not, is dedicated to God, as if God is a separate entity, a selfish entity and a crazy entity to hold the whole mankind's attention to Himself. Does one's mind get free from the concept of God whom no one knows and yet lives as if for this One Being only? Everything is done and dedicated in the name of God-in birth, in life and in death also, whether knowingly or unknowingly. Life looks like a mirage and so the God too. He is slippery. He always wants you to run after Him and yet beyond catching. God is a concept of a limited mind of man. Man for sure, having coined the word God, does not know what God is. Maybe He is the totality of the entire Universe including the microscopic dust that functions in its own ways, which cannot be comprehended by man at all. The very functioning of man's mind, which is not possible to comprehend too, is another function of the Universe, within its totality of function. Human race is another degree of function of Universe in its totality beyond the conceptual dimensions of time, space and causations.

Man with limited intelligence, unlike other species which cannot speak like man, coins words for the reasons to subjugate his own species to himself. In the process he can never be peaceful, happy, lest someone else may subjugate him and this process goes on and on endlessly. The end comes to everything that which had a beginning, at its own pace. Then what is that which has no beginning so that it shall not have an end too? Probably, it is the cosmic energy. I do not know. It is only my concept. While nothing can I understand about anything, even my very physical body and its subtle functions, the very subtle instrument which craves for understanding and ends up with un-understanding of that it can never be understood. It just functions. But how can never be understood? What is that which produces or holds our mind and intelligence as if they belong to that being? From where these mind and intelligence draw energy to function? Nothing could be known. These are the subtle instruments through which understanding has to come in; but, to whom? To me! Then 'Me' is not intelligence or mind. 'Me' is the holder of these two instruments, through which 'Me' works. These two are the channels leading me to infinity-the Cosmic Energy

—ɯ—

03ᴿᴰ January 2004 04 00 a.m.

The totality of God, if there is one, can never be understood by the insignificant intelligence of man. The Cosmic intelligence is beyond the understanding of the man's intelligence and yet the human intelligence-is a part of cosmic intelligence. Cosmic energy in its functions exhibits its intelligence. Man and its function in the entirety of his existence on the insignificant face of this globe within the panorama of the entire Universe is like a speck of dust on a particle of sand lying on the vast sea-shore. Maybe the quality of intelligence being the same with a microscopic facet of the Cosmic, man's imagination of the Cosmic is something like an ant on a hair in the tail of an elephant trying to gauge the enormity of the elephant itself and trying to understand the entire function of the elephant both physically (biologically) and energetically. And yet both, the elephant and the ant, being the creations of the natural energy move on their own without taking each other's support drawing energy from the Cosmic according to each of their capacity from one and the same source-the Cosmic energy; and as such they are the same in their functions but for their physical capacity. In the process ego of man finds no boundaries. He feels that he is the creator of the Universe and Universe exists only for his requirements and it is there because he is there. His individual ego is much bigger than the Universe itself. So his ego is the creator of the Universe and its functions. But ultimately the Cosmic plays on the level ground and brings his ego to a naught in the form of his death. Does the death of an individual make any difference to the race of the humans, let alone to the functions of the Universe? 'Birth-life-death', is a movement, a function of the Cosmic and its cyclic order. In fact there is nothing like birth, life and death. It is only a hallucination, a conceptualized hypothecation within another conceptualized dimension of time and another conceptualized dimension of space and one more conceptualized 'cause-effect' phenomenon. All dimensions are imaginary and of man's egoistic intelligence. In fact nothing can be understood of anything by man, even his own physical functions. The more I desire to understand, the less I understand; and yet of late, I understand that I 'can never, ever understand anything about anything'. This is a firm reality of not knowingness. When this understanding has dawned upon me, I have become calm, peaceful and silent in my innermost being, while the entire ignorance has evaded me. Ignorance is the key to understanding of 'not-knowingness'. Helplessness leads to go back to oblivion and to surrender one's ego to oneself, in which process one finds oneself and in finding oneself one finds the Cosmic.

2ᴺᴰ January 2004   04 00 a.m.

The greatest regret is that I could never be able to find out honestly and truthfully the meaning of life—birth, living and there—after. Is it possible to have any answers to these questions honestly and truthfully? Is it possible for anybody to know for sure the true answers, not conceptual, not hypothetical, not theoretical answers, but answers from experience of going through and knowing the truth as seeing and feeling the light of the Sun? To me these questions have no answers. The very fact I have no part to play on my own to take birth, and birth in a particular family, and birth as a male, while I have no say to my end and to a great extent to the time spent between birth and death. Combination of all these three, to me, is life. To me these are just functions of the Universe. Universe has its own functions to play and even the Universe is helpless other than to function in the way it is doing. There is a great urge, a chocking urge to find out the answers to these questions. But equally there is disappointment since I am unable to find out any answers genuinely and honestly. Deep regret follows, while the time is ticking towards that already fixed goal, about which I know not when I reach. I may reach it in my sleep, or I may see it before some days or just before reaching it. The time and the method of reaching it are not known to me. However, I am feeling that it is nearing. But before that I desire to find-out by myself and not by copying from any text books, whether those texts are from any great masters who have gone through these experiences, but I want to experience these phases, especially what is after, by myself. And is there God, whom the majority in the world believes and prays? Is not God the creation of a phenomenon of fear, conceptualized by men to keep the society in order and thus bringing the God within the framework of social behavioral pattern? I don't know? I too, as others, somehow picked up God along the way with the second hand influence and second hand knowledge of others, either through their words or through some books or through the behavioral pattern of others-visiting temples, following family and social rituals etc; while all along I have been feeling emptiness within me as regards to God himself. To me, God is Cosmic in all its functions, just from micro functions of a cell in a body to macro functions of the Galaxies and the Universe. In these functions of the Universe, I do not know where I fit in. And holding on to this physical body, which I desperately hold on to with all my force and energy at my command, lest any loose hold may throw it out, which I do not want to happen before I come across face to face with that Cosmic eternal Being. I know my energy and force are ebbing away as days pass on and one day the entire hold loosens and out I will be from here, but to where and how I know not. Somehow, I always contemplate deeply, honestly and truthfully with my entire being to find out the 'Truth' behind the so called life; but still I am empty without any experiences. Mind may answer and intellect may rationalize it. But there is something in me which does not accept unless it is concrete, real and truthful, which I desire most to experience it by myself. Any given pattern will not make me to arrive at it. Maybe there is nothing to arrive at. Even a cog in the wheel of the entire Universe cannot function without the Cosmic energy and intelligence, while it will not have any individuality by itself as I am to the Universe.

—⚋—

01ˢᵗ JANUARY 2004   04 00 A.M.

Observing a New-year by welcoming it and saying good-bye to the previous year is more a notional concept than reality. Every second passed is also a welcome to the next second. But in reality there is nothing like new or old. It is the past that has left an impression on the man's mind as memory. It is the past memory that brings the future. Every fraction of a second falls to the past only. But God is a future concept, a theory about which man is afraid of. You cannot stop a fraction of a second and say 'this is the present', nor can you advance it to call it as future. Future and present are projections of the past. Future is a hope to be different from the past. But man being what he is, he always hopes and this hope only creates the future. For man God stands in the future, always man hoping that he will realize God tomorrow. When tomorrow arrives it becomes past and another hope of tomorrow is created in the conceptual mind of man by projecting the conceptual present with the memory of the dead past. Experience is always of past left in the memory of man which the man uses for his benefit to face once again a conceptual future. So, time has no definition and is only a hypothetical dimension and so is the space. It is eternal, infinite, having no beginning or an end. So the cause and effects too, not as separate entities. They are one and the same. What appears to be a cause or effect is nothing but one function which again is only the function of the Universe. The sum total of all functions is the function of the Universe, as in a physical body the sum total of all functions of various organs, including the micro functions of every cell of that organ, become one single function of the physical body. Yet, there is something in you which witnesses these functions without functioning itself in the way the Universe functions and it is a particular cosmic function within its entirety, maybe that particular function is ME and the entirety is God.

—ɯ—

25ᵀᴴ/26ᵀᴴ December 2003   0000/ 12
MIDNIGHT

Time ticks precisely. I recollect my waking and watching the watch striking 12 in the midnight on many 25ᵗʰ Decembers, also 31ˢᵗ Decembers. Life slips between the fingers, but leaves behind the impressions on the mind as memories. I would always sit on those 25ᵗʰ December midnights and praying to Christ. So today after long years, I am once again sitting to watch the watch to strike 12 at midnight. On my table is a photo of the present Pope in his meditative pose, eyes closed, holding a cross to his forehead, completely surrendered to God, forgetting the entire Universe, probably even of his own self. What a personality he is! To that thought, to that meditative mood, to that complete surrender and humiliation, do I desire to surrender without a thought of my own merging completely with the entire Universe, loosing completely myself to that Cosmic Energy, to that Cosmic Silence, to that Cosmic Light, to that Cosmic Intelligence, which is the Ultimate in all aspects, which is the very Universal function, beyond time, space and causation. To that timeless, eternal, omnipotent, omniscient and omnipresent energy, I would like to merge myself and in the process desire to completely loose my individuality. I urge with all my soul's cry to experience that Cosmic Energy in me and I want to be magnetized by that Energy, I want to be lighted by that Light, I desire to be silenced by that Eternal Silence, be blessed, be loved, compassioned by that Power. In me I want to find Him or in Him I want to find myself, loosing self in Him.

I wonder if there is any measuring rod to measure a person's life as a success or failure or a percentage of mixture of both. There is no absolutism in any extremity of success or failure. They are only social concepts, a behavioral measurement, with reference to social/economical points. I feel, that nothing much to have been contributed by me to the life at large and to my own life, let alone to the life of others. Nothing worthy be counted upon from me. A peculiar man, I am. I expect certain norms, certain principles to be followed; the failures in this would always take me away from others, separating me. Somehow, I would rather get myself isolated than to be part of such persons without compromise and this I know and experienced a lot, that I suffered, sometimes, the social boycott. I would rather suffer such indignities rather to feel at home with such persons. At such times my tongue becomes sharp though my heart does not mean what my tongue says.

—⚋—

15ᵀᴴ OCTOBER 2003   03 30 A.M.

Is it possible to purchase death, while the life has already been there? And in this process can it be possible to purchase the functions of the Universe so that death and the Universal functions and also the Cosmic Energy can be your slaves? If they are to be purchased who is the seller and what is the value of the barter? While it is beyond the perception of any being to do so, what use would it be to purchase anything else that is superficial which may at best provide some luxury, materially for the comfort of body and to some extent to the mind too? To be out as an entity of this Universe and witnessing its performance with detachment, is impossible, while the very concept of being or becoming a separate entity from the entirety of the Universal functions, is impossible-since the very thought cannot be a separate concept other than the Universal function. All thoughts come to the mind as waves floating from the Cosmos, picked up according to the nature of that being's mind, rather these thoughts enter such minds which are conducive to them. So, irrespective of the being, the entire Universe is conditioned and controlled by its own principles of law, to the precision and can never be altered though here and there, now and then, an infinitesimal aberrations of nature takes place in the form of draught, fury of floods, earthquakes, volcanoes, typhoons etc; which have no bearing whatsoever over the functions of the Cosmic Universe. And yet, man with limited intelligence but abundant self-ego and vanity thinks that he is an entity, all together separate from the Universal function and he can control the Universe.

—⚋—

28ᵀᴴ SEPTEMBER 2003   05 00 A.M.

Is it necessary to know God? Is there a God to know or is God a mere word coined by some hallucinated men to conn others to make a profitable life of their own out of it? Is it necessary for God, whom it is described as omnipotent, omnipresent and omniscient, to advertise himself through these agents? Is

God a salable commodity? In fact, that is what it looks like. This word God is used, misused, abused, elevated, expanded, compressed, pulled and pushed from all sides and equally neglected and sinned in the name of God and also divined, named and unnamed and did everything from everybody in every manner suited to each individual, from time to time, as required, while none would have known God in His reality. Human race being a small entity of His creation, to know the entirety of the creator is like an ant trying to understand an entire elephant by sitting at the end of a hair of the tail the elephant. To me the question of 'what if?' arises. If He is the owner and creator of the entire Universe, including a particle of dust like me, 'what if?' arises in my mind. Since I am not an entity different from the entirety of this creation, what right do I have to differentiate something other than me? In the process of Universe's function nothing can be understood. Any understanding or knowledge is nothing but an exhibition of intellectual ego which again is like a speck of dust on a small grain of sand. To call oneself as 'God-realized' and a guide to others in the path, while there are no definite paths is like one blind leading the other, and ending up before a huge wall. Whereas, nothingness is the only path to the unknowable one

—w—

14ᵀᴴ Sᴇᴘᴛᴇᴍʙᴇʀ 2003   0000 ʜʀs.

I feel the emptiness deep within engulfing me entirely. There is something wanting, unfulfilled wanting. Nothing possibly satisfies me from within. What that is I know not. Probably, to run away, not physically but psychologically, from everything and reaching something extraordinary, unreachable, un-understandable, un-hold-able, is something beyond me and has never been attained by anyone. To be in that state, in that arena permanently without any physical ambition, rather psychological ambition, would be like a vegetable without being influenced by action-reaction phenomenon, while everything that is conceived looks to be illusory and meaningless. It looks like a dream. I know not anything, even the so called my-own-self. Who this 'I' is a mystery to me. Somehow, some voice, though very weak, says in a remote corner within me that I do not belong to this world, I am an entity, have come to this world by chance loosing the way and having not found any other way for there might not be any other way at all. I feel that I am pervading the entire Universe having been a part of the Universal Cosmic energy itself and yet have no individuality or personality of my own. All words of wisdom would rather remain as utopian conceptual words for me. Yet, I want to reach that realm, that platform, that arena which withstands beyond space, time and causational phenomenon. I want to be there. Sometimes I am there and some other times I am in the ordinary lower platform. Journey from here to there is a process of not either being here or there. Probably this journey is the reality.

—∞—

6ᵀᴴ August 2003   03 30 A.M.

It is said, for all those who have not anyone to help, God comes to help them. Is that so? First of all, is there a God, who is all powerful to do all good things and extend help to who ever needs, irrespective of whether that person approaches God or not? That person may not have any concept of God or belief in such unforeseen and un-known help. But, do-gooders with ultimate selfishness do exist in plenty. Some do-gooders take the whole crowd for a beautiful ride on a non-existing and imaginary horse called God only to extract money so that they could live in style of a 7 stars comfort with everything at their command, but without accountable to anyone, rather not even to themselves.

I have no conflict either with a spiritualist or a rationalist, since I do not understand either of them. They argue against each other with limited knowledge of their own. While I do not have even that limited knowledge of their sides, it makes no difference to me and as such most of the time they become displeased with me since I contribute nothing to either side. Somewhere along the line I pick up their dislike to me and to some extent they are also influenced with the way of my dealing the things especially about God. Anyway, that is their market and there are buyers. Let God speed them.

—∞—

6ᵀᴴ January 2003   05 00 A.M.

Why do I need God? Why this craze to hear, to know and to follow about God? Is it not the fear of death that leads one to God, to falsely create a sense of security while death will have its ultimate say? However, what 'death is', no-body knows, for none has come back after dying to explain about after death as it really was. Maybe all the gross functions of the gross body may stop and it may be replaced by other subtle functions of bacteria, worms etc; if kept for a long time. These bacteria and worms too are lives expressed at different degree and at different level.

Suppose, I overcome the fear of death, then, would God be necessary for me? Is not God the very function of the entire Cosmic Energy? Is not God the entire Universe in totality and its functions? If so, am I not a part of this Universe and its functions? Can I understand how the Universe functions except to know that it is functioning in a particular method? Suppose, I say why earth should not spin in the other way round rather as it does now and why Earth should go around the Sun; why all these systems should function in the way they are functioning? Nobody can say for sure why. But they would only say 'that is how they are'. When so, is it possible to understand the entire functioning of the Universe? None can understand the ways of the Universe and the Cosmic Energy.

—∞—

21ˢᵗ DECEMBER 2002   03 00 A.M.

I think, of all the things the Universe holds for a man-for that matter for all the animate objects-is 'FEAR-OF-DEATH'. If a person is informed either directly or indirectly that his death is at the threshold, he rapidly sinks from within for, he does not want to die so early, he feels, though he is hundred years old. The desire to be permanent is permanent in the man's mind. But it cannot be. Nothing can stop death. It cannot be bartered or purchased. It can only be faced and you can make friends with it by welcoming when it comes, for death may take you to new horizons unknown to you, maybe for your good. But man being what he is, he wants to hang on to the present life. He holds his life in his fists. But that fist is broken by the death and life vanishes to nowhere. Man is forgotten, in spite of all philanthropic works he did on earth to make other humans and may be, some animals comfortable. But it cannot hold him. So, what is the way out? The way out is only to accept the inevitable. But is it possible? Yes, by training one's mind for long time and by keeping that status of mind always, it is possible. However powerful a man might be, economically, physically, intellectually, or even for that matter spiritually, he shrinks at the very thought of death, let alone the very death itself. The fear of death seems to be more fearful than death itself. This fear is equally more powerful to hold down the mighty powerful person. Nothing can stop it.

Though the birth, to some extent, is in control of somebody, death cannot be controlled by anybody. What is birth and death? They seem to be the obverse and reverse of the same coin while the thickness of the coin may be compared to life. It is easily said than observed. A man can talk and do everything when in good health, but when he is down and sick, he makes those days not only cumbersome to his life but also to others. Or otherwise he becomes a recluse. The truth being that as the birth is beyond oneself, so the death is. When born, death also is born though it takes effect afterwards. Death is a sure and definite and no amount of any means to avoid it keeps the death away, but the only thing is—nobody knows when and how it comes. May be, some people recognize it a few minutes before its arrival. This play is a wonderful play, but still the wonderful part of it is, 'fear-of-death', but not the death itself and still wonderful part of it is, that every person thinks he will be permanent though he sees death all round him.

—⚮—

26ᵀᴴ November 2002   03 30 a.m.

'Seek the divine grace through prayer' says an article in the 'Times of India' dated 25/11/2002. My question is: when you go for divine grace, what for it is required? Is it to seek ultimately the material benefits to enjoy the physical desires? To me, there is nothing to seek. The whole Universe is 'ONE HAPPENING'. This happening is just a function of the Universe. No seeking has any place in its functions; let alone what is called as 'divine' and further the 'grace'. Whose grace? No grace of any external being is required while the whole function is one happening and with the understanding of 'what-is', seeking comes to an end. The correct perspective of the Universe would be that 'I know that I do not know anything about anything-total ignorance of everything'. Like an ant on an elephant trying to understand the entire system-both physical and biological functions—of the elephant. In the totality of abstractness, functioning of a small grain of sand, a drop of water, are included in the functioning of entire Universe. Their functions cannot be different from the functions of the Universe. In the functions of Universe there is neither 'divine', nor 'devil' let alone the 'grace' nor it's 'seeking'. But to arrive at this understanding of 'not knowingness', 'not knowableness' and 'there is nothing to know', it takes you all round for a ride on every philosophy available in the world.

To be aware of your state of not being able to know or 'nothing is there to comprehend, or to understand, or to know' is the 'real awareness' to me. This brings to an end of seeking the duality of the seeker, the seeking and the seek-able comes to an end. And you become aware that you are the very functioning of the Universe while you don't know anything about anything of your own self, if there is anything like 'yourself' as a separate entity of the Universe. In the process, you come to a definite conclusion that there is neither seeker, nor the process of seeking, nor the one who to seek. All remain to be one in the process of functioning of the Universe in which when 'you' is separated, it can never be understood and at the same time even when 'you' is not separated from the functioning of the Universe, it also cannot be understood because you are also a part of the functioning of the Universe. It is like a thought to understand itself. That understanding of one thought is nothing but another thought of different degree. So the entire functioning of every individual is the totality of functioning of one Universe.

—⚟—

24ᵀᴴ NOVEMBER 2002   03 30 A.M.

Something deep within urges me to stop reading but to start writing. There is a very small voice within me which pervades the whole of my being at such times and somewhere along the line, while writing, the same voice, sometimes, urges me to stop writing and to keep quiet silently. And so I do. Whenever I hear this voice I act accordingly which leads me to a better understanding, always resulting in some happy atmosphere from within; and tranquility and bliss, unexplainable setting. I become light in my mind and body, completely detached from everything that is going on around. The whole physical body looks like 'a cotton made', so soft, so light, so detached and some tiny sparkles, through this cotton body, show up tiny Cosmic rays the original of which is the central Cosmic Energy of the entire Universe. This 'I' stands separately and at the same time it looks as if the entire functions of the Universe is a part of this tiny force of 'me', which is inseparable, indestructible, though having different physical activities at different levels and at different phases of the activities of the Universe. In fact, there is neither time nor action nor reaction. It is one grand function with different facets of one and the same Universe. In this function there is no separate entity like 'me', 'mine'. They are one and the same. It looks that this 'I' is immortal passing through different phases and acting accordingly. There is neither 'I am' acting nor 'somebody else' is acting separately from the Universe. Everything is one single act of the entire Universe. While I am in this state, I feel that my entire physical body has fallen apart especially at the joints and some force within me is holding them together and a wonderful electrical white energy is passing through every limb of my body, in a tiny channel, as a thread and is playing within keeping my body's limbs together. Mind calms down, thoughts stop and yet this writing continues from some energy which I know not how. Even my hands become so light that the pen becomes very heavy to hold, but still it is not my hand which is holding the pen and I am not writing. It goes on by itself in a detached way, in fact, which is nothing to do with me at all. All desires, even the desire to seek, dry away. Desire-less-ness hangs on to me.

24TH OCTOBER 2002   03 30 A.M.

What is happiness or unhappiness? These are the emotions that arise out of desire, be it material or metaphysical. While there is nothing either material or metaphysical, the desire being the product of emotions too does not exist in the absolute sense. Desire is only a thought wave which comes in series on a particular wavelength. It fortifies the desire of that particular wavelength. Otherwise lot many desires vaporize even before they come to surface. Any desire is not only the product of emotion but also of cultural conditions imposed by the society as a whole. Nothing can be done to erase the desire whether expressed or unexpressed, whether tangible or intangible. It may be a condition of Cosmic Energy expressing itself with different facets at different levels in different persons and in the same person differently at different times. Human is incomplete without desires which are to a great extent mirage of Oasis on the canvas of life's desert. Human mind travels to un-traveled edges of the Universe but cannot travel within oneself, for mind does not know what one-self is. My mind, if you call it mind, is not an independent one but conditioned one, however one argues of its independence by its actions. It acts mostly in a subtle manner without being aware of its actions. It is an energy relating to both external and internal desires, deriving its strength from the Cosmic Energy. So, neither my mind nor my-self, as a whole, do have any independent actions. Though these actions are very insignificant, they do form a part of Universal function in totality and are not actions of an individual and also not by an independent entity. In the process, somewhere along the line, man changes his earlier perception of his individuality to Universality-and ultimately it dawns upon him that he is completely ignorant of all things including of him-self.

Ignorance, not knowingness, leads a man to the destruction of individuality. Probably, this condition is the Ultimate TRUTH.

20ᵀᴴ OCTOBER 2002   06 30 A.M.

Although it has no answer, still man being what he is, he questions-'why this so called creation?' Personally, I do not know. In totality nothing is known and nothing can be understood and nothing will give any answers. 'It' just is. Why, what, when, how etc does not arise. To me the whole Universe looks strange. I am a strange personality, the Universe is strange and at the same time I am a part of the Universe and the Universe as a whole is a part of me. I am incomplete without the Universe and Universe is equally incomplete without me. Here 'within' or 'without' does not arise, because they are the same. And yet I as an entity am different, aloof and I am myself. Though I do not know what 'I—am' or what 'myself' is. There is some uniqueness in me which rebels against all similarities, against all teachings, against all followers, against all such things which sets up the so called examples for others. There are no examples or icons to follow, for, there is nothing to follow. It is my slavish mind that compels me to follow the so called examples who without understanding themselves about themselves try to teach others to understand something un-understandable let alone understanding themselves. I am equally a part of the Cosmic Energy though of a lesser potency since I draw that energy from the only source as there are no other sources of Cosmic Energy other than the central one which pervades and controls everything of this Universe. It is self-propelling, self-generating, perennial and eternal energy from which, probably, the entire Universe is created and is functioning with changes and throbbing and living continuously from one phase to another phase vibrating all though beyond human perception and yet he is a part of the entire Universe in his own perception.

30ᵀᴴ AUGUST 2002

03 30 A.M.

Dear God;

Is it possible to address you as Mr. God? Are you an individual like me? First of all, I don't know whether I am an individual or not. What individuality is? I do not know. To me individuality is mere a word. Conditionality is me. I am conditioned and yet I am independent and individual entity. Is that right? Wrong. Physically I am conditioned so, to a great extent, mentally too. Thought process though look to be independent, may not be so. Thought being a wave of energy drawn from the eternal perennial Cosmic Energy, cannot be said to be an individual one. In a way nothing is independent or individual. Everything is a part of the entire eternal Universe which functions by its own natural laws. So, where do I fit in? I don't fit in to anything as I am not a separate entity but a part of the Universal function, knowing or even perceiving as to how and why it functions in the way it does has no answer. The only answer is 'that is how it functions'. Giving any meaning or rationalizing its function is only a futile exercise of a man's intellectual ego, though it is very limited.

—m—

26ᵀᴴ AUGUST 2002

03 30 A.M.

I feel completely tired of rat-racing both in material and in spiritual life. Nothing I have contributed either to anyone or to myself, a life without any real meaning in any respect. All seems to be a make belief. What purpose? I do not know. Morning dawns and night falls moment to moment movement takes place. An unfulfilled agony, a deep rooted uselessness occupies my entirely. I look to be physically well and yet mental aloofness occupies my mind. My sincere cravings for answers are not forthcoming. I am left helpless, because I seek answers while there are none. Not a single answer has come to my satisfaction. I sincerely crave that something (which I know not what) should happen to me to know the 'reality'. I want the cosmos to bestow upon me and to reveal the reality and to make me one with its energy. I feel from the bottom of me that I want to have cosmic companionship, cosmic love, cosmic energy to support me, to live with me to become a part of me and I want to be Universal in all its aspects. I don't want any theory of spiritualism, rites and rituals etc. I want it badly, as badly as a drowning man needs a breath of air and some support to hold on to and saving himself from drowning. Why it does not reveal to me? Why it does not come to me? Why I am not chosen by it; though I want it above everything? I don't know.

Please reveal yourself before soon. I want you with me always. Stay with me. Do not betray me. You are the only one I depend upon-you the Cosmic Force, the Cosmic energy, the Cosmic function. I feel I cannot put up anymore like this without you. I want to know, to experience and to be with you eternally, peaceably, blissfully, without anything other than you-the Cosmic force.

24ᵀᴴ AUGUST 2002   04 00 A.M.

Nothing is a big deal in the Universe, even experiencing God. The big deal is—you. Yet you are not sure about your own self. You don't know yourself, let alone knowing anything outside you. You have no option to be anything other than what you are and at the same time you don't know for yourself what you are. To me, I am just a part of the function of the entire Universe, but I do not know how I am functioning, let alone how the Universe is functioning. I cannot wish otherwise. Even if I do, I am helpless to be what I am with limited intellectual capacity and still cannot use it. And if I do, the border of the sociological terms hit me back to where I am supposed to be and where I love to be. I have neither the better nor the superior job to do than a grain of sand does lying on vast seashore of the Universe with its eternal cosmic function. Other than myself being a socially graded person, I have nothing of my own to say, for sure, that 'I am this' and 'I am not that'. And yet deep down in me a feeble voice raises its hood now and then to rebel and say that I should know 'who I am in reality?' And somewhere along the line, having lost the capacity to know, I accept that I can never know the Reality in all its facets. And then it dawns upon me that I can never know anything about anything and ultimately I have to erase everything, what all I hitherto thought to have been in the knowledge of all that I picked up through this mortal journey, which, in fact, are false for the Reality is unknown to me, so that I could be completely blank and remain to be so which, in fact, I am slowly becoming.

20TH AUGUST 2002   03 30 A.M.

It is an uncontrollable hunger for something that may be called as divine Cosmic strength to fill me up, I most pray for. Day in and day out I feel the urge of needing this Cosmic guidance, Cosmic knowledge to dawn upon me. I really do not want anything other than the universality of myself, to belong to the entire Universe and at the same time the deep unquenchable desire to acquire or even to pursue the mysterious facts of the Cosmic functions that is keeping me in an always hunger status. I am not satisfied, I am not quenched with anything other than some knowledge, some mysterious Cosmic strength to reveal to me. I need to know, to experience that inexplicable thing, that is be all to me. I am feeling the wanting, the incompleteness in me, void in me, without this experience of something beyond my perception of this life. Somehow, deep down in me, some guts feeling in me says: that there is something other than what externally exists and that I am in need of, though it may look to be only a concept, a perception conditioned. What it is I don't know. What I also want I don't know. But somehow I want to know and experience that which *Sri. Ramakrishna Paramhansa, Sri. Ramana Maharishi,* have experienced and were with, though I don't know what they have experienced or with whom they were. Is it possible? May be. Somehow, the life is slipping away and slowly the life is thinning out and before long it ebbs away.

—m—

09TH JULY 2002   03 30 A.M.

God, you work perfectly without any external show, since you are beyond karmic boundaries. Our helplessness has brought us to you with calls from deep down our hearts and souls. Man in his physical form always thinks his wants in physical forms only. When once the idea that he is physical vanishes, then his desire for physical forms too vanishes. And then, only the spiritual need comes in. What is the definition of spiritual need? I cannot explain it physically, but can conceive and experience it, non-physically. Is not the Universe and all that it holds are physical? Yes and no. Yes, when we look at the Universe through the physical eyes it looks to be physical; and No, when we open our third eye and look at the Universe, it looks completely spiritual, in the way God created it and God makes Himself present in His own creation. All creations are the manifestations of God's energy. God Himself being the Supreme Cosmic energy, there cannot exist anything which is devoid of God's energy. Everything, even the cancer in the physical body is a form of energy but with different reflection in the form of pain which is felt by other energy in the form of brain cells. Yes, the whole Universe is energy functioning according to laws of God who is the creator, preserver and destroyer too of his own makings. No one has any right to interfere but to pray to him to be with them in the crisis. While the crisis is human made, the salvation is sought from the God. It is just like a baby dirtying itself while it is the mother who cleans it up when the child cries or when the mother notices it herself.

—∞—

30TH JUNE 2002   05 00 A.M.

I feel so much intimate with the whole Universe as if it is entirely mine and it has nothing other than my welfare and the entire Universe is in tune with my feelings and would always stand by me. It has no conflict with me nor have I with it. Some force is always, though external one, with me and would not let me down and at the same time gives me courage to put up with the Universe. There is no strangeness for me with the Universe and as such there is no fear of future, even the fear of death is not there, for somehow, I feel, the function of the entire universe is a one continuous movement, and that force is very intimate with me and stands by me always as a constant companion, in my strength and weaknesses. I really feel and enjoy this companionship of some external force and yet it is with me and within me. Is it the reflection of my own mind and my own self? It may not be. This force, as a companion, is not physical, but a subtle, stays with me always and I am fearless, desire-less and I feel that there is nothing wanting, but only to be in bliss and happiness with this force, which has neither any religion nor institution, nor rituals, nor has any material acquisition. It is completely subtle but mighty and yet most lovable force or call it a strange Being. I talk to this strange Being, we laugh together and we understand each other and we are inseparable and I distinguish myself as a separate person from this force and still I feel we are the same reflecting each other in our very core of personality. There is duality between us and yet there is oneness. I feel that I belong to every nook and corner of this Universe, in its vastness of innumerable galaxies and the entire space, and in functioning of the whole Universe. With all this I feel I am an entity-a separate person though I am a part of the entire function of the Universe. There is nothing beyond my functioning with the functioning of the Universe and still feel some sadness is gripping me. There is sadness in the entire atmosphere, probably because of failures of expectations, failures of desire that bring more sadness in its degrees than the happiness of success of expectations and fulfillment of desires. Man is helpless. He becomes an instrument of production of both desires and expectations. It becomes impossible for him to be in balance in every aspects of life. Some desires are set aside, some are given certain degrees of values and some bring moderate joy or sorrow and some other bring extreme sorrow or joy. Though, these are just fleeting emotions, a chemical change in the body and electric wave change mind. These are the realities and to seek otherwise is utopian.

—⋙—

23ʳᵈ JUNE 2002   05 00 A.M.

The entire Universe being one, we human beings try to make ourselves individual entities separate from the Universe. But I feel deep down within me that though I am an individual, at the same time, a part of the entire Universe and in that relationship I find oneness, as if I know the entire Universe since its inception in the form as it is now. I feel so friendly with the entirety, that I, as an individual do occupy the entirety of the Universe. I feel not only in the entirety of the Universe but also the entirety of my inner self along with the central Cosmic Energy. I do not feel that neither was I born nor do I die. I feel that I always am with the Universal cosmic force. I do not feel any strangeness in the outer space world. I feel they belong to me and me to them. I feel the calmness, the energy, the natural functioning of the entire Universe where I am not only a witness but also a participant. I feel at the same time something unique, something superior to all the natural functions of the Universe, since I could see, perceive and enjoy the functions, which are methodically and naturally going on, on the mosaic of the Universe. It looks that the entire Universe is a canvas before me, to where I have traveled and have been traveling. I feel this travel, rather the Universal motion, is going on before me, while I stand and watch along with the central cosmic force, the entire panorama of the Universal function. That central force is so loving, so blissful, friendly, known to me since eternity, as if we are twins enjoying each other's company fully without any remorse without any split. I feel the companionship of that central force always, although I cannot explain what that central force is, how it is and how it functions, is with me and I am in perfect harmony and perfect understanding with that force and we are alone by ourselves without any interference or without any break. I always feel the eternal presence of the central force, its welcoming me smilingly with happiness and pure and perfect bliss without looking to any of my human weaknesses or any imperfection, as if I am an equal and at par with that central Cosmic force. It is not only a force inexplicable but an individual, perfect and pure bliss and intelligence in control of the entire Universe, playing, witnessing by itself. I am one with it. All fears, all selfishness or separateness vanish when I am present with that force. Somehow I feel I travel to meet that force which is eternally present to meet me and waiting for me. And yet with all these I fail to understand in its entirety. I do not know anything about myself let alone about that Cosmic Force. I am a stranger to myself, I feel. The entire Universe looks strange to me because I do not understand even an iota of its functions. Ignorance pervades me when I try for understanding. Ignorance dawns upon me, strangeness engulfs me, individuality melts, time stops and ego vanishes, when I am with that central Cosmic energy. I find myself everywhere in the Universe, as that Cosmic energy is, while the Universe shrinks and the vision widens.

22ᴺᴰ Mᴀʀᴄʜ 2002   03 00 ᴀ.ᴍ.

Tomorrow is never there, neither today remains. What the real is: yesterday. The past is always a memory in timelessness. Time is a man-made hypothetical space measurement between two assumed points, which in fact do not exist at all. You could see in everything the past by the result it leaves behind. From conception of a baby in its mother's womb to its final destination to the tomb, it is the past that is always in the front. Neither tomorrow nor the so called 'now' stand, since they have no ground to stand but for the past in the memory of man. But for the Universe by itself functioning on its own natural laws irrespective of the qualifications of the past, present and future, time has no relevance. In totality no-one understands for sure to say with authority and confidence as to what the future holds or what the unknown death holds. Is there, death? I doubt. Death seems to me a physical change while the innermost 'I' looks eternal. Somehow, deep within me I feel the eternity of me. I not only feel but also confirm to myself this eternity of me through all these external physical changes taking place. All these concepts are conditioned and fed to me through my religion, society, its culture and from teachers, parents and peers etc; to a great extent and yet somewhere along the line I do not shun them but proceed on my own and with my own conviction to live with the natural ego from within of my eternity which creates fearlessness to go for a change-death-in peace and bliss with a pleasant looking for

—ɯ—

1ˢᵗ MARCH 2002   04 00 A.M.

There is no goal and hence there is no path at all. All goals and paths are creations of an illusion mind. However there is 'you' who is always witnessing what all is going on with and around the World including within yourself. Thoughts are like uncontrollable, fathomless, eternal waves rising from deep within you only. You are that very thought itself. 'Thought-less-ness' is 'your-less-ness'. The peace, the silence, the re-thinking of the past, all go in vain for these are only the process of thought connected with the future, while there is no such a thing as future in actuality. Future is illusory, projection of past through memory. If this memory is lost all dimensions are lost and everything becomes new learning, new expression at that moment and once again these new learning, new experiences are to be stored as new memories, for them not to be lost. With the loss of memory man is born again and again at every moment with new thoughts and new experiences.

—ɯ—

27ᵀᴴ FEBRUARY 2002   03 30 A.M.

Somewhere along the line, man starts hating God also, whom he has created through his conditioning by the social structure, cultural structure and religious structure, while man is supposed to love God unconditionally. Man being what he is globally, he loves God provided God grants him his prayers at least to some extent. When God does not grant the desired wants of man, man presumes that God has failed him while it is the man who failed God. God comes to man only when man is happy but then man forgets God. Only when man is in distress he seeks God but then God neglects man to know the sincerity of love of man to God. This is the play that man and God play with each other—a game of love and hate. Here there is no difference between man and God.

Somehow, I feel that it is always the man, in the name of God, divides his own race so that man should remain in the helm of affairs on all sides. God needs man's undivided attention with devotion and slavery by surrendering all to God. God is the most selfish person ever known to human race. A piece of bread He throws to man to subdue him and to be always in remembrance of Him for life; because man wants to enjoy through his physical form all his imaginary joys, dreamy happiness, unsuccessful and slippery peace. God slips away from man the moment the man does not desire anything from God. However, God cannot live without the attention of man, though God pays very little attention towards man, especially when man is in distress. God creates man to attain His achievements in Himself. But God puts spokes into the progress of man so that man should turn to God and pray for help. God should die for man to live, but the reverse of it is true.

15ᵀᴴ FEBRUARY 2002   03 30 A.M.

One of the most lovable subjects on this earth, I think, is 'LAW'. It brings to you the innermost reflection of the society-the people-their mind, their behavior, their greed, their lies and equally their sense of equality, balance of thinking, the sacrifice, in inner quality perceptions, belief, disposition of their lives etc. One sees both positive and negative aspects of the society while dealing, you feel that it is you who is a part of it, but when finished you are completely detached though it did have some sort of influence on your life while dealing with it. Law becomes a second nature in you. You find yourself standing before the vast deep ocean even without comprehending it, let alone, taking a spoon-full of water from it, as a Judge or as an advocate. You feel that you are too small before the Law, a grain of sand on its vast beach. The entire Universe, you feel, is en-composed with Law-the nature's Law, the man made Law and the divine Law. No one can live leaving the Law aside whether he is aware of it or not. At every step of your life Law is protecting you, physically, economically, socially and even mentally too. You dare not trespass or overstep on it. If you try to break it, it will break you completely. It is the most powerful one. God, if you call it so, is Law. By Law, the Universe came into existence, is functioning and may after billions of centuries destroy itself within the ambit of its own Laws. But man can never understand this Cosmic Law which is perfect, pure, unalloyed and functioning at every breath and yet beyond you. You can never reach it. The moment you try to hold it, it engulfs you, chokes you and you realize all together a different dimensions of life hitherto unaware of and unknown to you. Respect and follow Cosmic Laws and as well as man-made

Laws to live in peace and harmony which will be the foundation for the realization of God

—⟋⟍—

18TH JANUARY 2002   06 00 P.M.

To me it is still a mystery to hear that a departed soul (soul of a dead person), however divine it was, in union with God, comes down and enters into the body of a living person and gives messages, though they seems to be divine messages on many previously appointed days and time, year by year. But I am completely ignorant of the other aspects of the soul entering another living person's body that too in union with God. First of all I don't know in reality what the soul is, let alone God and how they together combined come down to earth and enter into another living person's body. I have no arguments either with the believers or with the non-believers about this phenomenon. I had had the privilege of witnessing and hearing the divine messages from this person in whom they say that that divine soul with God has entered that person's body while that very person would not be aware either of such entry or any divine message passed on through that person. I really adore this phenomenon since it is beyond my intellectual understanding, for it is the nature of the ignorant to adore that which is beyond his understanding. Why It should not enter me?, I ask myself many a times. May be, from what I hear that the person It chooses should be qualified spiritually, for such entrance and as such no one else may be qualified from the point of view of that Divine Being. However, I am equally not bothered whether such a thing is prevailing or not. I have nothing to do with it. But my desire, may be a selfish one, somewhere in the corner of me, shows up and asks for it. But I know for sure it will never be fulfilled. Probably, it may bring, power to dominate, power to enjoy the reverence that others show, power to be in the midst of large believers and followers, powers to command men, materials and money and the power of so called divinity. All powers gather in the person in whose body such an entry takes place. And yet an uncomfortable life thereafter prevails in me. I would rather be myself without exhibiting such an entry of such a soul into me, if at all it happens. But I am sure that such a thing will never happen to me. Why should I desire that to happen to me? Why, sometimes my mind is depressed and I feel that no help is forthcoming from anywhere however I deeply need it? Why should I be deprived of it? I cannot say. There are no authentic answers to these whys. Somewhere along the line, maybe almost at the end of line you realize that you are most helpless creature in the order of the Universal function. Maybe, it is due to want of being a separate entity of yourself. The expectations, the desires, the wants in combination with selfishness and strong urge for the things to turn out to your selfish desires, bring equally strong disappointments, for the things are not going to be the way you want them to be. They have their own ways and in actuality there are no such thing existing, let alone going in your way. These things you create out of your own concepts and further dream and imagine to follow your line of thinking. And in the end your own mind which created them is kicked by the much created concept and the mind becomes agitated and disturbed. So the creator is made to suffer by the created-the concepts—and the mind hangs on to these concepts helplessly hoping that one day these concepts will help the mind and in turn you. But nothing like that happens. The instrument of mind goes along with you to nowhere and to nothingness you go ultimately.

11ᵀᴴ January 2002   03 00 a.m.

It is beyond my comprehension as regards to any aspects of the Universe, even a small movement of an ant. The life, even in such an ant, though looks natural but un-understandable. You only understand that 'it is just there and functions as it does'. I look at, sometimes, with awe and wonder, being an ignorant person, with all my humilities and ignorance, even of such small event of the life. What life is? I know not. 'Who am I'? Even that I know not. All egos, vanities, prides vanish when the Universe with all its naturalness reveals even an infinitesimal part of it, which again is beyond the comprehension of the best of the human intelligence. And still man tries to hold the entire Universe within his fist of intelligence, but in vain. And in the end to that which is beyond him, he qualifies it as God. This God becomes the resultant of the human helplessness in comprehending the Universe through his intelligence. And such a feeling of God gives the man an understanding of his own limitations and still man's nature being what it is; he struggles to go beyond his limitation to find out what is there beyond and ultimately accepts that he can never know as to what is there beyond him. He becomes a beginning and the end to himself. And in the process he continues to be 'him' alone. He stands as a separate individual entity, an indestructible individual entity, feeling that his entity is there eternally without birth or death, in the meanings of the mundane world, and feels that his entity is a part of the Universal entity and the Universe is his entity's reflection and sees himself in the whole of the Universe and realizes that the entire Universe is known to him since eternity and the end result is : the fear of unknown vanishes. Time becomes a relative factor with hypothetical measurement and comes to a standstill losing its powers, space becomes limited, causation becomes meaningless and thus man transcends beyond time, space and causations and he realizes that he is only a happening along with the Universe which too is only a happening without qualifying any attributions. All qualifying attributions either to himself or to his conceptual God are only social necessities which in turn are conditioned both socially and geographically and confined to the dimension of time. When a man thinks of time, space and causation, they could only be relative terms. But in the order of the Universe's function there is no absolute relativity and as such the entire concept of time, space and causation are lost and go to oblivion losing all meanings and eternity, though beyond the concept of human intelligence, stands as the only reality. And that is the only real cosmic natural function. The energy for such cosmic functions is eternally self-generated and perennial in itself, for the entire Universe is at its eternal central Cosmic Point. Man is equally a part of this function. The quality, the intensity of this cosmic function is immeasurable and un-attributable and can never be qualified or quantified and yet it can be felt, it can be experienced and it can be enjoyed as bliss and happiness which hitherto was absent. It is a great blissful joy to be one with this Cosmic Energy. It is in the nature of man to adore God, for man adores that which he never understands. God is always adored for the simple reason that man always remains ignorant about God whom he never understands, since God is only an adorable concept of man.

Anything which is beyond the comprehension of man's intelligence is attributed to God-a word coined by the man. And yet everything is tried to be comprehended. Nothing could be understood in its true function. Nothing is known and nothing can be known of beyond, at least to me. To crave, to know, in itself cannot be known. It just happens. Everything is naturally happening. The reality is: telling lies, cheating, doing all that which is taboo to social orders in the name of God. There is nothing called falsity. The very falsity is reality and it cannot be other than what it is. 'What is' cannot be understood and this inability to understand 'what is' is making man restless, to seek something other than 'what is'. Nothing can be arrived at. It is said that space is within the boundaries of time. The time is only a conceptual hallucination, so the space is too. Actions and reactions are one and the same set of functions of the Universal phenomenon. In totality the whole Universe is one set of function though it appears to be different. In the process of this function man thinks he is a separate entity having an exclusive power of his own either to function differently or to dysfunction. But he knows not whatever he does it will be within the Universal function he, being a part of the Universal function. Birth, life and death as concepts are nothing but the same functions of the Universe wherein nothing can be separated as an independent or individual function. They are all the only one process of function and can never be understood in the reality of the Universal function. Nothing for sure can be understood in the real perspective as they are. The Universe in which a man is a part, functions with everything that man can conceive with his limited intelligence. When the man's intelligence is limited compared to the Cosmic intelligence, it is impossible to understand the unlimited intelligence of the entire Universe and its functions. Everything is contained within the Universe's function. My function from my conception in my mother's womb to tomb wherein I am going to become a chemical composition of carbon is contained with in the Universe itself. Universe looks to be limitless and without boundaries, either physical or subtle. Giving meanings, qualifying them would only make man still small in his intelligence and shrinks further before the eternal and unlimited intelligence and the functions of the Universe

05TH JANUARY 2002   03 30 A.M.

I personally feel that the whole spiritual writings and speeches are only hogwash-a brainwash. How can you understand God, which is a conceptual word, the knowledge (jnana) etc; that are found in Holy Books? Are not the body organs working normally? If this world is a hallucination, if this body is a delusion, and if everything connected with the body and the body world is an illusion, is not reading, writing, hearing, talking too are bodily functions? When so, to say that Vedas and Upanishads are also nothing but hallucinations and illusions including this very writing, in as much as any other text book which deals with the so called material world. Hence, to me, I feel that it is impossible to understand anything about anything especially of such conceptual knowledge. Of late, as age advances, I am coming to the firm conclusion that 'I do not know or understand anything about anything'. I have neither the positive nor the negative attitude towards anything and more so towards such conceptual spiritualism, because I have no argument with anyone on either side, while I do not understand any of them. The whole thing looks to be some sort of intellectual somersault. He who desires to spend his time to acquire the ego of his conceptual knowledge, gets probably a type of kick from within. This kick, maybe, like a drunkard gets when he drinks alcohol etc; or a narcotic drug addict gets when he inhales or consumes narcotic drugs without which he would go mad otherwise. Probably those kicks whether due to intellectual, spiritual, alcoholic or narcotic etc; maybe the real hallucination since they create such situations from within leading to brain washing that one cannot live without such kicks.

I feel that I am an expression of the entire Universe though in an infinitesimal part of a low degree but of the same kind. I am not a separate entity from the Universe with all facets expressed through its natural phenomenon. And yet, feeling deeply from within, that I have a separate existence as an entity, liable for destruction from the 'point-of-no-return', loosing everything physical of me in the end, is making me to compromise myself to an unknown conceptual entity, which has been attributed to have omni-potency and omniscient, infinite and eternal existence. The feed, the conditioning, which a man gets from the birth, somehow puts a subtle fear in the man to answer that unknown beyond this life, for all that to which he did not adhered to now, in this life. Everything creates a subtle fear and greed for something conceptualized wonderfulness of life in future. This beats the man to submit or surrender to the other human being who claims to have the powers to make the man blessed like himself and who claims to hold all answers to that unknown future that happen to come into existence after the death. To some others he promises paradise here in this life itself. Every living creature including man, does not want even a small physical pain let alone death, and craves for permanency in this very physical body irrespective of its condition. Living, rather existing physically, becomes the goal of man than ending. And to draw away the attention of man from this inevitable reality of the physical end, somehow, the other man tries to build conceptual emotions in another so as to make the existence of another a bit utopian, offering unattainable state with sweet and melodious voice to reach what is not reachable and to attain the unattainable, but still he promises attainment in this very existence itself.

There is a *sholka* (aphorism) in *Srimad Bhaagavatham* stating: 'The mind alone is the cause for repeated births and deaths'.

Now, what is mind? Is it not some type of energy with electrical impulses or waves of energy? Can mind exist and functions independently without it being expressed through the physical body media? If mind can exist by itself without the physical media, then can that be called a mind or can that be recognized as such? As for me, there is nothing called mind. It is only an expression of the same physical force functioning at different degrees at different facets expressing itself through the physical media of different human beings. Further, in the eternal order of the functions of the Universe, births and deaths are only part of the natural functions of the Universe while it creates a hallucination of birth and death as separate functional entities, while in reality they are one and the same movements in continuity of the Universe's function. However, nothing is comprehendible; nothing is understandable because that which functions cannot understand its own function, that which is functioning and the act of function being inseparable, while in entirety it is only the expression of the same Cosmic force. Hence I feel there exists no-mind and when so there is neither birth nor death.

Nothing is going to reveal the Ultimate, while the Ultimate is a mysterious concept of the human conditioning as, may be, there is nothing like ultimate. Every moment of this functioning of the Universe, in totality, is the ultimate by itself.

While it is said that this world, this physical life is an illusion, is it not that which is expressed and experienced including such spiritual ones, are equally illusions, since these expressions and experiences cannot be separated as different entities from their media—this physical life? When these expressions and experiences become illusions, the very human concept of God also becomes an illusion since God is an expression of illusion's physical life's concept. Hence God becomes a mystery through this physical life of illusion, because this illusion's physical life has created that mysterious and illusory God.

Nothing explains anything. Even if explained it could only be skin deep for the man's intelligence cannot probe beyond skin deep in the order of the Cosmic Knowledge and Cosmic Intelligence which is the pivotal force of the functions of the entire Universe in toto. Having said this, every function cannot by itself function as a separate entity from the totality of the Universe's function. What the Universe's function is? Nobody can explain. Hence it shall be impossible to correctly and absolutely perceive or experience even these small functions of the human being by himself. How do I function? I don't know. Even I don't know whether there is anything like 'I' and further what functioning is?. It is just a movement-an eternal movement-beyond time, space and causations. And it cannot be other than 'what is'. But 'what is' cannot be explained or experienced; but has to be just taken in the way it is conceived. Yet, what is conceived may not be the reality of 'what is'. The reality may be something else. But I don't know for sure. Finally nothing can be known in its originality and in its reality. Ignorance dawns and that is the only reality. I am ignorant. That is sure and certain. Nothing other than this is sure and certain in its absoluteness. Absolutism in any aspects is unreal. Reality or unreality of absolutism ends with the results of ignorance, which is the reality. Limitation is reality, incapacity is reality. In this reality, there is neither pessimism nor optimism. These words have no reality. When a man lives physically, his physical wants like food, shelter, clothing, and security are the realities at that particular point of time. His physical pain and disease are realities, his desires are realities, his emotions are realities-which include greed, jealousy and selfishness etc. His wanting to hold to his physical body irrespective of its conditions is reality. And apart, every other thing of ecclesial concept is unreal and in the end everything remains unreal especially when the physical body fails.

08ᵀᴴ OCTOBER 2001　　　　　　　　　　03 30 A.M.

Today I read about 'Death'—a subject, I feel, nobody can exactly, authentically and authoritatively say what it is all about. To me it looks like an eternal passage of the Universe's function. Nothing for sure can be said about anything. The very 'Me' is unknown to me. In the correct perspective I do not know 'myself'. This 'I' as a separate entity with the ego to understand the whole Universe's functions when, ridiculously, it cannot understand the simple function of its own physical body, as it is. If death is a dimension of time, time itself becomes the functional process of death. But time is hypothetical one, a physical dimension, but in fact of subtlety. In abstract there is nothing like time. The process of time, the resultant of functioning of every aspect of the Universe, to the mind of man is the physical time and yet, time cannot be held to be shown as to what 'time is'. In the process, I now realize that this physical time too is running out of my physical existence. It is short and nothing can be said as to when it ends. And nothing has been achieved so far and nothing could be achieved in the future too, and in a way, I feel, there is nothing to achieve at the same time. To achieve is to set a goal, which is a precondition to some concepts and in the process every step is judged to know where the goal is-a hypothetical, vague, hallucinating, non-existing, non-achievable and unknown. It slips out mostly there is no real goal but an ephemeral one. Physical body, due to its use and abuse over the years, wears out and cannot be regained or cannot be replaced. Slowly but surely, somewhere along the line, the body picks up its own dysfunctional forces and maybe due to some of its original organs being genetically defective. But 'why' has no answer. And yet deep within the realms of thoughts man thinks his permanency through his physical body, while for sure it is going ahead towards his own destruction whether in slow process or suddenly, only the time and the end will tell. In this process of self-destruction by the physical body where do this 'I' stand? How come a person stands as a separate entity from the entire Universe, still being one with it and its functional forces? All types of qualities are attributed to this force, which is the Central cosmic force and to that this 'I' belongs and to this 'I' the Cosmic force belongs and in a way this 'I' is that Cosmic force and that Cosmic force is this 'I'.

1ˢᵀ AUGUST 2001   05 00 A.M.

Where do I stand in the vastness of the Universe? Is there anything like 'me', on the canvas of this eternal Universe? It bothers me for sometimes, and some other times I brush aside such ideas. And still all these ideas seem to be unanswerable. Questions are there but answers are not forthcoming—for reasons that there are no answers to such questions, hence such questions burn out. And yet, human mind is the only one that cannot be quenched. It is always thirsty to know that which can never be known by this limited intelligence which has unlimited thirst. Somewhere along, this struggle between the unknowable answer and the thirst of mind to know, man looses himself and slowly but surely it dawns upon him that in spite of all achievements he comes to become the most ignorant one and his ignorance cannot be pierced to the other side of the Universe, if at all such an other side exists, which in reality does not expect in the mind of man. Mind is an instrument that catches cosmic energy and expands itself into the form of thought waves, sometimes subtle and most of the time in gross forms reflecting itself in physical form. Man wants to subdue his mind, by creating desire-less-ness as a goal and to achieve this he desires to choose to walk on the path of meditation, in a way it is a medication too. He thinks, that more he spends time on this path of meditation he will be more nearer to reach the goal. But what goal? He knows not. It is only his concept. In fact, the goal he sets to reach is his own making, through his hallucinated concepts, while in reality he is ignorant and at the same time it is a mirage, which is not there to reach and there is no path to this mirage. Maybe I am a mirage to myself since there is no such an entity as 'Me'. The only one entity in this 'Universe' is the Cosmic Energy as its life. I am an in significant part of this vast cosmic energy with its own expressions as it expresses itself in the form of all visible and invisible, animate and inanimate objects the entire Universe holds. When so, neither 'I' is born nor die. 'I' is an expression of the Universe at different degrees in different facets beyond time, space and causation-these being only hypothetical ones. So, the 'I' too is a hypothetical one, but with some form of expression of the same Cosmic energy and still, 'I' do stand aside and look at the Universe as a separate entity created for this 'I' and for 'I' alone. And yet 'I' is an insignificant grain of sand on the vast shore of the Cosmic Ocean.

—ɯ—

27ᵀᴴ APRIL 2001   03 30 A.M.

This Universe moves. The mover is the Central Cosmic energy, through the medium of time. They say time is only a relative term in this part of the Universe. I do not understand what time is, except to see something is heading for its end and also something is heading for a beginning. In the process it is impossible to understand where the beginning begins and where the ending ends. To me, both are the one movement beyond my comprehension. The physical and metaphysical are being the same and inseparable, the human intelligence tries to separate them and conceptualize them but these concepts remain only as concepts to me, for it is conceived with limited knowledge and limited intelligence of human beings. Hence, it is impossible to comprehend, let alone understand anything in its true functioning in the Universe. For me, it is impossible to separate anything from its function and from the function of the entire Universe. It is the only one function of the whole entity in its entirety. It is the pure energy that functions with different facets in the entire Universe. The sum total of all the functions of all these facets, are within the realms of the Universal function in different degrees; like electrical energy while being of the same kind but functions in different degrees in different mediums like in a tube light, in a running motor vehicle, in a pump lifting water, in a flour mill, in looms weaving clothes, in manufacturing, in ships and airplanes etc; in the material world; and in the waves of ocean, air, flowing rivers, lightning and thunder and rain, earthquakes, volcanoes, light of sun, moon and stars etc; and the electrical impulses of heart and brain of the animate objects in nature. The energy cannot be separated from any of these in their functions. So, it is the same energy expressing itself through different facets. It is this energy that holds together certain things in totality and at the same time the atoms of such things; while it is the same energy that separates certain things and atoms of the same thing to zoom and project the same type of energy further. So in totality, the whole Universe is one of energy which can only be comprehended through different mediums functioning at different degrees; but neither can such an energy be seen nor be held. But that naked energy when touched gives shock and the object may be burnt out depending on the intensity of the energy.

I desire, very strongly desire, with cravings to touch this Cosmic energy in its nakedness and in its purity, irrespective of its intensity, for that energy is a pure intelligence, a pure knowledge, a pure power, a pure mover of the entire Universe and it is the ONLY ONE without a second one like it. This energy is there in a very subtle state. Can this energy become latent, intense to be tolerable and yet gives me a shock to awake me from within? I need it. I crave for it. It is the only ultimate thing I need and nothing else.

24ᵀᴴ FEBRUARY 2001 03 30 A.M.

It is said that 'man is trying to play God', but to me, the reverse of that 'God is trying to play man' is right. God cannot play by himself except in the garb of man because man is the real instrument with which the whole Universe is expressing itself through its functioning. But that is not how God expresses himself through man. Man is an essential media for God to express Himself to the very same media-the man. No other animate object recognizes God's expression except man. Hence God expresses himself through man. It is a circle of play between God and man while the entire functions of the entire Universe consists of both animate and inanimate objects of every kind the Universe holds, and man is one of the most insignificant objects on the surface of another insignificant object-the earth-on the vast panoramic canvas of the Universe. As such, God's expression through man is only a small facet of God, while the God has innumerable facets to play with the Universe. Hence God is in the center of Universe who plays all round, wielding the cosmic energy. This Cosmic energy is potentially self-generating and eternal one. May be, subtly flowing from a central point. This point is the very core of the Central control, may be, attributed as God.

—◠◠—

12ᵀᴴ FEBRUARY 2001   04 00 A.M.

Some people think that their contacting the departed souls by astral travel is the ultimate definition of spirituality-that is reaching God. May be, we do that in our dreams, sometimes. Is the dream, a subconscious experience? May be. Dream is a status of mind at that particular point of time when we are asleep or half asleep. When the gross consciousness goes to sleep the finer-the subtler-consciousness starts working in its own method, voluntarily, without any external effort or influence. The job of the external consciousness is always to transact with reference to material and gross emotions of the material world. It is an internal thought process of external gross objects. Mind, to a certain extent, can also be defined as consciousness. In the entire process of life of a man, he hardly understands himself and his functions, both physically and mentally. Functioning is something beyond the comprehension of man's intelligence. Comprehension has a frame within which man functions. Probably having thought to have arrived at the edge of this frame, man thinks he has reached the other edge of the Universe; while the Universe does not have any edge at all. Even the very knowledge of eternity, infinity, timelessness etc. are the concept of man's functioning confounded within the framework of his mind and his conscious intelligence. Man complicates his life and this complication gives him a kick to further complications. Man desires to function in complications of his own making. Slowly but surely, somewhere along the line, as the age advances, he comes to his own conclusion that though he had been thinking of himself to be the most knowledgeable person, so far, but he now for sure realizes that he knew nothing about anything including of his own self. He becomes a mystery to himself and a stranger to himself. He, for sure, knows now that he was and is only a straw in the tremendous forceful stormy flood without any destination. It makes him no difference whether he reaches the bank, or continues to be in the midst of floods. However, the reality is the fear of his functioning coming to an end. His consciousness coming to an end. He sees this end taking place to others but hardly affecting him. When it comes to affect him, he will not be there to experience it. Maybe, the sum total of all his experiences, both conscious and sub-conscious, are compressed to a tiny concentrated point within him and accompany him to take effective results subsequently and accordingly he comes to act once again on the gross surface of the Universal function. This process goes on eternally. Everything is an influenced concept of man. In this process there is neither superior nor inferior functioning. The totality of all tiny functions is the one whole gross function of the Universe. In this I am a tiny ebb trying to understand the eternity of this function which I am sure, I will never do while I know hardly myself for I am NOT MYSELF.

—⁓—

06ᵀᴴ FEBRUARY 2001   01 00 A.M.

Some questions like, 'why should there be this creation?' that human nature produces, have no answers. Hence these questions would only reflect the status of man's mind. The Universe is just created and the human is a tiny part of this creation but not the whole creation, as he thinks he is. The entire creation, its entire functions and the entire destructions, which are also its functions, are the natural phenomenon having no answers that would satisfy man. Man wants answers to his way of preconceived thinking. Only when answers reflect his pre-conceived questions which fortify his thoughts, would man be satisfied and thereupon new questions arise in his mind. Arising of such questions is perennial. It does not stop. Both question and answer are being one and the same, though at a different degrees, are already existing in the Cosmic and it is only drawn through the instrument of mind in small quantities, by many, in different shapes, as people draw water from a well, which is already available in the well, through different shaped vessels, while water has no shape by itself. Water is not the creation of man. It is a natural source held in different shapes in a pit, in a well, in a tank, in a river, or in an ocean. The shape of water takes the shape of its holder. So also, all thoughts have no shape, but when drawn from the perennial source—the Cosmos-it takes the shape of the mind of the person who draws these thoughts. One can never question anything, which has its natural source. Nature cannot be questioned, but conceptually maybe, but it has no answer.

God is a conceptual conceited understanding of man, which is always subject to variations, for whatever the man had thought about nature, is not the emphatic final analysis of the nature. Nature can never be understood in its finality, for the man and his mind being a part of nature, it is impossible for a tiny part to understand the complete, the final and the everlasting one. It is beyond the intellectual capacity of man to know his maker, completely and finally. Man can never understand himself, let alone something external to him while it is beyond man to know the entire natural Universe and its functions. As man travels in these quests, he stands and looks at the nature with awe at the enormous and colossal spectacles of the nature, its vastness without boundaries, its functions beyond his understanding. All his intellectual concepts so far held by him about himself vanish and there comes the humility of his ignorance and limitations. Before the vast canvas of nature, he recognizes himself to be a speck of dust, though he could be able to look at this canvas of nature within his limitations. He dies from within and a new person of ignorance and humility is born. And thus he becomes aware what all he had held so far, about himself, were only his vanity of knowledge while the true knowledge can never be perceived, let alone understood, with his limited ignorant intelligence. It dawn's upon him that he can never know anything about anything of the Universe including of his own self. In ignorance and emptiness from now on he travels towards the light of the Universe and maybe a particle of a small ray may touch him for a fraction of a second, and lo! He thinks he is an enlightened man. It is like a blind man searching for a black ant in a dark room at the midnight of the new-moon-day. His thought of his enlightenment blinds him and he searches for that black ant of that material power in his conceited mind of dark room and thus creates and instruments himself for his self destruction in the end. That is his black day. This will be a history of a man who tries to behold the Universe in his fists of intellectual vanity, which destroys him ultimately.

—ഇ—

2ND FEBRUARY 2001   04 00 A.M.

Some people think and act as if they are the absolute owners of God and they can trade Him in any manner they please, since they feel that they are the only ones on this earth who are the exclusive owners of the God. They also feel that God being a perennial power is under their superior power and can release His power, through them, in installments according to the benefit they receive, or according to the slavery of their followers towards them. But to me, God is available to everyone, whether a saint or a sinner, equally. God being the cosmic energy, He is available at all times and at all places and His presence can be felt when we think of Him.

Now, at this point of time I could feel this Cosmic Energy penetrating into my body through the tips of toes and fingers, passing into my body through nerves and slowly spreading bright light and unparalleled energy all over my body. I always feel His presence in me, asking nothing from me, but at the same time giving love beyond expressions, assuring that He is the best companion in my best and worst times. My mind becomes calm, the body slows down in its functions, time too, I feel, slows down and slowly the Universal consciousness pervades and Absolutism encompasses me in which state I go beyond time, space and causations. In this state (of being) all dualities vanish and there remain the Eternal, Infinite Absolutism. In this state I become one with everything the Universe holds, such as sun, moon, stars, earthquake, volcanoes, storm, floods, all engulfed in space, which slowly compress them so that the intensity of these multiplies geometrically and I become a player, a companion and a friend to them. I feel that I have been with these forces and they with me in a very understanding friendship, eternally playing with each other, for they too are the expressions of the same Cosmic energy as I am. In the functioning of the entire universe, they are individually very insignificant ones, having no impact whatsoever on the universe since they are the part of the universe's natural functions, but with separate identity. In such a state, I feel, the eternity of my own self, my own divinity, my own function and still I cannot be a separate entity but a part of the entire function of the Universe which neither has any positive nor negative qualities, we human beings try to subscribe. They are just as they are, in their own natural status, without any relative comparison.

All religious doctrines, dogmas and even the scientific theories like relativity, black holes etc. shatter and there is only one universal function beyond the understanding of the human intelligence. When man stands at the border, realizing the Cosmic Energy's functions, he feels himself to be very insignificant but with awe and aghast. Humility occupies him and it becomes sure that he knows nothing of anything about the universe and goes into deep silence and finds God ultimately in that Silence.

29TH JANUARY 2001   04 30 A.M.

Why is it that something sometimes ends up badly while on the contrary it should end up finely and friendly? The desires, the expectations and the values we set up for others, but not to ourselves, end up because of bad means. When the means are bad the result too must necessarily be the same, which cause frustrations, mind disturbing and soul stirring. And at the same time they are all man made ones—a prisoner of one's own thoughts. Freedom from ones owns prison is to free the thoughts from within. Let thoughts raise high and wander all over to understand and to know how the universe functions and finally come to the conclusion that it can never understand or can never perceive anything about anything, for the thoughts are conceptual and conditioned moulds of the human society. Thoughts can never be other than what has made the thoughts to function in a particular mould of doctrines, dogmas, religion, social order, external influences etc. though against internal convictions. Thoughts have a limited area within which they operate and function. Thought, though a part of the cosmic energy, it restricts itself to the capacity of an individual mind to reciprocate to what are all fed to it from womb to tomb. Thought creates birth, life and death. Through thought a person is aware of his being, though it looks to be a conceptual one by looking and thinking about the death of another but not of oneself. Death cannot be touched, cannot be experienced, cannot be defined or understood and can never be explained since the instrument through which a person touches, experiences, understands too dies. It does not live to explain death. The capacity to explain the experience of death too dies. So, there cannot be an explanation or experience of death to reveal itself. Since what 'death-is' cannot be explained, and death being a part of the universal function, it is impossible to say with this limited instrument to understand, to experience, to touch the infinite, the unlimited, and eternity about death. All these remain only as mere words, words of conceptualization which are conditioned according to ones capacity and capability.

In conclusion, no understanding, no experiencing, no touching of the Reality could be there, for there is no such a thing as Reality within the framework of human concept, since Reality is the product of falsity, hypocrisy, negativity and duality. While there is no duality but one single existence of function of the universe which is unknown and un-understandable to the human limited intelligence.

—ɯ—

27ᵀᴴ January 2001   03 00 a.m.

Man's nature being what it is, he always wants to reach new things without giving up what he already holds. Man wants to reach death but still desires to hold to this life in this present physical body. Experiencing the death and coming back to the present life is impossible. Probably, man can hold both new and old in almost everything except in death. To feel what is beyond death in the present life is impossible, but still the intense desire to reach beyond death will not leave me. Death is a natural phenomenon but no person; rather the entire animate and inanimate universe cannot escape death. It is the natural function of the universe. Fear of death and the desire to continue to be in the present life creates God. Those who believe in God think that somehow God will save them from death and they will continue to hold the present life perpetually. Irrespective of a man's belief in any religion or in any form of God or in any philosophical theory or the so called spiritual attainment, he in his deepest inner being does not want to die but to stay in the present life with all its miserablities. Sometimes, from deep within I feel that there is neither birth, nor life, nor death. The whole thing is: there is only one single process of the function of the universe wherein neither time, nor space, nor cause-effect functions as they do on this earth.

I hardly find any difference, in the absolute sense between any objects of the universe be it an animated one like me, or the inanimate objects like the galaxies, or the stars, the sun, the moon etc. I feel, all animate and inanimate objects are the one expression of one and the same Cosmic Energy in different degrees. All the dualities, such as, light and darkness, saint and sinner, pure and impure etc.; that are contrary or opposite, are only of different degrees, but not of kind. When so, there is neither any hallucination nor any reality. These words remain un-understandable and incomprehensible. While I do not know anything about my own self it is beyond me to understand, in its absolute sense, anything outside me. My mind does not belong to me-rather I do not belong to myself-since I am not an entity to belong to any thing, or any thing belonging to me. I am just like a dry leaf in a whirlwind and thus become a part of the whirlwind of this entire Cosmic Energy. It, to my limited concept, is functioning in its own ways and it cannot function in any other way than how it is functioning. Even, whether it is functioning or not, I do not know. A scene is brought about on my mind's stage and my intellect accepts it. But however deep within, I know that I do not understand what the scene is and what this intellect that accepts it. In fact I do not know the reality or the falsity of the scene. Slowly the so called science and technology is perusing that which cannot be seen or felt or held, is also becoming a reality especially in the communication areas. Man sitting in his drawing room can reach any person in any corner of the world and not only converses but also see his living picture, which was impossible a few years earlier. This happens through the medium of nature. But nobody knows how the nature has such secrets in its bosom. So, nature holds mysteries and surprises to man. The surprise indicates man's limitation both in his physical and intellectual capacities. Anything man does is for his existence and much more for his physical comforts and his physical longevity. And in the process man treads on many others and his own species. Name, fame, physical desires, greed makes a man to march on with least concern to any other issues. All issues of others do not become his issues. The power, whether metaphysical or material, is the goal of man, even the so-called spiritual man. He thinks that with the power of God in his hands he can subjugate gullible persons and further empower himself over men, materials and money. Slowly such a person becomes a law and to himself ultimately destroying himself and also his followers where God comes the la

—ɯ—

26ᵀᴴ January 2001   03 30 A.M.

Why God becomes elusive although it is said that He is perennial and available to everyone at all times? Is not God a gate to escapism from everything? I feel ultimately I have to escape from the God too. Since there is nothing to escape from or escape to and there is neither here nor there, God is just an excuse for all the things a man does. God is 'just-is'. What that 'is', is not known to me. Life is one eternal function where there is neither escape nor staying back. The reality is the fear that grips the heart of every man of his moving out of his own physical body. In the process of this fear man desires to hold on to some conceptual idea so that escapism is given a different color and the mind is hypocritically assured of making the escape more pleasant, more looking forward too and more sought after too. The base of all these is fear. Fear of something unknown and hereafter what etc. that creates God in man. And to God all attributions are made that the human desires to have for himself and in turn he looks towards God to receive these qualities and powers so that this person in turn may try to subjugate others to his powers-power of knowledge (though not real but that which is in lack in others), the power of money, the power of holding large number of followers, give such a man a kick, as if he is on the seventh cloud where nothing touches him. So called spiritual man thinks that he can even subjugate death to his wishes. However, the reality being that death subjugates everybody and it is the leveler of everything. Death plays on the level ground. The mighty come to the death's level. Everything, the name, fame, money, even the God's power in man is leveled in death. Nothing can conquer death but on the contrary death conquers everything and in the process God in man too meets the death. It is a process neither liable for stopping nor postponing. The feel of God at such particular time, may at best, give a little courage to face the death. Facing death has no meaning for before one could realize what is happening, death snatches man from himself. For, death will not confront you since you are only a small fly before the gigantic power of death. Confrontation takes place between equals but not between un-equals. Death is not an end all and be all. It is only an external functioning of man. In death the physical functioning stops along with mental functioning. While the physical cannot witness its own stoppage mental function may witness the death. Mind may get connected, depending on the habit created by man, to God, to give a hypocritical strength for the mind to witness the end of functioning of the physical body. However, it could only be said that death is the birth of new life, while the concept of God continues to be held.

4ᵀᴴ JANUARY 2001   03 30 A.M.

God is the most exploited word that man has ever coined. It can be sold like a hot cake by anyone who has the ability of marketing it to every gullible man who wants to save himself from himself. The society creates problems for man to run for such marketing persons selling God. God is not an entity but the entire energy of the whole universe in all aspects of its functions expressing through every facet. In those expressions they are no dualities. It is one expression conceived differently by different persons. It is one movement beyond time, space and causation, while these dimensions are hypothetical concepts created by human ego and within the limits of time, space and causations. Somehow, my intellect creates hallucination on me that I am a separate entity from the entire universe. No I am not. I am one and the same expression of this, one and the only Cosmic energy. When so, there is no such a thing as 'me', 'my mind' and 'my heart' etc. My thought, in the real sense, is not mine but caught, as an antenna does, from the Cosmic waves. My thought cannot be other than the thought of every other person, who has the capacity to think and project it to convert into action, when required. It may differ probably in degrees, being of the same kind and from the same source. The source is the eternal, perennial Cosmic energy.

—⟋⟍—

02ND JANUARY 2001   03 30 A.M.

What is experience? Is it knowledge of past-event's memory? Is it a measurement or a movement? No. I emphatically say no. It has no dimension; it is not a present one. It is not a happening but that which had already had happened but spilled over as memory. It is an after-thought from memory. If a person has no memory, or after-thought of any event that has passed, it cannot be called as an experience because he is not aware, rather he does not remember in his memory of that event in spite of having undergone the event. So, experiencing God, experiencing self-etc. is only after thoughts. They have no present-ness. It is a movement, and movement has no dimension. May be, it has an arbitrary dimension of time, an artificial one made by man and a relative dimension. Otherwise it has no meaning by itself and it cannot express by itself. It is man's thought that gives meaning and value for such experiences because they are measured relatively. And relativity is a subjective matter. It is not objective. So experience is a subjective measurement related to an individual memory of thought. Experience has no expression by itself except through the thoughts and words of the experiences. It is dead and past, because while experiencing he will not be aware of it. So, any experience of God is only a memory and an after thought, which is the dead past and the experience of God is a dead experience and God dies with that dead experience.

—⟋⟍—

1ST JANUARY 2001   03 00 A.M.

It is just that everybody wants to be 'some body' and 'nobody' wants to remain to be a no body. In this, where does a person like me stand? I am a 'no-body' and I desire to remain a 'no-body' till the end. Time, a hypothetical measurement, is just pacing itself. Time is a comparable one, the physical phenomenon of this earth, probably. Physical world changes, but not grows may be, negatively with disgrace and indignity. Time is the span measured between the two points in space. It is also a measurement from freshness to sloth and decay-womb to tomb. Anything that begins has the birth of an end and the end has the birth of the beginning. In a way birth is the beginning of death and death is the beginning of birth. It is a chain reaction—a time within time-a physical phenomenon within another physical phenomenon. The inner phenomenon expands and bursts, like a ring wave when a stone is thrown to a calm pond. The moment stone touches the surface of water, waves are created without waiting to know how the waves are created and it just goes down to the bottom of the pond and settles itself there without absorbing water on its way, though it comes in contact with water. So are we to be. When we are thrown as a stone into the pond of this world, maybe we create a wave on the surface and yet not having absorbed the water (the material world), we should go down in our mind and settle down at the rock bottom by our self, though surrounded and submerged in the water of the mundane world but untouched. Why we are thrown and who and when, are not the questions. If we are strong like a stone of pebble we go down, if we are not strong we float and water seeps into us and no wave is created and we are carried away by the wind, the ways of the world.

Nothing answers anything about the functioning of the universe. It could be the conceit of the limited intelligence that echoes the false ego that plays the hypocritical part of understanding the universe. Universe just functions. Even, as for me, I don't know whether it functions or what exactly it is. I do not know anything about anything including about my own self, let alone the universe. As already said, I feel time is only physical; it is neither mental nor metaphysical. Physical change creates the concept of time. And behind this physical change lies the subtle force, which is dynamic in its energy, which is the throbbing expression of the same Cosmic Force and Cosmic Energy in different degrees through different facets. So, may be, I am that expression, my so called intelligence is also that expression, my physical needs, physical pleasures and pain are also that expressions. There cannot be something separate from that expression. Birth, life and death-all physical-are one and the same expressions. Is not emotion too, though subtle, born through the instrument of physical body, the expression of the same energy? All emotions are physical, all desires are physical, even mental waves and thought waves are physical, fitted into the physical framework of time. These emotions cannot be independent of the physical body. When the physical body is functioning, emotions too function, and express themselves physically for the other person to understand. Man thinks that the entire universe has come into being for his necessity. While his ego knows no boundary, his intellect, though limited stretches to the so called edge of the universe, hoping to contain the entire universe within his knowledge forgetting that what little ignorant knowledge the man possess is only a subtle wave of Cosmic intelligence. This Cosmic intelligence, which is a pure energy, manifests itself in every function of the universe and the man's existence on this earth is of no significance while the earth itself being insignificant in the order of the universe and its functions.

—◊◊◊—

31ST DECEMBER 2000   03 30 A.M.

I don't know why this happens. Somewhere a small voice within me, with firmness opens up and says to leave everything I am doing and to sit quiet contemplating upon myself. A type of 'let-go' occupies me. I lose interest in everything, may be a lethargic attitude. All nerves loosen, muscles relax, mind becomes calm and thoughts slow down. It looks that the journey is shortly coming to an end and I am going to step into an unknown arena and still there is courage and a type of joy in 'looking-forward' to a better something unknown. I feel that something better is waiting for me, which I know not what. I feel that I am going to meet a long lost friend—the Cosmic energy, in its central seat from where the entire universe is controlled and its process of function. It is such a comfortable and blissful feeling that I shall be with my companion and sometimes wish to hurry up and deeply desire for the present to move fast though there is not much to walk. In the functioning of the universe time has no limitations, time being a hypothetical creation of man. Universe functions despite of human race. Human race has not created the universe but it is the other way round. In totality everything makes up for the completeness. Here, the question of the presence or the absence of anything from the completeness is only a hypothetical one. Man's nature being what it is, he always ponders on the hypothetical relationship in the universe, while in actuality everything is related to each other. The birth, the life and the death are related to each other and are inseparable. They are, in fact, in the abstract sense, 'one and the same'. They function at different degrees at different times but with continuous relationship with each other, which is a natural phenomenon of the function of the universe in totality.

In spite of understanding and being aware, there lurks in a remote corner of the mind, the fear of death-the fear of coming to an end of the memory and the present. The imagination of the present and future, whether the future turns out to be pleasant or not, or even whether the future comes at all, nobody knows. Future is only a projection of the past experience hoping that it will not be worst than what had been and what is now. There is no such a thing as tomorrow. Tomorrow is never born, it being only a concept, remains to be a tomorrow only. It is the hope of tomorrow, of conceptual thought, that tomorrow comes to exist. God is the concept of tomorrow which never comes to exist now and tomorrow never comes. Tomorrow is only a hope and so God is only a hope.

—ᴍ—

22ɴᴅ Dᴇᴄᴇᴍʙᴇʀ 2000   03 00 ᴀ.ᴍ.

As the days are coming nearer and nearer, the degree of ignorance of the functioning of the entire universe is increasing. It is being confirmed of 'not knowingness' of anything about anything. Of late, I wonder, for any number of reasons, whether there is anything like birth, life and death. Are not these the same concepts of human ignorance? If I separate myself as an entity from the universe, perhaps, then these concepts may acquire some qualities. But when that 'I' is not separated as an entity from the functioning of the entirety and from the totality of the whole universal functioning, then I feel that this concepts of 'I' and 'me' remain to be only concepts at a lower level. I still cannot understand how that 'I' in me be separated from my consciousness and also conscience mind, thoughts, awareness etc. without the sum totality of functioning of both gross and subtle of me; gross, in physical body and subtle, in mind. For this 'I' to manifest, a physical body is very much required. Without physical body this 'I' cannot function and at the same time without 'I' physical body too cannot function. It is supplementary and complementary to each other. They have to come together for the function of 'me' to take place. When these two are together, 'me' comes into being and functions through them in co-ordination and express through them. Thought is an expression to oneself. It is a dynamic energy within, whether it ultimately expresses itself, physically or not. I look at the whole universe with aghast and awe and at its enormous functions without attributing any qualities whether positive or negative. I expand myself to the entire universe. I feel that every particle of the entire universe is contained in me and they are me only. The volcanoes, the avalanches, the floods, the famines, the earthquakes, the life, the birth and death etc. which look, to me, to be a very insignificant function on this insignificant earth, compared to the entire universe and its functions. The entire planetary system, the galaxy with its milky way etc; is infinitesimal part of the entire universe, which is beyond time, space and causations. In this function I am functioning and it looks as if I am that very function itself. At this level no dualities remain. I only become aware, at the subtle level, of the functioning of the universe, which is rather under its own control, in a subtle way, with the Cosmic energy emanating from a point. These are, maybe, my concepts, since I do not understand any of these in their true and correct perspectives. Whatever anyone has established to have known is only very insignificant, which leads to understand his limitations and ignorance. With these understanding of ignorance, silence prevails. Deep silence engulfs me and in this deep silence I arrive at myself and in the process I become aware of the Cosmic intelligence and its energy and also its functions but without understanding anything of any of these. In this silence, I awake to my ignorance and incapacity to know anything including of my own self. Silence is the language of the universe and the Cosmic energy. I know the silence present in me and thus I know the language of Cosmic energy which is also present in me. I am the Cosmic energy itself, in a way.

—m—

18ᵀᴴ DECEMBER 2000   04 00 A.M.

Standing at the cross roads of life, not just two, but umpteen number of cross roads, causes complete confusion and dilemma. Life is meaningless and empty, both from within and without and stares with naked eyes. The entire walk till now in the life fills only with emptiness having no useful meaning what so ever. The time is ebbing away and the life is slipping out. There may be more things that could have been done the other way than what has been done. In these confusions and dilemmas deep down a subtle voice of strength is heard. It is very feeble but still strong. The voice of silence, it may be called. It is the voice of understanding, the voice of eternity, the voice of feelings and the voice of permanency. But this voice, though given some support, is not enough to pass through the rest of the left over time.

I feel completely from within no more can be done to fill it up, for there is nothing that could be filled up with. Probably the remaining time too goes with emptiness. I feel that I am slowly but surely surrendering myself to this inner emptiness. 'What next' is facing me? There is no next at all. The same emptiness continues. So far I was thinking that I was the most intelligent person who has understood God. But, of late, I know, for sure, that I know nothing about anything, let alone the unknown entity called God. These feeling arise only because, I feel, I am a separate entity from the entire universe. When once I feel that I am a part of the universe, which is functioning in every aspect in its naturalness, this very emptiness may become a part of the naturalness of its function. From the emptiness comes peace, attitude of surrender, deep silence, and detachment to oneself and to one's own ego. I cannot hold myself permanently and perpetually to this bodily life. It has got to deteriorate and destroy itself by coming to an end having had the beginning. But the path I walked has not been satisfactory when I look back. But now, I can do nothing about it, nor would I be able to do something during this small span of life left over. Probably, this is how everyone's life has been and probably such thoughts arise when some persons are taken as examples, not knowing whether such persons were really what they make us to believe or we have projected our concepts of them without their knowing of their qualities. God has become an empty word to me, because I have no capacity to know anything of such an entity called God. I do not know whether such an entity is in existence or it is only a hallucination and mental aberration of such men. I have no capacity to judge anyone while I have lost, rather do not have the capacity to judge myself. To me there is nothing like 'myself', since I do not know what that 'I am' is. The awareness and the consciousness intensely desire for its expansion to universal consciousness, which may be my illusion coming out of the conditioned imaginations. Imaginations that were conditioned lead to faiths and beliefs. These faiths and beliefs that may seem to give strength are really hallowing ones. Man in his greed to take more than what he is capable of, craves for permanency. This craving leads man to every type of staunch beliefs assuring that somehow one day he will be reaching the permanency of this bodily activity. I do not know anything about the intensity of someone's belief and faiths, because I do not know anything about my own and once again 'I AM COMPLETELY EMPTY FROM WITHIN'. May be, I am acquiring that emptiness, rather I can say, I am becoming that very emptiness itself.

4ᵀᴴ DECEMBER 2000   03 30 A.M.

It gives me immense strength and happiness to feel that the Cosmic Being is my close companion. Nothing matters. The whole world's wealth looks like a grain of sand, compared to that companionship. Somehow, the feeling of that eternal companionship is deeply made aware of in me. It looks as if I have been in eternal companionship with this Cosmic Energy in all times. The future, after this physical body disintegrates is something wonderful to look forward to, wherein no desires, no wants, no expectations remain. It is a deep silence, a wonderful and blissful peace that is coming after this life, that very expectation brings the content of that silence and peace now itself. And it is now being experienced as such. Alone—myself alone—with that Cosmic Being in close inter-twain companionship with full understanding with each other, finding no un-towards feelings, is almost the reflection of my own self in that Cosmic Being which is something unimaginable. So deep is this commitment that no longer there will be any fear that 'I' will be separated, come what may, from that all pervading Cosmic Being. It looks, that in the whole universe we are the only two witnessing the entire functions of the universe in all its facets and aspects with no attachment what-so-ever, expanding my conscious universally in every iota of its function, enjoying by being a partner with that Cosmic Being, to eternity. Nothing matters to either of us-me and the Cosmic Being-as long as we are together. But for this togetherness, all other theories, experiences, whether material, or metaphysical, or spiritual, by what-so-ever name it may be called, makes very little consequence. Yes, it is a body-less experience and it is the reality. Bodily experiences are simply illusions, for they are played with insignificant acts in this Cosmic Eternal drama on the stage of the entire universe while only we the two are both the actors and spectators. This spectacular participation I feel, is the Reality, beyond every human knowledge, human rationality and beyond every human emotions. There is neither any static nor dynamic entity which is equivalent to, let alone exceeding, this Cosmic Dynamism. Everything in this universe is a small reflection of the resultant functioning of the Cosmic Being, which in fact, with blissful happiness is witnessed by both of us together. It looks that by a single thought we move together from one end of the universe to other end in a fraction of a second. The very thought takes us anywhere and everywhere. I feel, that there is no place, not even a small remote corner of the entire universe which is unknown to us, which is unfamiliar to us and which is strange to us. The whole universe is in complete harmony, even in its small turbulence, with us. The entire universe belongs to us and we belong to the universe. All the dualities are very insignificant ripples on the surface of the vast eternal ocean of the universe which does not affect the ocean at all. Maybe, I take part in this eternal drama in which that Cosmic Being remains to be the only one Spectator and equally an Actor, and a Director too in His own ways. As, I am both the spectator and an actor of my own drama, which is within the grand drama, that Cosmic Being creates, directs and enacts and witnesses too. However, in the end I remaining with that Cosmic Being alone, though looks to be selfish in terms of the material world, we are the only two who remain together always without leaving each other's company and it is beyond the human knowledge and perception to understand the relationship between myself and that Cosmic Being. This is the Reality. The reality is: we are the only two who remain with each other eternally.

—⚭—

1ST DECEMBER 2000   02 00 A.M.

Fear of death, let alone the death itself, brings even the most powerful and daring person to his knees. The fear, I feel, is responsible for the creation of God and faith on which man completely depends and ultimately has to inevitably die. Along with the present birth the future death too takes birth. It is certain and inevitable. No one can escape it but still the deep desire to live somehow, irrespective of the bodily condition, is the topmost in the mind of man. Physical pain and disease lay the foundation for the fear of death. This fear constantly keeps the company to man, whether the man is aware of it or not due to his daily struggle to keep pace with the life. All theories about God will not eliminate this fear though it may seem to have reduced for the time being. When man grows old, becomes lonely and gets up during nights due to physical discomfort, the practical reality is: there is fear of his being dead before dawn. The night and loneliness-physical as well as mental-coupled with physical diseases and weaker economic conditions definitely wakes up the latent fear of death in man. But still, if a person has been holding on to God and willing to feel that He is with him and His presence is joined with someone like *Sri. Ramakrishna Pramhansa*, this fear, to a great extent, converts itself into calmness to face the death. Some type of courage and peace engulfs such a situation combined with calmness of outside atmosphere.

To me, I am being aware that the time is slowly but surely closing the gap of physical life. I am becoming sometime restless for I have not still realized God. I desire, it is becoming very intense, as the days pass on, that I want to physically experience God and hold Him and understand Him in His true perspective. I need God; this need is becoming intensely sharper, not for living perpetually with physical body but to be with Him perpetually without the physical body. I do feel that I am with Him and He is with me. And yet I am not satisfied with the quantum of His companionship. I desire to have Him entirely for myself. I want Him in my selfishness, weaknesses and at the same time in my selflessness and strength. I desire to expand my conscious to that of His universal conscious and be with Him in all aspects of universal functions including earthquakes, floods, volcanoes, storms, avalanches and destruction and reconstruction of the entire universe, unattached as He is and be with Him in deep SILENCE, PEACE AND BLISS TO ETERNITY.

—ɯ—

28ᵀᴴ NOVEMBER 2000   05 00 A.M.

God is the only perennial and freely available commodity to any person. Once he catches this word he can go on and on till his death either to have it to him or at the same time hypocritically sell it to any thirsty person for a huge amount, like, probably, drugs. Once a person becomes addicted to this word he cannot keep quiet but to purchase it at any cost at any level making himself a slave to the sellers of these words day in and day out and try to consume it though he cannot digest it. It is a mirage in the desert always shifting ahead of the thirsty man, for he cannot catch it while in fact there is nothing to catch. Recently more shops have opened in the market each has decorated this commodity called God with different colors, competing with each other to sell this commodity to gullible, self-hypnotized persons so that such a person can completely be brainwashed in such a way that he should not go to the next shop but always comes back to the same particular shop only to claiming that his shop alone is the original manufacturer of this commodity with latest technique and research done only by that shop while the next shop has an obsolete and dirty commodity which would rather harm the buyer. All tall claims shouted into your system in the name of this commodity so as to acquire a big estate with enormous power over men, money and material all in the name of this commodity. The man who is intoxicated with this word having lost all rationalities, since having felt that he had committed sins in his past days in the absence of this commodity and to appease his left over days, makes not only himself but also every other person nearer and dearer to him to become a slave to these shop runners, but not to the commodity itself. When he first entered the shop it was this commodity that had attracted him with a sweet and hypocritical and brainwashing words of these sellers and slowly but surely without his own knowledge he becomes a slave to these shop runners for they somehow acquire the capacity to make him their slave while with auto suggestions he hypnotizes himself that for the love of this commodity only he goes to that particular shop not for the sake of the shop runners knowing that he cannot do away without these shop runners and knowing fully well that he has become a pawn in their hands and with a fear in his heart that in the event their dropping him he will be completely destroyed and shattered into pieces, which fear in fact was put into his heart by these very shop runners, slowly but surely, lest they go to oblivion and hence they increase their onslaught with all new ways of expression towards this commodity, called God, day in and day out involving Him in every aspects and extracting everything from him before he comes to his senses and run away from them. In the end after having known that he is no more be of any use to them, throw him out, sucked to the last pie and laughing through their sleeves and making a ridiculous person of him and speaking all ills about him which once again gives impetus for the other new-comers that they should not be looked at like that person and so the leftovers will continue to be the slaves of these slaves-the shop runners-having lost all individuality and having become bankrupt both economically and intellectually. Beware of these shop runners and have this commodity called God directly and store it for yourself but do not sell it and if possible distribute it freely, since it is perennial and freely always available.

—m—

27TH NOVEMBER 2000 0330 A.M.

What is thinking? Thought concentrated in a particular wave length may be called as thinking. Deep thinking involves thinking more and more of less and less subject. And the product of deep thinking is something of intangible conclusion, which more often rises-up in further deep thinking. It takes a person beyond the frontiers of tangible thoughts, beyond inexpressible boundaries, while in the depth of silence answers are found, rather realized. Silence too is a thought but of extreme subtle nature. Awareness of silence through one's conscious is almost a mirage causing illusions and hallucinations, because it is beyond the boundaries of rationalism. Rationalism is physical while silence is metaphysical. Metaphysics is something that does not fit in to the framework of rationalist. Once again rationalism being logical it cannot understand the mysticism of metaphysics.

What I am doing now, by writing my deep thoughts, is that I am thinking loud so that someone could be a party to my thinking. To think loud is to make other person a party to my thoughts whether through words of mouth or through words of writing. When a person is alone he may express his thoughts loud through his mouth, but only to himself-to talk to himself. Here another person is not involved, so it cannot be called as 'thinking loud'. The life is almost filled with thoughts. A baby just born also might have the capacity to think and so a man on the death bed, while both would not have the capacity to talk-when the baby is still to acquire that capacity, the man in death bed having lost that capacity. From birth to death thoughts occupy man, rather thoughts only become the living. Even the dumb may have the capacity to think but the normal man cannot understand dumbs ways of thinking, while he can understand another man's line of thinking because that man has got the capacity to 'think-loud', however gross 'these loud thinking' might be compared to the real thinking which is very subtle in nature.

The capacity to 'think-loud' has coined the word 'God' and attributing all such qualities beyond the comprehension of man, naming these qualities as divine while man himself basically remains a devil in nature. The urge to become divine remains only as an urge with a few exceptions here and there. In the process, man becomes a 'demy-god' and 'demy-devil' too, since absolutism can be attributed only to the absolute truth which remains only as a concept of human thinking. As for me, understanding of physical knowledge itself being infinitesimal, it is beyond my comprehension to know what metaphysics is. I know nothing; I am completely ignorant and admit it fully realizing, for sure, that I do not know anything about anything. This is my loud thinking. I do not know how even a particle of sand functions and which part or the whole of that particle of sand plays in the functioning of the universe. I just do not know anything of my own self. I am a mystery to myself and this mystery takes me to a deep silence and I find myself and God in this deep silence.

—∽∿∽—

26ᵀᴴ NOVEMBER 2000   05 00 A.M.

Man is completely conditioned in every aspects of life whether material or mental or metaphysical. The very fact that my birth is conditioned by the family I am born to, by the society, by the religion and by the very humanity itself through its economic, social and spiritual orders. It is but inevitable to be born in a particular family and to be born sometimes to a family-less person.

Slowly but surely, somewhere along the line of my life, my mental attitudes towards all things get conditioned. There cannot be such a state of mind which is unconditioned. The very thought of becoming unconditioned is conditioning oneself to another aspect of life-replacing one condition with the other. These conditions are fed to the mind from the very moment of my birth itself whether I know it or not, whether I invited it or not. It is a continuous process of conditioning and in the process, the concept of God, suited to that particular religion, that particular family, or to that particular institution is fed through rituals, scriptures etc. So God finds a division of himself by these conditions and still man can never even concede the divided God, let alone the undivided one. One never knows for sure what undivided God is like. Even while the very word God itself being a concept projected by these conditions within the framework of mind, it is beyond this mind to project itself to eternity, while the eternity becomes a mere word by the limited intelligence of man who considers himself to be the most intelligent of all species of the universe. So, where does this lead to? To a limited conditioned concept of God that suits and sooths the mind. That brings lullaby to the sleeping mind and in this sleep we walk to nowhere like somnambulist do-with a stupor. And we call this state of mind as God-realization or by any word suited to the comfort of that conditioning. We quote, misquote, elaborate, twist, use and misuse, explain and do everything of the second hand knowledge acquired from these somnambulists to show that we are the 'somebody' and take steps on the foot-prints left behind (or erased?) on the vast sea shore of the universe. To me, personally, there are neither any footprints nor any shore to walk on, for I do not know anything about anything. The more I seek, the more ignorant I become and the more blankness occupies me. I am blank and incapable of receiving or giving; a bundle of nothingness, a bundle of gross ignorance-a speck of dust on the vast canvas of the universe. And yet, the ego in me—(rather I am the very ego itself)-says I am a part of this universe having a spark of cosmic energy and ultimately I am the very cosmic energy itself, but covered with the past results, in the process of time, space and causations. But deep within I find the bliss of silence, an ignorant sweet, beautiful and blissful silence-the Epitome of 'Me'.

—ᴍ—

25ᵀᴴ November 2000   03 30 a.m.

Mind is the projector of thoughts. Thought is a subtle wave of Cosmic Energy expressed through the medium of mind to make the awareness of itself. Thought, sometimes, produces actions. In a way thought is also an action or a reaction of consciousness on the screen of mind. It is through thought awareness expresses itself. Awareness is the expression of conscious. Thought brings everything this universe holds. Even the God is the product of thought. Everything, for that matter, is the product of thought. Deep thinking on any subject brings a breakthrough and there will be a psychological mutation that explodes the truth of that subject. Only when all the original beliefs, doctrines and dogmas are shattered completely, does the psychological mutations take place to reveal the reality of such thoughts. With this psychological mutations, the mutations of physical cells too take place and no more originals, either mental or physical, remain. By seeking it, no such mutation takes place. It strikes by itself without choosing any particular person and without any definite formula. It just happens, which is beyond the human rationality or intelligence. It may not strike a saint with one hundred years of meditation on the Himalayan peak, but it may strike a worst and hardcore criminal in prison. No one knows why and how this happens. All books, talks, experiments, striving etc are like predictions of rains in an almanac. When you wrench an almanac, which predicts rains, not even a drop of water comes out of it and further the predictions would, in majority, go wrong. It is beyond human understanding. Man is helpless in spite of his advancement in science. Science is the product of deep and concentrated thoughts. There is mutation of mind for break-through in science. You may observe the great scientist who had breakthrough in their subjects having gone through both mental and physical mutations. They come to look physically neither as a man nor as women which is the result of physical mutation. They look at the universe with awe; for they cannot understand the functioning of the universe. They become more aware of their limited intelligence, their ignorance and small achievements in presence of the whole Cosmic Intelligence. They become childlike persons having come to be aware of their ignorance and limitations. Their vanity vanishes. They become humble. Humility reflects in their behavior and on their face. This is what results in psychological mutation (of mind). God will not come through seeking especially in the institutions-mass seeking, mass believing, and mass meditation etc. The best these Institutions do is: to prevent some people acting criminally at least during those hours of their participation so that there will be some social order during such times of their attending such institutions. Seeking in these institutions will be just a brainwash that cages our thoughts in their doctrines. Nothing, as for me by going to such institutions, has happened, as I thought that it would. But now I am sure nothing could happen, for there is nothing to happen. Even if something is to happen, I am completely ignorant of it and I know nothing about any happening, except for an insignificant psychological mutation, which resulted in my awareness of incapacity to understand anything about anything. Now, I know for sure that I know nothing and also I will not know anything. This understanding of self-ignorance, leads me to deep, very deep SILENCE within wherein I find myself one with the Cosmic Being.

—⟋⟍—

20ᵀᴴ NOVEMBER 2000   03 30 A.M.

Power is the name of the game. The power with the economic, intellectual, physical, military, political or even for that matter, spiritual, would give a big kick to holder of such powers., so that the power holder would make the lesser privileged person to subjugate. Some people who may lack everything but for the power of speech—words—would equally get such a kick to subdue others. It becomes impossible for any being to live, rather exist without wielding some type of power at some time or the other. Even the lowest person refuses to do what he is supposed to do for which he is paid, just for the heck of a kick it gives him to confirm himself that he is equally an important person in a given circumstance. All types of power would push-up a person's ego. Ego is what one thinks of oneself while the vanity is what one expects others should think of him—an imagination projected on others to think about him. The whole universe, a man thinks, depends on his thoughts and actions. But if a small, very small cell in a part of his brain malfunctions then it brings him completely down and he thinks no more of others and to some extent about himself. And that is the end of his universe. A small tumor in his brain makes him dysfunctional and brings pain and misery to his life. In the process all his egos and vanity fall like a 'house-of-cards'. Life slips away between his fingers and he can never hold, let alone control his life. So fragile is the man and his egos. And still that is how the universe functions naturally in its own ways reflecting itself through the various facets of the lives of men making him a history—a dead past. Dead live in the memory of the living and so are the living in the memory of other livings. Memory is the living and throbbing energy only of the dead past, which influences the present and the future. However, time (the universal functioning movements) is fleeting away without turning back or looking forward to. It just moves from one second to the next. Neither does it limps nor jumps nor stops nor goes back. It has the forward movement to precision. It does not care as to who would role under it. Everyone has to come to be crushed by its movements. There cannot be any person or anyone event that could be mightier than this movement of the universe in its function.

Movement as such does not have either the past or the present or the future. It is just a movement—in space with pace and peace.

—∿—

23ʳᵈ November 2000   04 00 a.m.

God is one word which brought many risks in many parts of the world. People become dogs in the name of god of various beliefs. Everyone think that what he believes is the only faith and all other beliefs are wrong. God is available only to him and not to others. And only in his faith the god is available and not in others. God is made a limited commodity. Fear of death creates God and in the end to find perpetuity to life, men follow different faiths, disappointed ultimately and his fear of death having multiplied. While 'fear' is the reality of human life, God is the concept to fight out this fear. The war between the fear and God occupies the human mind which has become the war field. Fear of failure, fear of becoming poor, fear of ridicule in the society, fear of being lost—and becoming 'no-body', while the ambition to be 'some-body' always pre dominates the human desire—whether in spiritual or material life. This deep desire to be 'some-body' is the real creator of mischievousness in the human life. Nothing exceeds than to be 'somebody' and desires to live in others mind as somebody does on our mind. This is the upper most desire of man—to be 'some-body'.

—∿—

19ᵗʰ November 2000   03 00 a.m.

Nothing has the ultimate answer. In what all that is done so far in every field the human being can think of, including the so called philosophy and the applied spirituality, the answer, I feel is not found. The ultimate answer is; that there is no answer. For the answer we seek is the answer to our conceptualized questions. And whatever the answer is, it is not the answer, for the question itself is the answer and ultimately the question and the answer are the obverse and reverse of the same coin of the human mind. Human mind being restless, being a living one and a throbbing one, needs strength to go on. It has no satisfaction with anything, the moment the mind is satisfied, it finds its own death. The death of mind would be the death of human race itself. The human mind is a voraciously hungry but bottomless stomach. Any thing put into it, vanishes without digestions leaving it almost empty. It can never be fulfilled. So, no answer can be arrived at. Framing of question is limiting the mind. And naturally the answer too would be limited. Time has no sentimental values. Neither the time is harsh nor has any kindness. It has its natural phenomena of movement—time I feel is physical—a physical dimension to measurer physical things including the physical position of the body, though it is hypothetical one. The reality is that there is this movement—the accurate and precise movement which never can be influenced either to jump or limp or stop or to go backwards, even to a fraction. This movement, what I conceive, is the manifestation of the universal movement. The universal movement is also the universal functioning. The universal functioning is the functioning of the cosmic energy manifesting in its totality and its naturalness. Even a cancer cell functions naturally to its qualities. Cancer is energy. It neither by itself has any positive nor negative aspects. When occasion comes to function with other cells do the war takes place and once again the stronger survives naturally. The higher the potency of energy the higher is the survivor. It is directly proportional to the potency of the energy, both physical and latent it has, which decides its survival. This is of the physical world. So would be with the subtle world too—if there is any such a world at all. And if at all it exists, it does within the universe. In all aspects of the universe and its functions, I being a part of its inevitable fraction of function, I can never understand whatever may be my intellectual capacity, of the universal function. I just know that I know nothing of anything about anything. This knowledge of accepting 'I don't know' is, I think, the ultimate answer is to everything. The desire to know something has its answer. Your imagination of something is the answer to your imagined question. I am sure, now, and I know for sure that I do not know anything about anything, is my ultimate answer to myself and my own questions. So, the questions and answers burnout themselves within me, leaving emptiness and deep silence in me as my answers. The ultimate answer is the 'deep silence is me'

—m—

17ᵀᴴ November 2000   04 00 a.m.

Why this feeling of 'let-go' engulfing me? I do not know. Somehow, I feel completely at peace and at the same time confused. Confused because temptation to be other than what I am, a desire to improve the status even at this age in the profession, probably to earn more, and at the same time to give-up everything and to run away from this desire. Not physical running away but mentally to give up everything. I feel that I am tired and at the same time am running away as I have not achieved anything so far in terms of so called spiritual life. I somehow want to catch that Cosmic Force soon or else the time will slip away. The intense desire to catch that energy and be with that energy internally is the desire in me. There are lots of pulls from many sides in different directions. I want to stop this. Somehow, I want to be myself. I should stop running around for improving my status—physical worldly professional status. The intense desire is to give up everything—but where to next? I know not. There is no escape. Escape is only a word, because there is nothing to escape from or to escape to. Escaping involves running, that is movement either physical or mental within the framework of space, time and causation. The body in which I live has somehow became 'me' and without the body I am not 'I am' and also in its activities. Activity, whether tangible or intangible, whether visible or invisible is the energy. Energy is both physical and subtle. Universe is dogmatically functioning in its natural ways, both as constructive and destructive, as the man differentiate to his liking and disliking. That which is against the desire of man becomes destructive and that which is desirous to human is constructive.

However, there is an intense desire to escape. This escape involves two factors, one is the past and the other is the future. Past being unpalatable, forces escape from the present to some imaginative better future to where escaping to is desired.

—m—

8ᵀᴴ NOVEMBER 2000   02 00 A.M.

Well, I have been talking to Shri Ramakrishna Paramahansa—my *Guru Mahraji*. I always love to talk to him who gives me thorough instructions and guidance, he is the greatest. He is the complete divine personality. He always stands by me in the worst and the best of circumstances. He is always there with me. Whenever I feel something wanting he fulfills my desires, with divine love. I am receiving the divine love from *Guru Maharajji*. He seems to be everything to me. He is impressed of my both physical and subtle actions which includes subconscious thoughts.

—m—

3ʳᵈ November 2000   03 00 a.m.

It is inevitable for everybody to go through his life span between birth and death, with no excuses or no expectations or expansions. The only defense to struggle is, to make it more peaceful—which itself is contradictory in terms. For any attempt to make the life other than 'what-is', is definitely not peaceful process. Peace comes in accepting, rather being natural without calling for any defense of ones own actions or thoughts. While either defense, or struggle or even the process which involves to be other than 'what—is', definitely is not peaceful. 'To—let go' is the best defense with no struggle at all. But 'let go' is arrived at on having compromised thoughts and experiences of not achieving what the concepts of conditional social order sets—which includes God. The background of all these are ambition of permanency to eternity while fear of death is the foundation for this ambition to be permanent. What is permanency? It is nothing but an ideal created by mind with hypothetical dimension of time. When once the time is removed there stands nothing but permanency, which has neither past, nor present nor the future. All these concepts of past, present and future are within the realms of time. Eternity dissolves time. Time is only a movement, a product that is slipping away, a process through which infinity and eternity project themselves dissolving without any trace of time. And yet, the only permanency seems to be the past—the dead past—in the memory of the human mind, while the present cannot be held—it being only a word and the future is the projection of the past and also the future is a shadow of the past-projected by the conceptual mind with the experiences of the past. The fear being in the present, while the experiences and knowledge are of the past and the death is in the future. Observations and feelings imprinted deeply upon the mind of the past wherein the death of others have taken place, creating self-fear for the present for the self-death of the future, produces God, to hold on to thinking that somehow God will help me to my permanency and remove the fear of death from me. While I always think that I shall never die and yet, the fear of death lingers in me. This becomes conditioning. Everything is to condition—including religion and God. Religion conditions human race to act and behave in a particular fashion while the God conditions the very mind of humans. I can never escape conditioning. At best I can give up a particular conditioning, only to replace it by another. My very thoughts are conditioning me. Freedom, individuality etc. remain to be only phrases—mere words. The sum totality of my life is one continuous conditioning with different degrees though not of kind, replacing one by another. There is no escape from conditioning. I am bound strongly to my or to others ideals who are too bound to such ideologies of others. This bondage is a chain reaction.

—⚎—

1ˢᵗ November 2000 03 00 A.M.

Nothing matters about the human attitudes and the results thereon, to the totality of the natural functioning of the universe. The universe functions taking in its stride everything that happens to our earth where—upon only (and probably) the intelligence exist—rather living organisms exist. Living or non living makes no difference to the functions of the Universe. The living organism is a part of the universal function. I feel that the entire universe is only one complete organism functioning in its own natural ways, beyond the comprehension of any limited intelligence of human beings which may be compared to the human body which has trillions of cells having their own characteristics and functions as living organisms. The manifestation of the entire function of all the cells of all the organs of an animate body is ultimately the one function of that body. The sum total function of every particle of DNA in a cell being the function of that cell, which in turn is the function of the whole body of a man or rather any living organism. Despite of all such functions going on in their own natural way, there is something that functions un-touched or un-mindful of the functions of all the cells of the human body, may be that (awareness) is 'ME'. While the entire lot of cells on reproducing one like themselves, die-out unaware and uninfluenced by the other cells. But the individual being aware of oneself of one's existence from and to eternity, accumulating, in certain ways, the results of all previous functions which further guide the future functioning of the individual which is being called as 'KARMA'. But are not all these philosophical definitions within the realm of human limited intellectual interpretation of the so called divine knowledge?

Human beings have given themselves very high position—super intelligence position than the cosmic intelligence while the humans are only a speck of dust compared to the cosmic function. I have come to the conclusion by myself and for myself that I know nothing and understand nothing of my own self, let alone that which are beyond me. So, the only way is to know for sure that nothing can be understood in the correct perspective and in their natural functioning. Acceptance that 'I know nothing about anything', I feel, is the first step and them comes the 'defense less-ness'. When I want—want being a perspective concept—things to happen in my way and when it does not happen, I start fighting within me with everything external to me. When once I stop to fight I become defenseless in the circumstances and nothing other than 'what—is' will naturally function. 'I' being a part of the whole universe, functions with the universe with least resistance and only then would I function naturally, even though I would not know I how function or rather how the universe functions. My struggle starts from me and ends with me without any least impact on the functioning of the universe. In the end I destroy myself. I am very important to myself, since if I exist the universe exists to me, and not the other way round. My functions, so far, on the vast beach are wiped off without a trace by the waves of the sea of time except a few wasteful memories that are dead, making no impact of what so ever.eithr on the waves or on the sea, while the wave is not a separate entity from the sea. Best, I find, is to stop struggling either internally or externally, but to accept without defending myself externally so that these acceptance and defenselessness becomes a part of me internally.

—⚏—

21ST OCTOBER 2000   03 00 A.M.

Is there no way to escape permanently from everything including me from myself? That is to free myself from my own self. Somehow everyone desires to escape from his own self and free himself from everything. Escaping from money, material, name, fame etc. of the physical world could be understood from the philosophical way of thoughts. But escaping from one's own self is the ultimate one. Becoming, day in and day out, a prisoner of one's own thoughts and then running after mirages, knowing fully well that all are mirages including oneself is the human nature. May be, even this very thought of escaping is a mirage; since there is nothing to escape from or to escape to and there is nothing that requires escaping. Thoughts produce tremendous energy and this energy binds oneself to oneself through thoughts. God is a thought, conditioned from birth. It becomes impossible to escape from these conditions and these limitations. My God is a limitation. Why should anybody condition oneself to the limited framework of God? Beyond God lies independence, I feel. Self is limited; God is a bigger limited frame. We are conditioned in every way. There is no escape from these conditionings. Social order is to condition, though externally, for the welfare of the whole society, which in turn slowly but surely conditions the self from within. And somewhere along the line, the thin border of external and internal conditioning vanish and they look to be the same and in an abstract way. And in the process, one limitation expands to another dimension of limitation. Probably the body and mind represent these two dimensions of limitations. It is impossible to segregate these two. One cannot function without the other and ultimately they are only one and they are not two and together they create a bigger dimension of limitation. Nothing could be really understood in the real sense of functioning of anything through these two instruments—body and mind. Everything is beyond understanding. Understanding is a limited faculty within limited and conditioned knowledge—second hand knowledge acquired—a conceptual knowledge projected from the limited intelligence, a person possess. Hence, infinity, independence, eternity etc. remain as mere words within the framework of these limitations of knowledge and yet there lingers within me a small ray of knowledge which knows for sure that I am eternal, indestructible and untouchable from everything; since I am a part of that cosmic energy having all the qualities of that cosmic energy and finally I am that very cosmic energy itself, as a spark of fire is the fire itself—'I—am-That'.

20ᵀᴴ OCTOBER 2000   03 30 A.M.

When I look back upon my life now, at this late noon of my life, I find that *Sri Ram Krishna Paramahamsa* had been, and of course even now is, with me at every turning point of my life.

There had been many tangential turn which then I felt them to be for my disadvantages, but later turned out for my advantages only. At every point of my life he has been with me. And his presence was more felt, having sought, when I was in some crisis or the other guiding me, consoling me, giving me strength by standing with me at every turn in my life.

9ᵀᴴ OCTOBER 2000   01 00 A.M.

What is wisdom? Is it not the opposite of ignorance and foolishness or some other things? Anyway, mostly everything has opposites. Those that are acceptable rather enjoyable freely without obstruction to one's self are taken as positive and others as negatives. So the duality continues. Positive or negative, in terms of absolute, make no meaning. By themselves, both sweet and poison, are perfect in their nature. It is the acceptance or rejection by the body or the mind makes the quality change. And so with the so called spiritualism. In spiritualism God is Sweet and devil is poison. Both God and Devil are the creation so the mind's concepts accepted and substantiated by the human society so that even the weakest, whether physically or economically or intellectually, being survived. Survival in the physical body, despite of diseased organs, is always the permanent desire of the animate objects including human being. This desire is unique, for it imagines, having known that this physical body comes to an end. This desire to be permanent extends beyond the present while there is nothing called either the present or the future. The past projects itself to the future through the present and hypothetically the time creates the past, present and future, which in turn are nothing but the hypothetical ones. The past is the history in memory of the human society; it is just a memory fading out slowly. So when there remains no past, it cannot project itself to the future. Hence the present and the future remains a fallacy since the past is fading in the memory. So the whole concept of time becomes illusory and hallucination, a mirage and an aberration of mind. When the concept of time collapses, the concept of space and cause-effect too collapse and in the end there remains 'NOTHING'. 'Nothingness' survives, 'Not-knowing-ness' survives. So the human mind is pervaded by this nothingness which is beyond time, space and causation; in spite of all tall claims a man may make with his so called knowledge, especially the spiritual knowledge. Knowledge is to know and to understand that very knowledge including the knowledge of God is only ephemeral. Almost all thoughts are subjugated to the thought of God. Manifestation of thoughts mould an individual and project him as an entity through the very thought itself. While the thoughts are very subtle waves, the individual is the result of the projection at different degrees of these thoughts, which is a continuous process. The very imagination of the state of thoughtlessness is nothing but a thought at a different degree level. Thoughtlessness is death, death is silence and in silence the death reflects itself and in deep silence death finds the God. So silence goes beyond death and that silence is immeasurable and is the truth and in that silence all the potentialities of the cosmic world exist. And into that silence I dive and ultimately I become the very silence itself to find myself reflected in that Truth.

30ᵀᴴ September 2000

03 30 A.M.

There is neither to celebrate nor to mourn anything in the life. It is a continuous process of functioning. It is by itself has no value system. It is the society that gives values according to its conditioning of social and religious orders which are once again changeable from time to time. The whole universe by its own nature functions as naturally as it should. But human nature being what it is, tries to interfere in the functioning of the universe which makes least impact for the reason that whatever human do is only for his existence not for the functioning of the universe, while universe does not require the help of human, but reverse is the true with the human. Man tries to control external nature but fails to control his inner nature. Being very much sure that the nature of the universe is immensely strong, man desiring to subjugate the universe, invents some other non existing force making his own statement that the other force invented by him is superior to the entire force the universe, and that man is very close to the superior force to draw solace to himself for his failure to control the universal force. Man can never control the universe for he is only infinitesimal part of the whole, though he has the same qualities of the universe. Man's consciousness, rather awareness that he is one with the universe should bring him the sense of making peace rather to confront the nature of the universe. Silence, the silence within oneself where neither the mind nor the intellect nor even of one's self exist, would bring peace and bliss to man for he becomes the very universe in his qualities and an inseparable entity. And yet, in his thought man separates himself and becomes thirsty for unification. The creation and non creation are the thoughts of man of his dissatisfaction and wanting. Dissatisfaction in the present status and wanting to become other than 'what he is' is one of his problems, but sure he continuous to be 'what-he-is' because to become something other than what-'he-is' is only mirage in his mind which he chases and drops dead in the end neither realizing the reality of 'what-he-is', nor the illusion of his mirage.

—⚏—

29ᵀᴴ September 2000

03 30 A.M.

As the age of this body increases, so the attitude of 'let-go' too increases. In every matter 'let-go' comes in. The fire that was once inside is almost cool and may be it turns out to be an ice cube one day. Nothing matters anymore, even my own body coming to an end. Looking forward to an imaginative 'after-life' gives a kick to the present, as if I am going to arrive at to a new universal phenomenal consciousness and occupy to comprehend the whole universe, recognizing myself in every aspects of the universe. In this state of being, there stands, in a very subtle form, the awareness of myself, which is something inexpressible and in a way this awareness of myself forms separate entity—the ego of oneself—stays on permanently and obviously. Thus, subtle ego of self looks to me to be an eternal one passing on from one phase to another phase; from one level to another level; from one degree to another degree without loosing its originality. May be, this ego, or self, or whatever it may be called, go through eternally, hoping that the next could be more important, more pleasurable than the present one, while in actuality there is neither past nor present nor future. These-the dimensions of time, cause-effect, space etc. are only human illusions created by the mind due to its conditioning—socially, religiously and even economically to some extent. In spite of this attitude of 'let-go' there is some thing deep with in, a desire in a very subtle way, to attain that something, to arrive at that something, to hold that something, to gain that something. But what that something is? I do not know. That something is definitely not at all those things which I know and which are already experienced by me or which I perceive physically and mentally. This 'something' which I desire, is beyond my comprehension. This 'beyond', may be, once again a concept, may be a hallucination equally. Slowly but surely somewhere along the line I have lost, in reality, the knowledge—the ego of knowledge, the ego of 'I know'. Now, I know that I don't know anything about anything. I am a complete ignorant person. It took many decades of this life to understand for myself and by myself that I am the most ignorant person knowing nothing about anything and not knowing anything about anything, while all these years I was thinking that I knew everything. However, whatever I knew were not what that 'Reality is' and whatever I knew were only empty husk which has burnt out and ashes scattered by winds living the emptiness of ignorance in me. I am now completely empty. This knowledge of emptiness is dawning upon me at the dusk of my life. Probably great men like *Sri ShankarAcharya* and *Swami Vivekananda* must have realized this emptiness very much in the midmorning of their life which perhaps might have led to their death before noon, while men like me of the emptiness with false knowledge live till the end of dusk, when the bubble emptiness bursts

28ᵗʜ September 2000   03 30 a.m.

Nothing explains anything. Any explanation of anything is only a rough concept of the individual's understanding of that thing. When so, how could it be possible for a tiny cell in a tiny brain of a man can explain anything? Man cannot explain about his own self, because he does not know anything about himself and he is a total stranger to himself, so I feel. I don't know anything about my own self, let alone of other things of the universe. Universe does not stand on the understanding of the man about the universe. Man is only a grain of sand on the vast sea shore of the universe and its functions. The birth, living and death are just other functions of the universe, as the universe spins around by itself which includes the vast space within the universe. The energy of functioning of this universe is the cosmic energy and the cosmic intelligence which produces by itself perennially and eternally. Everything is really dynamic derived from the universal cosmic energy. Not an iota of sand can exist as a separate entity by itself without it being contained in the universal cosmic energy. Neither anything be added nor taken away from out of this universal cosmic energy. It is all pervading, omnipresent, omniscient and omnipotent in its nature. Birth of an insect and death of an elephant also are the manifestations of the same cosmic energy at different degrees but not of different kind. If birth and death are understood in their real perspective, fear of death and the desire to be permanent vanish, for there is nothing to be called as temporary, but one of permanence in different degrees. When this understanding comes and reality dawns, it brings peace, tranquility and bliss, all in deep silence. And still having confined to the limitations of body, though not separated from body, this 'I' functions through the body, which, once again, is nothing but the expressions of the same cosmic energy at different degrees with many facets. However, human being is a peculiar expression of this cosmic energy. It is only the human who has wide range expressible emotions. No other animate beings can come anywhere nearer to the human's nature of emotions. They are unique and peculiar to the humans. From this human nature of emotions the world is discovered by man. These human emotions have created and sustained God, irrespective of rationality or argument or philosophy on God.

20ᵀᴴ Sᴇᴘᴛᴇᴍʙᴇʀ 2000   03 30 ᴀ.ᴍ.

Human society lives in fear as the animals do. However it is peculiar to human for which he depends upon God and also he fears God. It is the fear of mighty and the unknown. This unknown being the creation of human mind, it fears its own creation—rather it fears itself. The known and the unknown are the emotional creations of the human mind, an expression of energy, derived from the very cosmic energy, while neither the so called known nor the so called unknown exists. They are just waves of the mind. Only, if and when human mind arrives at the conclusion that its function of thought is a natural phenomenon of universal force and its functions, only then would the human mind unshackles itself from all its perceptions and drives to the deepest silence beyond the nature of the human mind itself. And in this deep silence man is reflected of his true nature, recognizing himself with that of universal cosmic energy which is infinite and beyond the limitations of space, time and causations.

—ɰ—

28 Aᴜɢᴜsᴛ 2000   01 00 ᴀ.ᴍ.

Some people advocate that unless one empties everything of the past the future cannot be filled. In abstract sense, I feel that time, space and causation, the past, present and future, in terms of time, the emptiness in terms of space and filling that emptiness in terms of causation, are all just void words. To me having known nothing, having realized that I know nothing of any of these so called universe and its function, being myself a part of that very function itself, getting the knowledge of function as a separate entity, makes no difference what-so-ever to me. All may be the same in different degrees but not in kind.

God, religion, life, the universe, the society have no meaning to me since I do not understand any of these. As, sweet cannot taste itself its sweetness, so I cannot understand any of these functions being myself the part of this universal function, however small that part may be. The conceited ego and the simplicity, the hate and the love, the sorrow and bliss, are the dualities that have not been influencing me, of late. And yet, deep down there lies a crazy feeling that I should become the whole universe in every aspects of the universe and I desire to find my reflection in every thing the universe holds.

—ɰ—

12ᵀᴴ AUGUST 2000   03 00 A.M.

In the order of functioning of the universe comprising of everything, the known and the unknown, there are no roads, no paths because there are no goals, no destiny, 'not-to-be-arrived at'. It is a hallucination of mind to find a path to an illusory goal. It is like a mirage in a desert. In desert there are no paths or ways to the mirage and mirage is an illusory goal. It is just an illusion of mind created by the heat of the desert. The heat is the philosophy that creates a mirage the God, in the deserted path way of this society. The whole thing I feel is a hog-wash, a brain-wash of those who want to live out of the weaks. They lead a comfortable life by taking these weaks on a beautiful ride creating sweet and encompassing words to which these weaks fall pray and when they are sucked completely, they are thrown out and discarded as dirt. They would have sycophants, flatterers, and cronies around them, who not only sell away all of themselves but also become slaves to them. When such hundreds of weak men fall pray to one person, that one person becomes so rich to control these hundreds of men with whose gratis that person became rich to have his own vast estate and God manufacturing industry to suit the individual, creating illusions of 'experiencing-God', and ultimately this weak person becomes an addict to such illusory experiences and dies in illusion like a poor dog on a street.

—ɷ—

11ᵀᴴ AUGUST 2000   03 00 A.M.

Man is the creator and destroyer of everything including the so called God. Man's mind runs astray beyond its control. Most wonderful part of mind is its capacity to imagine, imagine what is not there, what is beyond, its power to comprehend. And still, it reaches where man cannot. However, with the death of man the mind loses itself. Life in the body creates everything including the mind and its recognition. Whether the mind can be separated from the thought? Mind is a thought and intellect is its functioning at a different degrees. Thought is reflected in another thought. Thought creates, in many subtle ways, the existence of inner core of man. Thought works like waves of ocean, non-stop, while mind may be called as ocean and intellects its depth. The depth of water being intellect and the mind being ocean, the thought as waves, they cannot be separated and they are one and the same. Deeper the ocean, lesser the waves. Waves have no separate existence other than ocean.

So thought has no separate existence other than mind. At the same time thought has no independent existence. It is the product of the cosmic thought. The sum total of entire universal thought energy is the cosmic thought energy which in small quantities with lower frequencies is received by the human antenna, the brain, to reproduce in the mind that make the cosmic thought to appear as thought of the individual, while there is no such a thought which could be called a 'Individual thought'—even this very writing is a cosmic thought energy that is in low frequency on the surface of my mind which is written though the intellectual operation of my body, in such subtle ways and with such high degree of speed and competence, that the very thought cannot comprehend its own production.

—◯◯◯—

7ᵀᴴ August 2000   12 15 a.m.

I feel I am the sum total of all my body's cells, may be trillions of them, and thus my body is a universe by itself and I am the center of this unifying body. And the entire universe is the sum total of everything and the center of it may be called as God. All the trillions of them die on producing one like them, so this universe replaces itself while the center remains eternal beyond space, time and causations. I feel, that there is this unbreakable, indestructible, eternal connection between the 'real me' and that 'center' of the cosmic energy of the universe. Deep down I feel and experience this eternity of 'me'. There is no fear in me to go to the next life and leave behind the present one. I always feel the eternality of the journey, the destiny-less, an aimless, a goal-less journey. The idea of destiny, aim and goal have a time frame, also a definite space-span and upon arrival a definite causation. But, here in this journey to eternity it has no such definite element; it is infinite and eternal and I am riding this eternal journey. But in reality there is neither journey nor I am involved in the journey. They become the way of expression and brain washing words, mere words having no meanings. Qualification or nomenclature made and calling them as spiritual, Godly, divine etc. and also to opposite of them, have no value system to me. Everything is the same and nothing is what it looks to be and nothing could be understood. I am sure I know that I know nothing of anything. This awareness of not knowing, not comprehending, is the reality to me. Some where along the line of this life, I realized that there is nothing to know, for it can never be known in the way 'as-it-is'. Probably this is the greatest blow to my egoistic intelligence by which awareness I am becoming empty and the intelligence till now I had, as 'I—know', has come to a complete naught and I am now being empty upon the burning of these knowledge, is very refreshing, blissful, joyful, the happiness of which I had not experienced till now. This emptiness is vast and deep beyond sound and beyond mundane qualities—an eternal sweet silence of bright tiny light, enlightening the whole universe, spreading bliss and joy to all. I am one with that blissful sweet deep silence of light.

—⁂—

4ᵗʰ June 2000   05 00 A.M.

Somewhere deep within me, a feeble voice echo's the feelings that I am a part the universal consciousness, and myself recognizing and becoming one with the whole universal functioning, I being a part of the cosmic eternal energy. I would rather feel that this feeling is the cosmic love. The whole universe is me and I love myself, which means I love the whole universe as myself irrespective of its social qualifications, in the absolute sense. I don't know how I expand to the infinite eternal cosmic consciousness which brings bliss, joy and the divinity in me. Everything vanishes and only consciousness remains without a second one. Nothing touches me while I am in this state of consciousness. All material, spiritual knowledge vanish. Only awareness of the universal consciousness remains. It looks as if my chest is expanding to a limit-less boundary. Everything, the millions of galaxies with their milky ways, billions of stars etc. vanish and I am with them and they are with me in the most natural ways. The volcanoes, floods, storms, catastrophes are most friendly and play their part as insignificant phenomenon in the functioning of the entire universe. They are natural, blissful, joyful, divine in their own ways and functioning unaware of anything except to function in the way they do. To me everything looks the same without qualifying them without naming them and without any result of either positive or negative nature from their functions. They are most perfect, natural in every aspects and complete (**Sampoorna**) in their characteristic by themselves. In every function I see and feel the manifestation of that cosmic energy—call it as God or by any name. It is like calling the rays of the sun as a separate entity from the sun. Sun is the provider of heat and light and it functions in its most natural ways bringing heat and light to everything that faces sun. Light cannot be separated from the sun. Sun without light cannot be called as sun. So the heat and light and sun are one and the same. They are not different they cannot be separated as entities. So God is projecting and manifesting everywhere in different degrees. This manifestation cannot be an independent entity from God. God will not have any existence without these manifestations. Hence God and his manifestations are one and the same; and as such God is attributed to be all pervasive—omnipresent—omnipotent and omniscient. But still it is impossible to qualify or to understand what qualities are like. God can never be understood in the way man tries to qualify God; if at all done, it is with reference to man's concept and social values calling it as positive, divine, virtuous etc. which are conditioned by man's hypothetical concepts. In the real sense, having no other capacity to understand myself expect through my own conceptual conditioning, my functioning is possible. It is the cosmic energy and its functions through its manifestation in different degrees, which could be perceived by my limited, tiny, intelligence, is impossible because these understanding comes only as a part of that cosmic intelligence, of that Cosmic Being while I am the very manifestation of the same cosmic being though a tiny one. My fear, my selfishness, my enmity, my anxiousness etc. are the manifestations of the same energy in different degrees. All these are, whether of divine or devilish, only because I create a separate entity of myself from the whole and I am afraid of my destruction as separate entity, on recognizing myself having a beginning and an end. But when I think that I am a part of the whole rather I am the whole of the entire functioning of the universe from eternity to eternity, the separateness vanishes and so all qualities whether divine or devilish become one with the universal consciousness of the entire cosmos.

—◇—

30ᵀᴴ May 2000   04 00 a.m.

I am sure that the time is short and the D-Day is nearing. Nothing could give back what has been spent as my life so far. This may be a phrase of life. Life, I feel, is eternal beyond time, but, eternal cyclic life where each span of physical birth and death is only a phase just like one step in the eternal journey. Lifting of one leg to tread a step is both the death of previous step and birth of the next step. And the distance between the two legs is an empty space which may be called as life. But in reality it is full of cosmic energy with subtle organic lives, conditioned to time and cause-effect. So is the gross life of man. Man can go beyond the condoning of space, time and cause-effect. It is something to be looked forward to that when man also frees himself from every possible conditioning both physical and intellectual. It is more blissful, most desiring. I feel, in that state, the consciousness expands to the whole universe, it becomes a universal one, aware of its state and stage. Everything of the universe becomes aware of itself in which I see myself. The cosmic energy engulfs me and brings blissful joy. This universal consciousness cannot be caught within the frame work of my intellect which I may call mere physical. I feel, that I can never subject my awareness of my not knowingness of myself or of this universe to this limited intellectual framework of rationality. Rationality is being subjected to variations. But I know nothing about this. It is beyond rationality and it is eternal. It is the one central subtle cosmic energy which manifests itself with different degrees. No qualities or qualification can be attributed to this cosmic energy. Even the very thought waves that are produced within the intellect of a person, are the expression of that cosmic energy in different degrees and wave lengths. Nothing could either be added or taken away from this cosmic energy. It is all pervading and yet looks to be of different entities, each differing from the other. But in reality there is no difference. It is the same energy that expresses itself and manifests itself with different degrees, having its own intelligence. Energy is intelligence and intelligence is energy. It is not a mere word, this unknown and inexpressible universal cosmic Being. I am one with this cosmic energy. I cannot perceive myself other than to be this cosmic energy, but in reality what is called as an entity in me is not a separate one from the functioning of the Universe. I can never be aware of myself and still I could be aware that I know nothing about anything including my own self because knowing is to separate oneself from the known. Knower is not different from knowable and the known and also the process of knowing; all being one and the same of 'me

—ᗯ—

29ᵀᴴ MAY 2000   05 00 A.M.

My sojourn for these years has made me to realize that I should return to my home, hence as a prodigal son, I went back to *Sri Ramakrishna*. The three days of *mela* conducted between 18th and 21st of May 2000 has made me to realize that I really belong to *Sri Ramakrishna*. My days away from him had been a bad dream I can say. He is the real person, a realized *avatar* of God. But still I must go beyond being attached to him. I love him immensely as I do not do with any others. I have no such personal God as such. *Sri Ramakrishna* is the only icon to me whom I regard and love; and the other persons are *Mata Sharada Devi* and *Shri Ramana Maharushi*.

—ᗯ—

15ᵀᴴ MAY 2003   03 00 A.M.

I feel, I am a part of the whole cosmic energy. The matter which is comprehended is not the matter but energy expressed and manifested in different degrees. The whole universe is one eternal energy, which is beyond the dimensions of time, space and causations. Nothing is static. It is one and the only one dimension of dynamic energy. Even the most subtle emotions like love, anger etc. are nothing but the expressions of that very energy at different degrees. Whatever is seen—even the way of seeing is energy. Hearing, smelling, tasting, touching everything including this very writing is nothing but the expression of the one and the same energy at different degrees. So the God though manifested at different levels and in different degrees is the same, irrespective of how the human being conceives the God within the frame work of his concepts, God can never change but can never be understood.

—ɯ—

6ᵀᴴ MAY 2000   05 00 A.M.

More men were are being killed in the name of religion than in all wars. Religion, when taken into the hands fundamentalist, die and God runs away from them, though they profess that they are the messengers of God, while the rationalist denies the very existence of God. God, who is being introduced to the humanity through various religions, acts variously in their hands. While God himself slips away between their fingers, leaving them empty handed, so that they could kill others who do not fall-in-line with them. And God witnesses all these actions of men of religions and He goes hiding lest these men may kill Him also. God in hiding is of no use to his believers while He cannot help Himself from the killings by the so called believers of non believers or the believers of other religion. He cannot help others also though He knows they believe that He would somehow save them. If you need to know what I am writing about please read the writings by Cathay Scoot, Clark and Adrian Levy, appearing in the Readers Digest of May 2000 (Indian Edition) at page 132. The heinous crime being committed by men of one faith on the others of different faiths. In both faiths God has failed them. In one faith God failed to educate them and stop committing crimes and in the other faith God has not protected His followers. So to both God has failed.

—ɯ—

23ʳᵈ April 2000   03 00 A.M.

Nothing seems to explain the 'Life'. What is life? Is it the birth of the physical body, exist through and exit from it? What is this 'I'? Is there something called 'I'? Is it an entity separate from the whole universe? I know nothing. While in my younger days, by reading philosophical books I used to feel that 'I-know', but now as the physical age advances, I confirm myself that I don't know anything about anything. I don't know my own self. This 'not-knowingness' is taking the firm foundation in me. Still somewhere a small, very small, voice peeps out and asks questions and desire is expressed to know what 'Life is'. Somehow I should cut-off the small voice in me to confirm I do not know anything about anything, for sure.

However, imagination and conception have brought some sorts of calmness, especially on the questions of 'What is after death?' First of all what is death?, let alone after-death. Neither it could be said nor can say authentically as to 'what death is?' What afterwards will be? I feel that there is eternity of myself and my personality. That 'I ness' which has not changed though there are lot of changes in my physical body due to time it passed through. I feel that there is something of more divine peace, more divine pleasure, more divine bliss and divine companionship of the universal cosmic force, soothing, loving and taking me to the eternity after the so called death. Death is once again a concept. Death is an intellectual somersaulting due to bankruptcies of time and knowledge. What time and knowledge are? I do not know. These, though are conceptual ones, do bring a lot of courage to face death and some times I invited death too. For me death looks to be a phase in the life. I feel that I am in this universe, rather a part of this universe from eternity to eternity. My personality is one of the trillions of this eternal world. Fear, worry, anxiety of future etc. melt away as the ice do in heat, when once the true knowledge of death dawns in the mid of the human. Nothing bothers me, because nothing is expected either from me to the world or world to me and nothing is regrettable. And yet, bondage does exist in me. I am conditioned, probably through my physical body. Sometimes, desires, crop-up within me and shakes me, may be at the physical and external level. But deep within me, my personality, myself, my thought, my convictions and my knowledge—a firm knowledge that 'I know nothing of anything' is constantly moulding me to that phase of next passage to eternity

I do not nomineclate this inner personality of mine, because it has no reference point unlike the social mores, social conditions, and social and physical laws. There is no reference point in me. It is—my personality, myself, or call it my most inner eternal self, that is 'me', the unchangeable one which neither has birth nor death but becomes a witness to this physical function of me. At certain level I question myself about my own self and I become a stranger to myself. Eternity engulfs me. I am not myself as could be seen physically and eternally. I set aside myself and witness my own physical external functioning. It looks as if they are not mine—the physical functioning's. There is no internal connection between me and physical external functioning. I am something inexpressible, un-understandable and non-conceivable, but only be 'aware' of myself. This very writing is only physical, a rough, gross, base expression of my awareness of my-own-self which I experience and become aware of. May be I am a split personality to the outside world. My worldly functions are diametrically opposite to my inner functions and I am aware of myself. This inner 'me', is the real 'me'. But at the same time I do not know for sure what the 'Real' is. I feel that there is neither Reality nor falsity. These are physical hallucinations and mental aberrations, I feel. It may be like somnambulist, walking in sleep and being aware not to step on other sleepers and at the same time walking in darkness. A somnambulist neither knows himself nor the others, neither know the darkness nor light. He is neither aware of himself nor the outside world. He walks, blabbering something un-understandable and without harming himself or others. Nobody knows how he functions in that state for he does not know it for himself. It may be like him that I am in this physical body functioning as if I know I am functioning according to a set of social laws, but at the same time not understanding anything of my own functioning.

5ᵀᴴ APRIL 2000   03 00 A.M.

It is more than 20 years back when I refused a genuine person, (who I was told to be a 'God-realized' man) who promised to help me, in a way, to realize God, by pressing his right foot-toe on my chest while I lay flat. This way, I am told and also read, that *Sri Ramakrishna* passed on some of his spiritual powers to *Swamy Vivekananda* and also many realized souls did to their disciples. I have refused for such a realization because that person had put-a-condition that after this episode of my so called realizing God, that I should go around the world earning money by lecturing, which art would come to me automatically with my knowledge of English language and with philosophical back ground and above all as a so called 'God-realized' person.

There were many reasons for this rejection.

1) I was honest. I never wanted to earn money for any purpose let alone for the development of his or any others land.
2) I was not binding myself to any particular place or to a person or to any type of spirituality though that spiritual road might have led me to God, if at all it did;
3) I had no intention to earn money in the name of God and build an estate which I felt as very insignificant act in the arena of God's stage of this universe;
4) I only wanted God and nothing else and no bondages what-so-ever, even the bondage of God not wanting

He resided with his family in a thatched hut while a stone temple of six feet square with an open veranda in front, was built, a few feet away. The height of the temple, having only a *pooja* room, was seven feet and a five feet high door without any windows. I was told snakes were rampant around there and would not harm this man and his family. I would stay in this temple. Even to reach his place one has to go to a village by bus and walk about four miles on the land divider humps which they form for their agricultural land for holding water.

He had been testing me about my honest thirst for God; he did not give me any positive answers whether he would help me to realize God, during my first five visits. I simply was going and staying with him without any conversations. He was watching me and I would stay there for three to four days at a time and som times for a week. He would not ask when I would return to that place when I was leaving. He had left completely to me to decide my stay with him. There was no work to do. I was doing only meditation. He would do *pooja* and *bhajan* in his own ways. But though I took part with him in these rituals, he knew that I had no interest in any of them. One day he told me that he had to do these things for the sake of nearby villagers, or otherwise they would not believe in God and may go astray. He was a judge for the quarrels between the villagers, particularly about their properties, he was a doctor for some diseases, he was a priest, he was an astrologer, a soothsayer, a swami, a guide and a respectable human being on whom the near by villagers had full faith. They would come at any time for any problems and would go back with cheerful faces.

They were wondering and enquiring about me, but he would only say that I am from the city, staying with him temporarily.

After nearly six months, I asked him directly whether he would help me to realize God. He said he would, after having tested me silently for all these six months.

So, I told him emphatically 'NO' to his suggestions. He was taken by surprise at my negative answer, because I had been going to him for more than six months, but at intervals and would stay for a week or two at a time. To fetch water one has to walk half a mile to a ground level well with circular stone wall and with open 30 steps cantilevered in a narrow circular way having gaps between them and without hand-railing. I don't know how I fetched a bucket full of water. Not knowing swimming, if I had taken one wrong step I would slip into the open well and that would have been my end, since there were no persons working in the fields or any houses around at a shouting distance. Even this person who was the nearest would not have helped me as he was far away from the well. He was the only one person doing some lift irrigation work on his bit of land around there. I would take *Ragi* balls etc. as my food, a more rural food of Southern Karnataka—prepared by his wife. He had two daughters, the elder one ten to twelve years of age going to the nearby village school about two miles away and younger of 3 years.

However, it was fixed that on a particular midnight, after *bhajans*—I would be empty in my stomach—he would close the doors of the temple and I would lay with bare chest and he would place his right foot on my chest and press his toe on the middle of my chest and thus pass on certain spiritual powers which would trigger my *kundalini* and the power of light will enter my head leading to God realization. While everything was settled, but just before this ritual was to take place, once again he asked me whether I would go round the world, lecturing on God and earn money to develop his area and make my stay permanent there and, as I said, with honesty and sincerity and with frankness and fearlessness an emphatic 'NO', he opened the temple door and walked out without performing the ritual and said that I may go back in the morning, which I did and never went back to him afterwards. I never heard about him. I don't know what happened to him or if any big estate has come up in that place now and have no interest to know also. I was not prepared to sell myself and thereby sell God for any wealth of the world, since I had realized that God realization should not go with the earnings of the mundane material things. To me, way to God head is freedom from everything even from one's own self, probably, even from God Himself

—⟋⟍—

4ᴛʜ Mᴀʀᴄʜ 2000   03 30 ᴀ.ᴍ.

Something deep within me and unknowingly, all of a sudden, something forces me to take up my pen and start writing in the middle of the night. The writing is to be of something about the universal cosmic energy. Something makes me from within to shun everything I am doing and start writing. It is not me who is writing, it is 'that something' that inspires to write, that urges me to write, or, in a way, forces me to write.

These writings, though are not meaningful ones and does not help anybody including me, I get some solace, some strength, some unknown joy inexplicable by writing. While writing I forget myself, the silence engulfs me though there is heavy noise of automobiles, men moving even at that hour of the night. This deep silence, even while writing, takes me to a different plane and the whole universe becomes mine and exclusively belonging to me in a very intimate way, as if I am in contact with the whole Universe from the time immemorial and since eternity with deep commitment to each other, myself and the universe. My relationship with the universe is inseparable even while this mundane world around me exists, though it could be called as illusory, and still they too have the part of that universal energy. In this state of my being, fear of the unknown is lost. Birth, life and death become mere phases, a movement within the framework of time, space and causation. But beyond this framework is the Cosmic Being, who is intimate to me. That intimacy, cannot be found between the two human beings. The intimacy of the two of us is pure, on an in habituated world from where the whole function of the Universe can be witnessed with neither detachment nor attachment. Now there is a feeling for 'looking forward to' presently to an unknown event, though the previous and present ones were and are not unpleasant. Calmness with deep silence catches me and I am completely at rest with everything which goes on around me and still expectancy brings a type of joy and happiness in me though these expectancies are unknown to me and yet conceptualized by me. Slowly I am moving with full knowledge that I am coming nearer and nearer to that event. Somehow, I should shackle these that are getting attached to me while I am not attached to anything externally but internally and subtly, but somewhere in the corner of my heart I hear a feeble voice of my attachment especially to my daughter, Megha

—⚏—

3ʳᵈ March 2000   05 00 a.m.

It looks to me, that the whole human race is just a particle of sand on the infinite eternal cosmic shore. When so, how one person can comprehend the entire cosmic energy within his limited and tiny intelligence? This morning I read an article wherein the author says that an individual is the center of the universe and the universe exist because he exists. The universe come to an end with his end, man is a referral point from where the dimensions start. Dimensions always, I feel, are within the realms of space and time and also cause-effect phenomena. These are only human dimensions, hypothetical ones, referral points on this earth. However, the urge to know something other than what is comprehendible is slowly being subdued, being put into silence. The wisdom dawns with the knowledge—'I do not know anything about anything including of my own self'. When so, how could it be possible to know something beyond me? I look like a stranger to my own self. Many a times I doubt my very existence. Am I an existing entity by myself? Is not the 'me' the whole? or 'me' a part of the whole? Strangeness from within occupies me, still, I feel, that deep within me, I know myself, but how do 'I know myself'? I don't know. The reality, I feel, is that I know 'I know nothing'. It—the whole universe is just functioning under its own natural laws which I neither can understand nor comprehend to explain them to myself. How, why, what and other questions do not arise in the functions of the universe. Only when doubts arise, these questions too arise. There are no doubts in me for it is beyond me to be analytical and even if I am to be analytical, there may not be true analogies as answers. For what it is—the universe and its functions—there are no questions, for there are no answers, the answers that satisfy men. In the final analysis it turns out to be 'that-is-how-they-are' and 'that-is-how-the-nature-functions'. All answers are permutations and combinations do not explain the natures functioning, the natural functioning of the universe. Let many theorize, make experiment give explanations and analyze the universe but the universe will not reveal, it is unmoved, it is unshakable, everything is 'un' with it, for its very nature is to function in the way it does. Every blade of grass, an atom of mud is a part of this gigantic function of this universe—a beginning less and an endless function which is complete, natural, and primordial though superficially looks to be different.

—ɯ—

03ʳᵈ Feb. 2000   03 30 a.m.

Who am I? This question seems to be the greatest foolish question ever asked by a man to himself. 'I' denotes a separate entity from the whole and who stands away from the reality—the reality is that nothing is known and nothing can be known. The concept of something called reality to me does not exist, for the reality to be is that there is falsity. There is neither reality nor falsity, they are just there. I don't know anything of these. Everything seems to me to be concept projected from the conditioned mind, social and the so called religious conditions to which a man is subjected to since birth. But nothing can be done other than being conditioned to. But internal struggle goes on to shackle these conditions. In the end these struggles subside with the dawn of the knowledge that 'there is nothing to understand'. The capacity to understand the universe and its functions are beyond the limited intelligence or the so called 'the most intelligent species of the universe—the man'. This intelligence is a speck though received from the cosmic intelligence. Intelligence is the energy canalized to attain or attributed to a particular way of functioning which once again is conditioned to the functions of the universe. Movement is functioning. But I do not call even that as a movement. Movement involves time, it is a measurement involving time and space dimensions while the cosmic movement, probably, is beyond any of these dimensions. It is the ego of the intelligence of the man which creates a concept of his separate entity from the universal whole and yet there is something wanting, something needed other than 'what is' and man is not satisfied with 'what is'

While writing these, I feel the immense silence, the deep silence, where everything stops the time, the thought, the knowledge and everything goes to oblivion and the entire Cosmic Energy engulfs me and takes me beyond this mundane world to an unknown and yet very well known and recognizable region to which I feel I really belong to. I feel I am here and also there and everywhere at the same time. From this region I could see the whole universe and experience it through my consciousness. I clearly see the innumerable galaxies with their milky ways silently, very silently, functioning. There is no sound—since the sound belongs to the physical body. When this physical body is not there, there is no sound at all, but deep, very deep silence which I am conscious of, which I experience as if I too am in silence and the light that could be seem to be every where without a shadow or speck of darkness but one sheet of light which is invariable and to this luminous light I belong, rather I become that very L ight itself.

11ᵀᴴ Fᴇʙ 2000   04 30 A.M.

Sometimes I feel that I am dry from within, neither love nor hate is there, but calm, eternal calm and deep silence occupies my whole being, in this deep silence the light of my soul shines, a few light rays of God are reaching and engulfing me. In this state of being, nothing is desired and at the same time it can only be perceived but not understood from the rational way. Only awareness is the experience. The desire to enjoy even the God is not there. And still, sometimes I feel that I am short of something which I know not what— the deep yearning to be one with the whole universal central cosmic force, is intolerable within. I want to catch something that no other has caught so-far, that energy must be the energy of be all and end all of the whole universal energy. That strong feeling to realize the whole and to be with it always, is very deep and I very strongly yearn for it. Fear of everything, even the fear of death, run away when I am in that state, since in that state there is neither life nor death, it is one continuity of movement from eternity to eternity neither having any beginning nor having any end.

There are no idealists (icons) to me and yet these very thoughts are conditioned thoughts. The concept of God is fed in to me and I have conditioned myself to thinking so. There is no escape from these conditioning. I am conditioned physically, psychologically, conceptually, intellectually, socially and universally. I am caught. There are no ways or place to escape to and yet I am free within myself being myself that eternal Being.

29ᵀᴴ January 2000   03 00 a.m.

Nothing explains that which is inexplicable, the one that brings some type of awareness of 'me', the 'eternal me' in spite of finiteness. Time, space and cause-effect, seem to be illusions, creation of mind, while reality is the functioning of the whole universe—the cosmic universe functioning eternally which can never be comprehended let alone understood and explained. It is the inseparableness or be one with the whole universe that establishes permanence, the eternity. Awareness of that Eternity brings unique bliss to me and I love the whole universe. I take into my fold, with deep unselfish love, the whole universe, and it brings the greatest eternal joy to me. Nothing would hold on to you. No words, no institutions, no person can claim you, for you belong to that eternal cosmic force which is a part of you. Ultimately 'you' is not there in the 'whole'. You become the very whole itself. And nothing can be understood through the thought process of human physical body probably, the only body through which one can have the process of thoughts and no other physical body other than the human body have the capacity to think. But I don't know for sure.

The totality of thought is you and that is your personal being—an unique being different from others since the thoughts that produced in you are unique to yourself and others do not know about your thoughts. And yet you don't know how these thoughts are produced, processed and proceed from within you. Thought is cosmic and that thought being produced and processed in you makes you a part of cosmos whether you know it or not, whether you understand it or not. You are part of the whole. The whole cannot be whole unless even an iota of you is not there. There cannot be whole without you.

—⚕—

26ᵀᴴ January 2000   03 30 a.m.

I travel, in spite of being the part of the whole, all over universe finding myself with companionship of the Cosmic Being. I am one with the universe, feelings of belongingness, feelings of bliss, feelings of love, feelings of oneness, as if, I am It and It is me, encompasses me, that 'me' is without this physical body; and still the awareness of seeing, the understanding, the thinking goes on also in that state of my being. It is only that 'me' without this physical body which travels everywhere in the companionship of 'That Being'. This universe has no edge, no boundary, no path, no darkness, no heat, no cold, and no sound. It is purely blissful, it is eternal and it is lovable. It is pure and it is peaceful without a second one like IT. I and 'That Being' are the only two traveling together from eternity to eternity to every corner of the Universe. We are the only two, as companions to each other. Eternally we travel together And nobody else is allowed between that Being and me.

—ɯ—

17ᵀᴴ JANUARY 2000   12 00 A.M.

Meditation is an auto-suggestion to which one is self brain-washed, so that the brain and the thought process are sublimed and sub limited. All words that create certain emotions within, are, in fact, influenced from outside. The totality can never be understood whichever the emotions that may be raised, followed and valued. To give value to anything would only be a comparative one, which has no standing by itself. Everything is inter-dependent and nothing can have its own independence. The whole in its function is at best be described but not understood in its completeness and reality. The reality is once again a comparative statement. Nothing, to me at least, is understandable, it can be theorized according to one's conceptual thought or so called experiences. The experience is also a thought of the past in memory. Experiencing is once again only a peripheral past event, it is not permanent. My thoughts even to myself are not jointed but broken while I am the product of my thoughts and so I am a broken person from within. I am the product, the producer and also the processor of such production of thought. In spite of my giving various meanings to my thought, I am not a separate single entity and still, for the world I exist as such and not the other way round.

—ɯ—

14ᵀᴴ JANUARY 2000   03 00 A.M.

I feel that I am neither a separate entity nor the whole. While I am functioning with the whole universe, the timeless ness creeps into my awareness and I feel that I am eternally functioning with the Universe, however insignificant part I may play. The awareness of my own self brings me a strange feeling of not understanding anything of the universe and including my own self. Internal renunciation is taking place, not out of desire for spiritual seeking, but because it comes naturally despite of everything. Physical functioning slows down, complete inner detachment naturally creeps and rises, but not by inducing. While in this state of being nothing matters, rather no value is created, no action is desired and nothing is induced. May be it is a natural state but I don't know what this state is, but only am aware of this state and go through this state for some length of time. Nothing is wanted while being in this state. Even the God is not wanted, all memories are lost every action looks meaningless, valueless and does not create any impression upon my mind. Nothing is absorbed and nothing is influenced. It is clean and blank, the mind would not allow anything to imprint upon it, however divine it may look like. This state of mind is only an experience of its own self without having any conditions or influences by outer reactions.

—⚊—

10ᵀʰ JANUARY 2000   03 00 A.M.

Everything, at this hour, seems to be in natural state and as the sun raises so the voices of the world raise. All activities start with the sun and slow down at some point of time after the sun sets and in the end everything comes to a naught ultimately.

—⚊—

6ᵀʰ JANUARY 2000   04 00 A.M.

I feel that I am in catch 22 and would very much like to get out of this clutch, I feel that by sticking on I am proving to myself that I am a hoax. I should have courage to come out of this hoax and I should not do anything with these mundane activities, I should stop everything with courage. There is complete spiritual dissatisfaction. Nowhere could I find what I am seeking, rather, what projections of concepts I make. I do know that I have no knowledge of anything. I do not know how and why this universe is functioning in the way it does. Absolutely I am ignorant of the whole universe including of me.

—⚊—

05ᵀᴴ Jᴀɴᴜᴀʀʏ 2000   03 30 ᴀ.ᴍ.

I wonder whether the man is so very important for the universe to express itself. I still wonder as to the man and his birth, life and death. Is it not the totality that counts in the world of human existence and that is important? Or, is there any importance to anything at all? Is it necessary for the universe to function in the way it does? Is there any other way the universe could or could not have functioned? Are these questions have any answers? Or, are these questions themselves are the expressions of ignorance? Is there any measurement of human intelligence? I feel, any question on the functioning of the entire universe ends up in 'not knowingness'. All rationalities, all talks of religion, God, spirituality etc. are limited to human intellectual concepts only. Concepts are generated from the mind thorugh thought waves. Thought is also a concept since it is very difficult to define, in the correct sense, as to what thought is. The power of man is his thought. It is not possible to say for certain, how thoughts are produced in a mind. I am the person both of one single subtle thought and the bundle of all thoughts, whether I am aware of them or not, from birth to death. With the birth of man thoughts are born, whether he could recollects them or not, whether he could express them or not and with the death thought too dies. The death of thought is the death of physical body. Even in sleep thoughts are produced and leave behind the results in the form of subtle dreams, whether they come on the screen of the memory or not. Memory in a way is a gross thought. Thus the loss of memory also will be the loss of thought production; or thought is produced in a distorted manner of which such a man is not aware of. Nothing could be sure. Awareness is not the proof of the existence of thought. Slowly, the thought slows down and the deep silence gets in. Calmness brings thoughts to a slow velocity. In silence nature too obliges man by subsiding sounds of many insects and flies making their 'kitsch-kitsch' sound, heard in the absence of all other sounds. May be there are sounds of air waves. Nature calms down in its functions as the man goes into deep silence, or he controls himself not to hear any sounds, or the silence itself shuts it doors to all sounds including the nature's sound while nature does not bother whether man made sounds add to its own or keeps to himself in silence. So the quality of silence is such that man's deep silence shuts all doors to all kinds of sounds including the subtle sounds man makes within his own mind in the thought process. So, this thought waves too slow down in silence and silence becomes very powerful to control the thought waves and in turn these thought waves control the man's mind through which man becomes aware of deep silence, only then his mind gets into the process of becoming 'empty'. An empty mind finds itself in the cliché of silence. Man becomes aware of his silence and he does not understand as to what silence is, in reality, for the nature of man is such that he cannot comprehend his own decibel capacity to hear the subtle sounds of nature including his body's blood circulation and other subtle sounds of his body while functioning. When a man goes beyond his body and mind and beyond material world then he would probably become aware of the deep silence of the universe, while this world is only a speck of grain in the whole panorama of the universe.

04ᵀᴴ JANUARY 2000   03 00 A.M.

In my deep thoughts, somewhere along the line, I lose the hitherto held opinion that I am born and reborn time and again. But it is to reveal to me that I stand myself eternally and firmly while the different bodies come to me as they were, according to the results of the cause-effect (*karmas*) of all the previous physical and mental actions of the physical body, both of gross and subtle. These parts of drama come before me, enact through me and pass on. It is not I who pass on from one phase to another, from one event to another in the same phase, but the other way round that these phases of lives and all events in each life come and pass before me and through me, while I stand eternally, as a witness, without any change or movement. We feel the movement and change of subtle to gross. I am definite that I am the subtlest of the subtlest, packed with all the potentialities of the Cosmic Energy, like a seed within which are packed all potentialities of a tree. As the energy in a seed—being subtle—manifest itself in the gross tree, so the energy in the subtle manifests itself in the gross body. When I know that the parts of the phases of events are like passing clouds, I stand there firmly and eternally in deep silence, with peace and bliss, untouched by any passing events. I stand and witness the whole of these parts, phases and events that pass before me, though they try to establish a relationship with me, I do not recognize that relationship, for I am not in any way related to a single event in any of the different phases. It makes no difference to me whether I am the king or the pauper in any of this phases for all these phase are passing ones while I am the firm and eternal being.

03ᴿᴰ JANUARY 2000   03 30 A.M.

Nothing seems to have any answers. Questions stop, for there are no answers, while I do not know anything about anything. It is probably the ego that expects answers other than 'what is'. 'What is' is also not understandable. It is probably my thoughts creating all mischief to project some concepts based on my conditioning for all these years. Questions stop arising within and so thought process slow down. There seems to be no dualities either within or without. All sayings, all writings, from any source, are only to fill up the gap in the measurements of time and that time is only a hypothetical measurement of movement. In fact there is no movement in the absolute sense. It just functions, a happening beyond the understanding of the human intelligence. Human intelligence though seems to have occupied universal expression, in fact is only a dot on the vast expanse of the universe. Of late there are no feelings either of sorrows or joys, may be, I look like a stone from within. Emotions do exist as emotions are chemical changes that take place in the chemistry of the body—the body being a chemical laboratory combined with electrical impulses generated within itself from the energy drawn from the cosmic. So, the body is the manifestation having its own metabolism and different from the functions of the other bodies, though not in kind but in degrees. Why and how of the functions of the universe is beyond the comprehension of the human intelligence, for the human intelligence too is a part of the whole cosmic intelligence and as such a part cannot understand the whole. Since there is no answer, there cannot be a definite question also. It is a feeling that I can never be correctly comprehended in this universe for I am the part of the whole functioning of the universe. And at the same time the concept of whole also has its limitations because these are the human concepts which have limited intelligence. To him, everything, even his own self, is un-understandable, it is inexplicable, as it is to a new born baby. The baby, probably, may not be aware of its own self but as a man, to some extent, I am aware of myself.

—m—

2ᴺᴰ JANUARY 2000   03 30 A.M.

Standing at a cross road not knowing which way to turn to and which leads to where and further not knowing whether they really lead to any place, is most devastating, thus encouraging a person to turn back and proceed to from where he came, for sure he knows the back ways. However, having courage and determination to proceed forward and to take steps on either way t to reach some conceptual destiny, is the human way of life, whether he succeeds or only meets disappointments that would only be tested or confirmed upon reaching. Or to go on proceeding since there may not be any reaching at all, but only involves in proceeding. May be, it is a pathless way. In the labyrinth of life, the goal is only a mirage. Mirage is created through mental aberration or hallucination. The desire to reach, the keenness to proceed than to stagnant, is the human nature. The human nature being what it is, there are no alternatives to hope, for the hope always remaining for the future. Hope is not for the present. Hope is in the future. Man makes and expects too much from the life, while it may not hold so much for him or may not hold anything at all. I strongly feel that in the order of things every individual feels his or her indispensableness and need to dominate on others either intellectually or economically or through muscle force with weapons etc. and if not, man invents God for others to submit to him. And yet, the universe functions in the way as it does. Expecting anything other than 'what is' is natural. You feel cheated, feel defeated, feel wronged but in fact you are not, because these movements, on their own, are natural. You want to escape but there is no place to go, so, you are bound to be a slave of some others opinions, of some others thoughts and of some others utterances. I feel suffocated, bound and thrown into the dense of pitch darkness into a bottomless pit in search of light and freedom from my own thoughts which are conditioned by my generic chemistry, by the social values, religious compulsions which were breaking me from within for some time and at the cost of some human relationship which have isolated me from the external world and still I continue to function as a normal person.

—·—

31ST DECEMBER 1999   03 30 A.M.

When man brings down God to his level of expectancy, God makes a trade—a contract, an agreement with man. God desires to be loved, respected and wants to be advertised. He desires that man should act in the way he directs and ultimately God wants man to surrender completely, unconditionally to Him and loose all the rationality and his very mind itself to Him. He desires that man should not think of any other thing other than Him (*mamekam yaad karo*). And also God wants man to serve Him through man's physical body, mind and wealth (*tan, man aur dhan*). Only then God would bestow upon man His blessings, His mercy, His power, so that this man who is a slave to God may acquire some cosmic powers, though very infinitesimal, so that this man in turn could enslave other men who hope to become like him to share some powers of God. God is like a politician, always to be on the throne as an absolute and ever lasting dictator. Whoever goes without God's friendship, let alone against God, that man will be punished destroyed and have to suffer physically and mentally and God makes that man to be reborn again and again punishing and equally rewarding that man for all good actions towards God. God is blind while punishing or rewarding man, as He assumes the part of goddess of Law.

—⁂—

December 1999 03 00 A.M.

What Death is? Nobody knows for sure and in reality. It could be non-functioning of both physical and mental activities. Body stops to function in death. It becomes like an inanimate object, like a piece of wood, but yet internally becomes a chemical factory for the production of bacteria which were not there earlier. If kept as it is, or even buried, it turns out to be a cesspool of worms with different chemical composition which may endanger other species including man.

Does death bring to an end to everything of that person? Is the death an end all? But having been deeply convinced, I feel, it is not. I feel though very vaguely for myself and by myself that there is eternity to me. What that 'me' is, I cannot exactly say. 'Me', I always feel, is a part of the entire universal functioning and is eternal in the same form or in the some form or the other without losing the basic quality in its naturalness. But what those basic qualities are? I do not know. I am only aware of the presence of me which is beyond all expressions—expression being gross and far from its reality. The reality of me can only be experienced by myself and through myself, while me and experiences are being one and the same and inseparable, about which I am aware. Awareness is the expression of consciousness to oneself that experiences 'me'. No rationality, no logic can stand before the awareness of 'me' by me. I think that this awareness of me for that matter myself, in a subtle way, continuous eternally despite of this physical body coming to an end. But this body being finite it cannot through any of its instruments—the mind, the memory. the intellect or thought, can come to catch the infinite. A finite element cannot catch an infinite. Infinite being only one and finite being several cannot share the infinite completely, but can only imagine and project the concept of infinite being a finite. Infinite, in fact, is only a concept of finite. In abstract Reality is neither infinite nor finite, and in the end ignorance of any of these concepts prevail. Not knowingness is the reality and all other concepts for the universal function remain to be the concepts only and as the age advances ignorance also advances in geometrical progression and desires vanish, simplicity catches, humility encompasses oneself, anger evaporates, but still the inner ME remains stronger and shines in its true qualities.

—m—

16ᵀᴴ DECEMBER 1999   03 30 A.M.

What is thought? Is not the very question about thought itself is a thought? So a thought is to be known only through another form of thought. Every function of the human being is the manifestation of thought. Where does thought come from? It comes from the thought itself. A thought is born from a thought and functions through another thought. The medium of function and also the instrument through which thought projects itself could only be the physical body, there cannot be any thought in the absence of the functioning of the physical body. Thought cannot function by itself. Even when the physical body is in coma, thought process subtly goes on. Does the brain produce thought? I am afraid not. Thought is a microwave that is already available in the cosmos, but the medium of expression is required and that could only be the brain. Thought is not the product of brain but brain catches thought and gives effectiveness of functioning by amplifying within. The manifestation of the thought at macro level through the movements of limbs, eyes speech etc, for the body to function externally. In the end when thought functions in deep silence it understands itself that it is beyond itself to understand by itself. It knows that whatever it understands is only its concepts cultivated and acquired through external influences of the society and the biological information gathered through its genes. Thought is the result of both external environment and biological genetic code.

The whole universe exists to an individual only because that individual functions through the process of thought. He cultivates to catch thought from the cosmos and thus becomes a part of the cosmos for he too in turn sends his thought waves to cosmos while he draws thoughts only from cosmos which keep the cosmos in balance. By themselves these waves of thoughts are neither positives nor negatives. It is the value system of the human society that creates the concept of the positives and negatives of thoughts.

—◊—

14ᵀᴴ December 1999 03 30 A.M.

It is the fear of death, the end of me in this body that makes me to hang on to something that gives promise of security, though false. Security of me and my family is the most important one to me. The continuation of this life is much more important than the end, although the end surely comes. No one knows for sure the distance of the end from the present moment. But still I love myself, I love my knowledge, I love my ego and I love everything about myself even I love my weaknesses for I do not consider myself as weak. At the same time fear grips me—the fear of the end, when I think of it. I feel that I am eternal in this body rather my body is eternal; it is an illusion and probably hallucination created by delusion.

—◊—

10ᵀᴴ December 1999 03 00 A.M.

Nothing is going to happen either now or in the so called future, other than what is happening or what is going to happen. To become (becoming is always in the future) something other than what I am, is only a desire conditioned by the culture and cultivated conditioning of my mind. Whatever that is, is not at all understood as it is, for the instrument we use is not comprehensible of its own self. First of all this instrument has created that 'which is not' and try to analyze its own creation thereby conditioning that which is. Our mind or thought power whichever you call, has its own limitations though such thoughts are drawn from the cosmic powers, the totality of which is 'what is'. 'What is' cannot be brought into the frame work of man's mind, however sharp it may be, however powerful it may be. Whatever mind may conceive, is always limited, for the limited cannot comprehend the unlimited, just like an ant cannot comprehend the whole elephant.

—◊—

08TH DECEMBER 1999 03 30 A.M.

Nothing could be farther from the truth that God is a personal Being of one set of people who alone claim to understand Him while every other human being has no capacity to know who the God is. What a tall claim! When such a claim is made from the so called words of God Himself through the medium of a particular person, it is still more a tall claim. They claim that they are the only one who have found truth of self and God and the connection between them. And further claiming that God combined with the soul of the dead person coming down and enter into the body of other living being and sending messages to be spread of His arrival to the whole of the human world and to receive the benediction from God. While they do not claim themselves to be authors, they say it is the God Himself who is giving the message through the medium. Their claims are

1. God descends from his permanent home—(*parm-dham*) into to a person who is claimed to be the only one person capable of receiving God.
2. Through this human medium, God is giving message of His arrival.
3. God giving lessons every day to this sect of people promising to take them to heaven and to abide by His messages calling it as the voice of God.
4. To know what the soul is and who the God is and the relationship between them.
5. To say that this world is full of sin and the heaven is awaited.
6. Only those who come to this sect and follow every word of it are the only eligible persons to go to that golden age of heaven and the rest upon their death will stay in *parm-dham* as *atma* in vegetable state and come back to this world taking another physical body according to their *purusharthas* performed during this age called *Sangam Yug*—the confluent period between *Kaliyug* (sinful and hellish period) and golden age (heaven).
7. The whole cycle is called a *kalpa* is covered by 5000 years divided into four equal periods (*yugs*) and each period having the span of 1250 years.
8. While the cycle is eternally spinning the present cycle is almost coming to an end and shortly coming to end this *kaliyug* is getting destroyed and a new age called golden age is arriving.

9. To that golden age, only those who are in this sect become eligible to take birth and not all of them but some of them who followed the message of God or in constant remembrance of God and who have sacrificed everything they possess to this sect in the name God, they profess. And the position or the status in that golden age depends upon how much we have sacrificed physically, mentally and materially (*tun, man & dhan*) to this institution which they call as giving to God for the future happiness.

10. They condemn everything man made law and calling it as illegal and even the institutions of other *Sanyasis* sects as false and ignorant and ill-informed

There are many such shops selling God.

—〰—

10ᵀᴴ DECEMBER 1999   03 30 A.M.

God has been the concept of human thought which brings lots of miseries to human being. God has been institutionalized by some, who make tall claims that God could be known, in correct perspective and understood as He is, only by going to their institution. God, if at all such a being is there, is universal and can never be caught and defined and also cannot be made a personal property of a particular institution, claiming all others as fools except themselves. They start bartering God in exchange for money, material and also complete surrendering by wo/men that follow them and slowly claiming that the follower should surrender to them before surrendering to God, meaning it is as good as surrendering to God himself. They try to bring in lots of theories with a bit of love, a bit of joy and more a bit of terror that if we neglect or not allow to be carried away of their sayings. They say you would fall and occupy a very low position in future, in the so called Golden Age (*Satya yug*). As for me I neither contribute to their way of thinking nor contribute to any other claims where only that particular institution shows the path way to God head while all others are wrong. It is a movement to take lot of gullible people for a nice ride and especially those who lead an immoral or corrupt life, so that they can see in themselves, having lost all powers of physical body, powers of office, mental powers some change which slowly and naturally comes and they attribute this change as a change due to their institution and those who do not fall in line with them are called as traitors. The institutions—a body of men and women desire to hold the intellectual reins, the independent thinking capacity of others to submit to their ways of thinking, thus causing intellectual bankruptcy and thus over powering the capacity of these followers thinking and curtail to act independently. Such institution wants to create a mass of slaves to their way of thinking, to follow them and in the end to pay them so that the institution can enrich at the cost of the poor followers while the god-men/women, as owners of such Institutions, travel by airplanes and air conditioned limousines all over the world, the follower, having emptied his pocket, walks bare-foot, in the hot sun, in a desert towards the mirage believing it to be God, as so shown to him by these god-men/women. It is a type of robbery and dacoity in the name of God.

—ᴍ—

11ᵀᴴ Oᴄᴛᴏʙᴇʀ 1999   04 00 ᴀ.ᴍ.

Deep thoughts bring me to a point of 'ignorance' and 'not knowingness' and away from my own self. The self loses its entity and there remains the whole in which no 'me' remains. But the whole is inclusive of me. Thought of time is a hypothetical concept of man. I find that time loses its dimensions in the eternity of the functioning of the Universe. Somehow, with the limited intelligence, if it could be called so, I hardly understand anything whether conceptual ones or what goes on around me. There is no difference between the material and the spiritual life. It remains to be a speck of dust—the knowledge of material or spiritual—before the whole functioning of the Universe. Man has not touched even one outer layer of the cosmic intelligence and its functioning. He is still exploring. All that the knowledge the man has acquired, whether it is material or metaphysical, are within the realms of the Cosmic Intelligence and man being an entity of this whole, though not a separate entity, is a part of cosmic intelligence. The totality of the cosmic intelligence can never be conceived but only a hypothetical projection of the whole (*Sampoornatha*) can only be conceived. For to know what that completeness is, one should have experienced at least a part of it, known it for sure to say that 'this is the completeness', but not by taking the example of someone else's completeness, since one can never understand whether that person is complete for he does not say for himself that he attained the completeness. The man who has attained can never know his attainment, because he will be in the state of 'NOTHINGNESS'

—ᴍ—

1ˢᵗ October 1999   03 30 a.m.

The whole functioning of the Universe looks to be a natural phenomenon including the functions of the physical body of all the animate objects. It is the combination of chemical and physical functions with electric impulses produced through the chemical functions within the physical body. If the process of every function, when seen as separate and individual ones, which, in fact, is not so, but one whole function, each relating to other and each within the whole, though looked to be separate. But at the same time each function functions at different level with different degrees, drawing the energy from the cosmic. Some where along the line, I lose the knowledge of my limitedness of being a separate entity and enlarge myself and my consciousness to the whole universe. In the central cosmic point of function of the whole universe is a force beyond explanation, but it comes as an awareness to me, as I cannot experience the functioning of the entirety but only I am aware of it. In this awareness of that point of 'supreme force', deep silence engulfs me and to a great extent I become the very silence in my awareness. Nothing matters in this deep silence. All the qualities we attribute to this 'supreme force' are not exactly there. Just silence and awareness of that central force exists. This awareness subdues the thought of material world. In this awareness I feel the dual functioning of my own self, that I do function both materially through my physical body and metaphysically or rather spiritually through my soul-'I'. But still I am myself. It is like one person performing different function at the same time, as a son, a brother, a father etc. Even in the functioning as a son though it is one part it assumes two sub parts, one as a son to father and the other to mother at different degrees, so also as a brother to a sister and to a brother, father to a son and to a daughter; while all the time I am being the only one person, with distinct personality but with a different facets. The inner core of me is un-changing and that is the 'real me', this core personality of me is the bundle of every function that I perform, each inter-woven, inseparable. Slowly the functions are becoming solidified and unbreakable—the thought process slows down, awareness becomes clear, eternity becomes a fact, not merely a conceptual one and the dimensions of time, space and cause-effects are lost, the separateness of material or metaphysical functions dissolve and the awareness of the whole function of the Universe comes to be realized and fear of concepts vanish since the death becomes another part of the process of function and in the end there remains only the eternity of oneself occupying the consciousness of the entire universe erasing everything of 'me-ness' and 'my-ness'. All separateness of 'me' with the outside world just melts away, heaviness, burdens of *karma,* whether positive or negative, too vanish, the ego melts, all questions are answered, and all dualities vanished. This One Reality is the answer to every question and hence there remain no questions and question being the thought process, while it is in the state of thoughtlessness the universal consciousness arises. So, I am the same without change of personality despite of having assumed different physical forms and at different levels in different degrees from eternity to eternity.

—m—

28 SEPTEMBER 1999   03 30 A.M.

While the death is inevitable, the fear of death is equally inevitable. However a person may put up the show of boldness, supported by many philosophical theories, but deep within the desire to completely eliminate the death of his life in this physical body, persists. It looks very ludicrous and equally lamentable, but the reality of the desire of a person to live permanently and not to age but to be an youth both physically and mentally is the inner most desire of all the animate objects particularly of human being. Most important is that everything, wealth, power, relatives, so called good deeds performed, even the knowledge of God will not make any difference to him who is suffering physically on the death bed. The upper most need of that hour is for the elimination of that physical pain. But death levels everything. The power of money, the power of intellect, the power of status and even the spiritual power also end with the death. These powers, I feel, are the energies and forces cultivated for the man to live for a long time and to be sane mentally and physically healthy. The deterioration of mental health reduces physical strength which in turn reduces all such acquired powers. And still one can never understand as to why such powers are needed to be acquired. Even for acquiring such powers man becomes helpless and becomes a victim of social surroundings and stigma attached thereto. He looks a beaten man. Even the so called spiritual person, who deems to show that he has completely surrendered to God without an iota of self, is subtly enamored by such powers. Such a person who easily commands the respect of others on the strength of this showman ship of being nearer to the conceptual God, yields to powers of other men, money and material and slowly succumbs to such a power, very helplessly. Having tasted such a power, such a person cannot and shall not give up any powers he holds even at the cost of his death. So is the enormous hold of such a power to which the so called 'God-man' becomes addicted to like an alcoholic. An alcoholic may sometimes give up alcohol, but a person addicted to such a power would rather commit suicide than to let go of such a power. Power is the name of the game; men play socially, economically, militarily, scientifically, intellectually and even spiritually. God is the invention of an intelligent person played upon the minds of poor and unintelligent so as to enslave such a man to his wishes and ideals and make him a bunch of auto suggested, brain washed sleep-walkers from which this intelligent man derives pleasure and powers. Freedom is mortgaged to the so called God. I have at least the freedom to think and convince myself that I am totally ignorant person so far as the spiritual world is concerned and I can never become bankrupt in the name of God for I know nothing about what they teach and practice about God, I have no interest in any of these institutions. Being and becoming completely ignorant after having studied so many so called spiritual scriptures, the sense of fear, at least the intensity of fear is weathering out. Nothing shakes me from within despite of the outer look as such

—⟋⟍—

3 July 1999   05 00 A.M.

I feel that I am not a separate entity in the order of the whole universe and yet I feel the individuality of my own self within me, though I do not know anything about my own self and do not understand of my own self. To me to understand anything other than the day today negotiations to live physically is beyond my comprehension. I feel that I am a part of the whole cosmic world drawing thoughts and intelligence from this perennial source of cosmos and to use it as my own to create a sort of self-ego within me. When I accept, rather deeply convinced, that I am a part of the whole, though a grain of sand, a small bubble on a wave of the ocean, it is not to be set aside just because I am a grain of sand or a bubble for reason that without this grain or bubble the universe is not complete. My mind and thoughts stop me to project any concept of the so called birth, life and death, which comes to a naught in their function, and yet in the eternity of the whole universe they are phases at different level. This level, to me, has no meaning since it is measured with arbitrary reference point while there is no point of measurement at all. So, even to comprehend let alone to understand 'what is', is far beyond me. In the course of comprehending this function all dualities drop out since every duality is only a difference in degree but not in kind. Attributing some qualities, however utopian they might be, are nullity to me. It is our conditioning from different sources such as geographical, cultural, religious, and family and other individual influences, have bundled and framed us to a particular pigeon-hole and we accept them with grandeur and pomp.

—⁂—

18ᵀᴴ JUNE 1999   03 30 A.M.

It is highly impossible to understand my own self let alone something abstract called God. I am bound and conditioned to all thoughts, feelings, wantings, desires to be something other than 'what is'. I am a part of the whole, despite of myself as a separate entity. And the whole exist because also of me. If a tiny part is lost the whole is not complete. Nothing could be lost in the universe. It functions as it should. All talks of heaven, the hope, and the virtues are all hypothetical ones, as to my way of living, if we call it living which looks to be hypothetical too. Awareness of something, that is transient, which is intangible, is to give hypothetical power to one self. Any power whether of money, material, muscle, intellectual or even the so called spiritual are just ego boosting, so as to enslave others, to dominate others and to give self importance to one self. The awareness of that power enslaves something else. I lost something from within. May be, other thing has occupied that place in me. Some independence is lost but some freedom is gained, independence of body and freedom of mind, may be. However there is no Absolutism in anything either in the bondage or in freedom. We are the totality of all conditionings both of society and of our own making. As such, I am both a separate entity and also bound to the whole and thus not a separate entity in the absolute terms.

My thought is to separate the self-created bondage. It is the thought that creates, it is the thought that translates and the very thought that brings back the past events as memories in the form of present thought.

It is difficult to reconcile to any doctrines or dogmas, or to the expressions of some one who claims that God came down and entered his body and through him the whole universe is being changed to heaven. This also I don't understand. Since I don't understand any of these aspects of God I do not argue about it and neither I accept it nor reject it. That person has right to have his own concept or experiences. That does not mean I personally should follow him thinking his experience to be the ultimate truth, for I know not what ultimate truth these people are talking about.

The one truth that I realize within me is that I am in constant connection with the Cosmic Being. This connection is there constantly for the simple reason that 'me' and that energy are related to each other having almost the same qualities and we are both eternally peaceful in nature. This is so, whether I am in constant awareness of the link or not. My awareness of this link makes no difference for the very reason that I am not an entirely separate entity and also that point of universal energy too is not a separate entity. Universe exists because of that Energy. Otherwise it has no meaning to that Energy. The whole universe is the extension, is the manifestation, and is the reflection of that 'One Energy' in different degrees, but not in nature. This energy that spins, rotates and controls the entire Universe is the same energy that sustains this physical body and mind, which keeps all the molecules and cells of different organs of my body together, for that matter all the molecules of everything this entire universe holds, be it animate or inanimate. Everything is dynamic whether conceivable or not by the human limited intelligence. In this process of link there is no medium, there is no media, there is no channel and there is no influence of others. It is direct, it is pure, it is original, and it is personal. It hits me directly with such tremendous force—that force is restricted, I feel, for my physic to withstand while that force is universal I am an iota of that energy and it knows my capacity to withstand the power of that Energy.

19TH APRIL 1999   03 15 A.M.

To me, the universe is something both known and unknown. I know the universe because I am one with it, in its all functions. I do not know the universe in its true functions because I do not know myself of my own functioning. These looks to be a strange situations, strange is my existence, my functioning, my departure etc. I strongly feel that there is no coming or going. 'I' is always here but under different situations, rather situations and events change and pass through, but 'I-am' permanent and eternal, remaining here. The whole universe including that central seat of universe looks to be my real and original home and I am all over the universe without any movements from me. I know myself to be eternal and I am a friend to myself. I know myself very intimately, passing through different situations and events which move by me while I stand still in deep silence witnessing every movement and event that takes place in me. These events, which pass through by me, have no influence on me and I witness these situations and events, untouched by any of them, without qualifying them, without putting any nomenclature on them. These go on eternally, but I am still (un-moved) and the same from the beginning to the end of the cycle of these events and situations. I do not count as to how many phases of these events take place and in each phase what events have what qualities, they move while I stand and watch them. Nothing could be more blissful and satisfying than to watch these events that pass by me, untouched while I remain to be the same to eternity without any change. These events, I strongly feel, happen by themselves. But I am not alone. I am with Him, who also is like me but without any such events happening to Him from whom I draw all the energy because He is the perpetual energy, pure energy, holding whole Universe in perfect order. The turmoil or changes etc. are not turmoil or changes, but they are the natural functions of the universe. I watch these turmoil and changes in the universe as I watch the phases and events, at a micro level. Nothing changes. Nothing happens. Everything is just functioning most naturally as I and He are very natural.

—◊—

15ᴛʜ APRIL 1999　　　　　　　　　　05 00 A.M.

It is said that to understand God, look at Him as He is and not what you want Him to be. While it is beyond the human perception to understand something that could not come to be captivated within the limited human intellect and it is impossible to understand that Being as He is and how He is. Deep within me, I feel, that everything this universe holds, whether seen or unseen, whether understood or not understood, all belong to me and I to them, in every element.

I feel that all the five elements of the universe, the space, the wind, the water, the fire and the earth are my friends and they are known to me since the time all of them came to be created for they are the creations of the One who is so well known to me from the time immemorial. Somehow, I feel very friendly with everything and I am one with them, I belong to them and they to me from the very perception to the creation and yet, I feel my intellect has its own limitations—the intellect of rationalism—but the awareness projects itself to something unimaginable and there is that region where nothing this earth holds exists. That world is full of light, peace, love, bliss, understanding but all in very deep silence. Communication do take place but in deep silence. Even silence cannot be understood in the way we understand in this world of sound. The capacity of our brain has limitations. That which we cannot perceive and also which we cannot hear do exist and yet, the very depth of silence, there in that world, is something very blissful and sweet. In that depth I find myself and the Creator of the universe, both being eternal and both known to each other and love each other in a way altogether different from the love of this mundane world. The strength, the love, the energy I hold is beyond this physical body. This physical body immediately perishes if all the strength and energy I process there were to be manifested here. This energy will be manifested only to the extent this physical body can sustain. And still I know I have the immense strength, love, energy transferred from Him for He is my Supreme Being and Supreme Friend.

26TH MARCH 1999   05 30 A.M.

Everything about God seems to be, for we human beings, only thorugh and in the functioning of this island, this earth, like a grain of sand on a huge beach and on this earth the human part, though very important, is again an infetisimle part of dust compared to all livings on earth, air and water together. When so, how little part an individual human performs and still how great he is for he can visualize the whole universe in his tiny brain through his subtle thoughts! The whole of cosmic energy is circulating around the universe in a perfect manner by which the whole universe functions perfectly. The value human beings give for their survival—bodily survival—and may be for their mental comforts, makes all the difference and scientific progress is only towards the survival, mostly, for the human beings at the cost of all other animate and inanimate objects.

When I leave the surface of this earth and travel up and up, hardly I find any movement on the surface of the earth except its spinning movement, which also is lost to my vision when I go still upwards and loose the significance of the whole solar system and further the significance of our whole galaxy and I find thousands of galaxies each like a little star in wide expanse of the whole universe. And then I find the central point of universe in deep silence controlling the entire universe and I stand without my physical body before IT with awe and aghast but with reverence and love for we know each other from the time immemorial.

—〜—

3ʀᴅ Mᴀʀᴄʜ 1999   05 00 ᴀ.ᴍ.

Nothing is farther from the truth to say that 'we understand'. Understanding anything in its true sense of its functioning is beyond any body's imaginations. We only infer with the so called logical rationalism from its past common result and once again with the same logical inference will change this inference based on different result, when the same function yield results differently. And yet, we could see some commonality in these variations of inferences in the continuum of the functioning. And ultimately we conclude that every function has the same quality or rather of the same kind but with different degrees.

The human nature being what it is, it shall become impossible to be satiated with anything whether about himself or of the outer world. The so called search goes on as long as human being exists on the surface of this planet. And somewhere along the line the man realizes the futility of his search and his helplessness not to have arrived at to say, for sure, that this is 'The Reality'. The Reality looks like a mirage on a desert. The Reality slips between the fingers for we cannot hold it to prove the Reality. The Reality is that man is conditioned by his own limitedness. Man cannot stretch his imagination with his limited intelligence to arrive at the Infinite Truth in its Real form, as IT is. Truth being the Reality is beyond space, time and causation. Space comes within the realm of time and so too the causation. The time varies—the time of the outer space is something different from the time of this planet earth. A person who enters space ages slowly both physically and mentally and if he comes back to this earth after certain 'space-age', probably, he would meet his great grand-children, as scientist proved. Man has limitations to go to space, physically. Beyond those physical limitations, probably, lies what we call the 'subtle-world', where the departed souls go in subtle body and after a span of time come back to this planet once again through a different physical body. And beyond this subtle world, may be, the subtle body too loses itself and only one which is immortal—the soul, the 'I' travels with its causal body, if it so destined to travel to the Central Point of Universal Cosmic Energy. At this point nothing exists, whether in physical or subtle form. It is something inexpressible, something unique, something beyond experience, something beyond explanation that functions at that Point. There is a central point from where the whole universe is controlled in an orderly way and in an orderly form and in perfection. All energy, all strength, all functioning of this universe manifest themselves from this One Central Point. It is an eternal, immortal, infinite one point beyond the human comprehension and understanding. One can only become aware of Its truth, if at all, by the one who goes there in his truthful form. To know It as It is, one should go without any blemishes and without an iota of these worldly memories—in a pure thoughtless state. One has to become the purity itself to stand before this Empowering, Majestic Supreme Being from where all powers of this whole universe flow. This point is an eternal, immortal, infinite, self-generating source and the only ONE source for the whole universe. The whole universe is the creation, the projection and the reflection of this One Source. But for this Source, this universe would not be existing and so I am. The sum totality of the whole universal energy stems from this point. The very awareness of this immeasurable gigantic energy, though comes from a tiny point, is very awesome, something very aghast and something unparalleled and incomparable. It could only through my very subtle experience I would become aware of such a point of universal energy. It is beyond the five elements of nature, beyond everything the man is known to have known. It looks to me that the whole universe is like a space-ball moving around this Point while This Point is constant without any movement. Very deep and wonderful lovable silence engulfs this vast arena wherein I loose myself and I am aware of myself being lost and yet there is no fear, there is no dream but only the Reality. Reality of timelessness, thoughtlessness, non physical and yet awareness, full awareness of my own self is revealed while that Point is always there. I become aware that we are the only two on this vast plane of this universe. Everything vanishes, melts away and my original and primordial personality is realized. My very origin is reflected and I feel that I am that in reality unchanged, unmoved by any external influences, whether physical or mental. And in that state I remain for long. And yet it is inevitable to come back to this physical world. These experiences of awareness make imprints upon me which helps further for me to still have experiences more and more of this Reality more and more frequently.

16TH FEBRUARY 1999   03 30 A.M.

Very deep thinking takes me to a definite realm of the universe which is very familiar to me, which, I feel, belongs to me and me to that world. Here I not only feel that I have been known but also I know that this state of my being has been eternally going on. And I am being a part of this and still having my own individual personality which goes on and on without any beginning or an end. In this individual personality of mine everything that have accumulated is resulted in a subtle manner and I am the sum total of all the results of these thoughts, words and deed that I made myself to undergo from time to time at different stages in different phases of lives. May be, I find, as a witness of my own self that there is both divinity and otherwise in my personality. However, this personality, which is me, cannot be destroyed under any situation. I do feel very strongly and very surely that this personality of mine is indestructible. I know that my personality which is my true nature can never be burnt by fire, drowned by water, held by earth, blown away or dried by wind or contained in space. This true 'me' is beyond the influence of nature (*Prakruthi*) and not bound by time, or cause-effect phenomenon; beyond every dimension and still comes within the realms of all these things having been in physical body; and yet eternally moves round and round from one stage to another in a cyclic manner.

This individual personality of mine is eternally and entirely my own, a unique one, unlike any other personality unparalleled and incomparable

My awareness of my own personality through deep silence brings me more nearer to my-self; deeper the silence my nearness to my own self is more nearer. And in the nearness of 'me' I find another Supreme Personality almost like me but infinitely superior beyond comparison and it looks that I am a very small branch of that huge tree. In this state of awareness of both me and that Supreme Personality, the entire mundane world including this physical body and its functions are scattered and lost.

I am just there as being here. All fears, all questions of the unknown future, everything vanishes, I am just I am without any dual personality and without any dual qualities. Everything looks to me to be a passing phase. There, in that world it is a stage of one level. While here I reach that state by peace and purity; and purity prevails and pervades me; and I feel stronger in my divine personality and equally my other personality slowly diminishes and vanishes altogether. I feel renewed to reach my original divine individual eternal personality. And that is the ultimate result of my meeting with this Eternal Central Point of Cosmic Energy

—ᴍ—

11ᵀᴴ FEBRUARY 1999   04 00 A.M.

In the human history, I think, there is no subject that has been discussed, written about or practiced more than the subject on God and spiritualism. Irrespective of what the modernity is, this subject has never ceased to be the main occupation of the human being, a subject which is more revered, a subject that is more divided, a subject which is most misused, for the reason of nations, on which, wars were fought and is being continued to be fought. And yet God seems to be elusive, or God seems to be the property of some people who ultimately claim themselves as God. From my point of view, even though I have heard and read and still do, about God, God is in one's own inner being, a self-conceptual projection, all that the society hold as good and wonderful; and what one experiences for one self, intangibly in deep silence, within in one self. All explanations, all attributes, all writings, all speeches, all discussions will not bring God by a fraction nearer to one self than the solitary deep silence one feel within one self and in this deep silence one comes very nearer to God. Sometimes, I feel, man is the greatest enemy to himself for he knows not what he is, he is not aware of his eternity and his real qualities, he knows not that he is beyond birth and death—the simple example being that man in his life remains to be himself despite of he being dead and rejuvenated every day through his three trillions cells and the whole body renews itself once in seven years and still he remains the same in his appearance physically though there are some changes due to time factor. But from within he is still a young man and desires to appear to be young, man spends a lot money, time and strength to remain to be so. If a man goes beyond himself, slowly but surely he will realize his eternity and even in that eternity he finds another like him. In that eternity man finds himself, his true nature and the eternal companionship of another Being too. This companionship is as eternal as eternity could be, inseparable, be it in any position the man places himself. But in whatever position man places himself, be it that man knows his companion or not, that Companion always stands by the man. While with that companion, at least to me, time stops, all *Karmas* make no effect, all talks have no meanings. It is beyond time, space and cause-effect. May be, this is what is called as 'karma teeth' (freed from all bondages) stage. Call it by any name.

During such periods when I am out of my body, the whole universe becomes a small place to play with, a toy. Nothing influences me; nothing brings me more joy and peace than being in that stage. No thought is created, no words come out, no Karmas are performed, no other human being including myself is present, even this very earth does not exist and it becomes a point of dot and so this galaxy of ours too let alone this solar system. In that state of my being, there is no galaxy, there is no sun and there is no earth. It is a vast, very vast, immeasurably vast arena and vista where there is no darkness; it is transparent, as if I can see every atom of those phenomena of this vastness. There is neither cold nor heat, there is nothing that this earth holds and yet it is the best. It has no dualities, it is beyond all the five elements and it is beyond all the twelve dimensions. I find in myself my true nature and He is with me and I am with Him for eternity without any desire. I am completely aware of this and when I return to this physical body that sweet memories linger within me which once again influences me to go back to that state of my being. This happens to me whenever I desire to be with Him and especially when I am alone irrespective of time, irrespective of all those external activities that go on around me with din and sound. I feel the terrific vibrations within me and around me. Sometimes I feel that I am electrocuted and yet I am in control of myself and aware of myself. I am aware of that deep silence within me. Silence is not darkness. In silence I find life everywhere and I find myself everywhere, enlightened.

Nothing brings me more joy, peace and strength, it is an experience of rejuvenation, an experience of fulfillment, an experience of love, an experience of desire to be always in that state. That state, I feel, is the real state and I belong to that state from eternity to eternity without stoppage and I am aware of that state and understand that state, but not this physical state, because I am that very state itself in my originality.

—◦—

29ᵀᴴ JANUARY 1999   04 00 A.M.

Whatever may be the theory as regards to God, soul etc. it still remains to be impossible for me to comprehend. I am a mystery to myself. Slowly this

'I' melts away and there stands eternity. I feel, I have a very vague knowledge of immeasurable past and the present is understandable and I know nothing about the future. Somehow, I feel there is neither present nor future. Everything looks to be only of the past. All my knowledge is of past. Even every second of the present having no stop becomes past and the future looks to be only a projection of the past, an extension of the past. In this line where do I stand? I don't know. Somehow, deep down in me, I experience my eternal past and the present is only a reflection and the future has nothing to do with me and if it comes, it takes care of itself and gets into the non-stop of the past. In the past I feel no fear. I have, I feel strongly, undergone many phases of life and all looks to be sweet memories though they are not explicit of every action of the past. Peace, silence and tranquility go together with an understanding of desire-less-ness. Nothing is to be desired, even the God should not be desired and if at all that concept of God is what others explain. Some—how, I feel, that having no knowledge or control on anything that goes on in the functioning of the Universe, including myself being a part of this functioning, nothing, I feel, can be understood in their reality of functioning, whatever may be the intellectual explanation a man many profound, for it is only the man who is capable of expressing in words, both orally and in writing. But this expression whether oral or written, having a very small part with its own limitations, imagination comes in. This imagination is a pre-conceived notion given to me by the society; it is not my original imagination. Imagination is a subtle form of expression. Beyond imagination is feeling. It is once again a very subtle form of thought. Where from and how thoughts are formed, is impossible to understand, at least for me. This very understanding, I feel, is once again another subtle form of thought. What I am clear about is; that I am aware of my being eternal. In this awareness, I feel that all the dualities have no place, because it is the so called rationality of human nature to give name to everything. But in that state of my awareness all such things have no part to play. I feel the deep silence, the eternal silence, the tranquil silence and the pure silence. And in this silence awareness comes in. And that awareness is: that I am beyond everything this earth holds. The time and the space dimensions vanish, rather all dimension vanish. It is in the dimensionless world I am traveling to and at the same time I am constant; for there is no reference point in that world, there is no relativity in that region—it is not a region at all, in the sense the mundane world understands. It is a state of awareness, a most soothing, most peaceful, most enjoyable and most loving. Peace, purity, silence and tranquility are the only dimensions in that world. Nothing is wanted, no expectations, no looking forward to or backward to, nothing comes in or goes out and nothing is desired. In this the state of awareness I am conscious of, the eternity of me.

A type of awareness of not being aware of anything that goes on in the whole of universe prevails upon me. I don't know what to call this state. It is beyond me to give expressions to this awareness. In this awareness everything stops and goes to back stage; and I would not be aware of anything of my own physical body and rather even the physical functioning of the universe itself.

I have a very strong desire to continue to be in this state of awareness. While in this state I am not aware of the physical state of my being. Strange it looks. That awareness being stronger may lead deep impression to continue to make itself of its presence even in this state but the reverse is not so, because it may be weak. This state (physical state) being very weak cannot carry itself to that state. In that state I am with the One Universe which belongs to me and about which I am very familiar with and as such I am not afraid of that state, since, I feel, that state of awareness is my real state of my being. And in that state I am always with the central cosmic Being, call it as God if it is to be so called. But I am alone with that 'Being' in eternity

—–m—–

26ᵀᴴ JANUARY 1999   03 30 A.M.

I really want to know about myself. Somehow, I cannot separate myself from the totality of the universe's functioning, as a separate entity. I also wonder whether I am born, alive and going to die. Nothing is clear. Everything looks to be un-understandable. I feel, I am a part of the whole function of the Universe. I am familiar with everything, even the functioning of the stars, all galaxies, why the whole universe. I feel I belong to them and they to me, very intimately. And being in such a state, fear of the unknown is lost since the known is friendly and I am of aware of my being with every function of the universe at every level. I feel that there has been neither birth, nor life, nor death to me. I am an immortal one not bound by anything. And there is nothing, at the same time, to be called as time, cause-effect etc; in the functioning of the universe. The destruction of anything is only a change from one state to another. Deep down in me, I am convinced, I am confident, I am definite, I am un shaken in this knowledge that I am as old as this universe is and it being eternal so I am. In the order of things of this univserset there no loss or gain or change etc. but it only functions at different level

I don't know how to put it across. But my awareness brings me a lot of understanding of functioning of the universe from its central point of cosmic energy which is familiar to me. In this state, there stands neither the past nor the present nor the future. It is a one continuous circle of functioning and I am riding this circle without any beginning or an end, while that center remains constant and it could be seen from any point of the circle. Everything I am processed with seems to be a hallucination, a mirage in a desert and yet when I function at some level of this world I function as an entity with all types of relationships of the so called life, keeping in knowledge that I am eternal, beyond birth, life or death. I really don't know much about the functioning of my own physical body let alone the functioning of the universe. I am only aware that they all are functioning, but how and why are not my concern and they have no answers, the real answers. A computer or a machine cannot question itself as to how and why it is functioning or rather not aware of its own functioning and it is being functioned through the external applications such as electric power and human intelligence. It is the human intelligence that is reflected in the functioning of these machineries. So, it is the soul's intelligence which functions in our physical body also. When the soul is out of body, the body deteriorates and decomposes itself, while the soul is eternal in its original form. I feel myself eternal, because I am the soul, and the Supreme Soul is also eternal like me, but will not take any physical body to be born or to die like my physical body, because that Supreme Soul is eternal in its formless function unlike me.

5ᵀᴴ JANUARY 1999   05 00 A.M.

Of all the powers man has, his power of speech is the supreme. Had it not been for this advantage, man would not have found God. It is the word rather the speech that has created God. Why *only* man could speak and not animals? This has no answers except to say that that is how the man is made of or born with. This one additional capacity has created lot many other capacities like writing, understanding, and communicating with the other human and forming society, we are living now and trying to impose and improve upon it. But for this capacity every bodily function of man is almost like an animal.

So, the creator, a common force, must necessarily be neither a man nor an animal and must not have had physical anybody at all. That must be the energy capable of being the creator of the whole universe and controlling it in its own ways under its own laws. However, it is beyond human understanding of this universal force—the central force, calling it as Creator or God. To me, at least, it is beyond understanding. It is like a seed with all the potentialities of a tree in it, trying to understand the completeness of the whole tree, while the seed itself also a part of the tree, wherein the very capillary force to grow runs through even in that seed. That is how I feel that I am a small seed of a big tree. But the absence of any one of the components of a tree does not make completeness of that tree. So with the universe, while the universe contains both animate and inanimate objects, each has its own functions and the absence of any one element, even a grain of sand, may not amount to completeness to the universe and at the same time no one particular particle can have the ego to say that that particle understands the whole universe, while it is incapable of understanding its own being, its own functioning, in spite of many millions of theories man has made in this behalf.

I do not understand, in the real sense, in the abstract sense, what it is that man calls as progress, whether social, economic or spiritual. All words look mystery to me. I am a mystery to myself; I don't know anything about myself, let alone the universe or its creator. I find this ignorance brings me lot of silence deep within me that leads me to peace and tranquility

—ᚮ—

2ND JANUARY 1999 04 00 A.M.

God is a word coined by human beings on conceptualization based on individual expression or his mental projection and experiences from within one self. The word has limitation but the concept has a bigger limitation while the experience too has limitation but beyond words and expressions.

The whole universe exists for man because he exists for the universe. Universe expands because man's conceptual consciousness expands and in this expansion of his own inner self to the universal expansion he goes beyond the dimensions of time, space and cause-effect. Man cannot see in himself his soul to be the eternal, pure, divine one; but detached man is aware of these qualities within himself which is part of the Whole. The awareness by itself does not have any qualification or quality or this awareness cannot be separated from one self—rather the self itself becomes aware of the whole universe and the central energy point of the whole. In the process of this awareness nothing touches man's soul and still everything including himself becomes a reflection of this whole.

Awareness has no fear for it is the reality of oneself. Man accepts that he ultimately, while being in a limited sphere of physical body, finds the process of movement of life from one phase to another and that becomes natural without attachment either to the past movement or to the present one or to his projected future. They are just happenings and an individual is a very infinitesimal part of this functioning. Acceptance, without wanting to be other than 'what is', is the only way for a man to be aware of the whole. I do not feel the presence of any other being in this state along with me. The presence is only of that awareness or the whole universe functioning in its own course. In the end no movement or functioning takes place in this awareness. There is complete deep and immeasurable silence. And silence is 'me'. Silence neither comes nor goes. It is just 'me' being aware. Silence becomes bliss, joy, love to eternity and I am that silence without dualities and this silence of peace, purity is my real self which has the original qualities as that of Supreme Being.

—⟋⟋⟋—

21ST DECEMBER 1998 03 00 A.M.

Some type of desire arises in me and I am out. There I remain in a plane very far above this galaxy and still be within the universe. There are no dualities—such as, sin-divine; heat-cold; pain-pleasure; sorrow-happiness etc. An inexpressible deep silence pervades all over, beyond thought, time, space, cause-effect. Everything stops; absolutely there is no movement at all. No presence of anything, but complete awareness of the whole universe with the knowledge of myself being not within the influence of anything, for there is nothing in that plane to influence me in any manner. But simple awareness fills me. I witness the whole universe. Only me and the universe exist and nothing else. This awareness knows no knowledge of anything, including the so called God. In that plane God too does not exist as an entity. I only am aware of the awareness and nothing else. I become aware of my immortal being, peaceful, pure without another being with me. I am alone and only one without any other being. Nothing exists and still the whole universe stands before me and I become aware of my belonging to the universe and still not belonging to its functions in terms of time, space, cause-effect etc. They do not touch me, and still I feel everything belongs to me, a friendly companionship but detached completely from any of the functions of the universe, because my awareness is absolute and infinitely eternal, not bound by any functions of the universe. There is neither any *Karma* nor any divine law which binds my awareness. Awareness cannot be qualified, cannot be expressed, and cannot be in conceptual understanding of limited intelligence of man. Awareness is becoming and being. Awareness lifts egoistical ignorance to naught and this panorama of eternal reality is beyond every conceivable values whether metaphysical or spiritual and beyond the knowledge of human.

—m—

20ᵀᴴ DECEMBER 1998   03 30 A.M.

I feel deeply within me about this universe—the universe which is functioning without the beginning or an end but perpetually, beyond time, under its own laws. Everything whether the best or the worst has to come to an end, though not an end but at least to a change; the change where no traces of the last one is left. In spite of such changes, I feel, that I am something that have never changed or changes, there is something of me that occupies these changes and yet unchanged. There is this awareness of changelessness, the permanent and the unchangeable of me, the continuity of myself, while the change—the external phenomenon—matters not to 'me'. It is the desire to be perpetual, to be permanent without decay of this external phenomenon (which is bound by the laws of change) not to change, brings lot of frictions between the changeable and unchangeable of 'me'. All external changes in the Universe are only with reference to the physical body I occupy. Otherwise neither heat, nor cold, nor any extremities of the nature matters to inside of 'me'. There are no dualities in that 'me'. The 'me' expands to the whole universe and becomes one with the Universal Cosmic Consciousness. Then no more 'me' remains, I become the very universal consciousness in union with the 'whole'. The more I try to understand these universal phenomena, the less successful I become; for the desire to understand, makes me a separate entity from the whole, which, in fact, is not there. That which is in front of me goes behind me, as I walk, because there is a real movement in 'me', while the one in front of me has not any movement or has a slower movement than 'me'. This is how I look at the future and the present. 'I' do not exist for 'me'. The existence of me comes with the memory of knowledge of the external physical world about which I do not understand in as much as I do not understand the internal 'me'. And still some type of understanding of my internal relationship with the universal cosmic force comes to me, and yet I cannot either understand or give expressions to an understanding of a relationship with that Force—the cosmic energy. Neither do I attach any importance to the changing physical body not to the unchangeable 'me' within. I feel, that everything is 'as it is' and as 'it should be', however otherwise we wish to qualify or quantify which are merely utopian projections of our mind that has been conditioned with dualistic approaches, while there is no way to approach at all. The only way to practice is to 'let go', and to try to understand the existence of extremities of both and to reconcile for 'what-is' than what should be. 'What-is' is a dim light of me and 'what-it-should-be' is the bright cosmic light of God.

—ɷ—

1ˢᵀ December 1998   03 00 a.m.

An inexpressible and unexplainable calm prevails within me. The calm, that never has a parallel, engulfs me. That entire din around me makes no matter and nothing seems to be significant. I wonder at the way the universe works. Slowly all types of interests are being lost. The very functioning of my 'own self' has no significant meaning to myself. Sometimes, I feel the very God becomes a burden to me, since the God is taken as separate functioning entity from the functioning of the whole universe. It is something that does not come within my restricted intelligence or comprehension or imagination which go wild within me and yet I feel the peace, tranquility, calm, the purity of which can never be compared within and without me. I become the very embodiment of peace and calm which are by themselves pure.

—ɷ—

10ᵀᴴ December; 1998   03 30 a.m.

It was 02.00 am since I got up and had been contemplating upon the ways of the whole functioning of this universe. It is the central point of energy of this whole universe that is functioning through each and every part of the universe. It has got to function at the level of every atom of the whole universe; otherwise the universe cannot be there to function at all; as the central energy acts through every part of a living body. I being a part of the whole, am I not that central energy functioning through me? Putting it in the other way, am I not a part of the central energy too? When so, I do not understand how that energy would be a separate entity from this 'me' energy? Thought is a subtle energy of the same expression with a different facet. When such thoughts cross my mind, my consciousness expands to the whole universe and I become expanded where in neither 'me' not 'that' remain. Universal consciousness prevails upon my consciousness. I, as a separate entity, am lost and yet awareness remains as a continuous process. Time stops. Time looks to be an insignificant measurement at the non-mundane level. The universal consciousness combined with the cosmic energy pervades the whole universe and it functions at different levels and with different degrees according to the capacity of the medium that has to withstand the cosmic energy. If any extra cosmic energy were to prevail upon this human body, probably the body gets burnt out to ashes and gases. It knows best as to how much of itself has to prevail through which medium. And that is the cosmic intelligence. The very functioning of the whole universe to the perfect precision is cosmic intelligence, whether that functioning is qualified as positive or negative or otherwise. It goes on, no matter what the functions of the other beings are. So I am slowly but surely try to be in rhythm with the functioning of this universal energy.

30ᵀᴴ NOVEMBER 1998   03 30 A.M.

I feel that I am least busy. Feeling of 'let go' comes in. Having nothing to do in worldly matters, mind bogs down to celestial mood. Eye lids become heavy, a type of drowsiness sets in and body becomes limp and mind, to a certain extent, becomes empty and still, while through the intellect I witness all these things happening simultaneously and very actively separating myself from all these happenings. While in this state, nothingness seems to have some resultant effect on me and looks very strange and still some force is acting both within and without me. That which encompasses me in this state, I feel, becomes the reality of me, though something triggers to get back. And yet some times everything gets burnt out and ashes of these left over fly out leaving a state of thoughtlessness in deep silence. The depth of silence becomes a bottomless pit into which I fall and ultimately I become that very silence itself. There is neither anxiety nor fear in this state of silence.

24TH NOVEMBER 1998   03 30 A.M.

I don't know how this whole universe within which we the human beings with the so called intelligence, have come into existence. It is just beyond anybody's comprehension as to why this universe is as 'it is' and not different. The totality of these universal forces, I feel, comes from one particular central force which is the mother of all forces, while the whole universe is the manifestation of this one central force. It is the same force that is spread all over expressing itself through different mediums consisting of five elements (space, fire, water, air and earth) and others. This force has its own laws, not man made nor that which comes within the realms of the man's intelligence and this manifested force works through these five elements very naturally, very accurately having their own qualities though different and sometimes, diametrically opposite from each other and yet, at the same time, each is not only a supplement but also complement to each other. The absence of any one of these five elements eliminates the other four elements also. However, keeping all these five elements within the limits of their functioning, the common element—the central force has to function in a very balanced and accurate manner. It is impossible for any of these five elements to function independently not only without the other elements but also fundamentally without the central force functioning within these five elements, which acts as a catalyst between these five elements. The function of this body consisting of five elements is very insignificant compared to the functioning of the universe having all the five elements within and subtle force acting upon the functioning of this body. This subtle force in all the five elements turns out to be the only one. But at the same time though this gross body may not be functioning in a subtle way, it gives out for different functioning, from the so called dead body certain bacteria and worms, surge out creating different type of life which functions within its own limited intelligence and at the same time having all the five elements added with the same force and in the same order. So, nothing can escape the force and nothing can exist independently without this force. Even the so called a grain of sand cannot exist without all the elements for every atom in that sand particle is held together by this force to form that grain of sand. And that very atom of a sand grain is nothing but an expression of that force. The force by itself is neither negative nor positive. It is the human nature to give nomenclature to everything and to value them according to his social living. To what all the human gives the value of negative too is a force of the same nature. To me, there are neither negative nor positive values. They are in their most natural state though I do not understand what this natural state is.

—ɱ—

22ND NOVEMBER 1998   03 30 A.M.

How helpless becomes a man facing the order of things!. He becomes helpless when he tries to reach that which is unreachable. He is disappointed when his ambitions are not fulfilled. Ambition is a type of competition, a desire to succeed, a desire to be somebody other than what 'he is'. Neither he knows what 'he is' nor does he know the reality of what he desires to become. This desire, this hope to be 'somebody' other than what 'he-is', is creating turmoil and disappointment in man. And this desire is just a shadow in front. If you chase it, it moves out at the equal distance. If you turn back it chases you. And still both can never be without the other except in darkness, when there is light shadow is also there. You and your shadow, while in light, are inseparable and it is natural too. If you understand the shadow but do not try to reach it, it stays where it should and you are at peace while the shadow is not a separate entity apart from you. So also when the light of God comes, there is no shadow. Your shadows are your *karmas* which cannot be separated from you and does not have a separate entity from you. Your *karmas* can completely be wiped-off when the Cosmic Light falls upon you. Only when you are in complete darkness without the Light of God, you are the darkness itself.

—m—

26TH OCTOBER 1998   05 00 A.M.

It is very difficult to understand how and why this system of the universe is functioning. But the fundamental question is, whether it is really a necessity to understand and is there a system as man conceives and is it functioning? Even take it for granted that one individual is an entity, though not a separate entity from the whole of the universe is it possible for this one individual to understand the whole? The whole becomes a concept; a projection of one's so called understanding of that concept. I always have been feeling that the more I go far from this physical body the more I am going to be nearer to the Central Cosmic Power that controls the whole universe and its functions. From this central point the energy is generated constantly, infinitely and transmitted to the whole universe. This very energy when manifested in different expressions creates different dimensions of the five basic elements. And beyond this five basic elements lay that which is indestructible, by any means, the eternal cosmic energy generating point. In the process of functioning of this universe, changes can be seen and yet, they are not changes fundamentally because they are the expressions of this functioning which is natural and inevitable too; and beyond human intelligence. I just stand and gape with wonder having lost all the senses of the material world including my own physical body. I come more nearer to this Central Cosmic Energy Point in its natural qualities and it is incomparable and only one of its kind, having no second to it. Still I feel I am only a hazy reflection of the quality of that cosmic energy, but yet, far away from it. In this process I loose myself a lot, but do gain in manifold the qualities of that cosmic energy. But I question myself why and what for this gain? Is it not a type of power? All powers, whether subtle, or divine, or of material things bring their own egoistical decay. So, I simply cannot understand what is gained, for I need no power. I am just a part with no negative or positive elements in me and I go beyond all the dualities, even the dualities of divinity and sin. Every qualification becomes a naught and I stand alone with that central point and we have been known to each other since the projection of this universe as a big bang and even still from earlier to that when both myself and that cosmic energy were in our subtle stage, and were in the seed form of this universe. We have always been there together and always will be there to eternity, that is the understanding between me and that Central Cosmic Energy and nothing else matters.

—〰—

23ᴿᴰ OCTOBER 1998   03 00 A.M.

Something deep down in me says that my days are numbered—rather this body's days are numbered. Slowly it sets in and I have prepared myself to take it in my stride. A type of happiness covers me because I am going to take up a new life, a new start, a new physical body. There are no regrets in me, no anxiety and no looking back. The past life was just as it should be and nothing would have changed it and now nothing would change it and there is nothing requiring change either. Sometimes, some inexpressible joy hugs me for the forthcoming change of events and I look forward to a new change, but not that I disliked the past. It looks good from this platform. Somehow, I feel that the next life would be far superior in its qualities than what it has been in this life. Looking forward to the new life itself is a joy of happiness during this life. There, I feel, I shall meet someone whom I had known from the time immemorial. A life of deep silence, the silence of joy and understanding, and the silence of desire-less-ness and the silence of fulfillment which is eternal and most important is in awareness and enjoyment of that silence. How wonderful that silence would be, that brings out everything that is mystic. The very projection of that concept of that life of silence brings the immense calm now itself, the immense satisfaction of fulfillment of this life, wanting nothing and yet wants to enjoy that song of silence this heart sings. It is a great experience to feel the singing of one's heart in silence—to capture that joy within, to feel elated, to embrace the whole universe to your bosom and to feel that the whole universe belongs to you and you to the whole universe. It is the very purity itself that elates these experiences from within. Nothing could compensate these experiences of bliss, joy, happiness and deep silence that leave behind an aroma to the nose, nectar on the tongue, song in the heart, joy to the eyes and a light body to the touch of hand. How wonderful of these things to experience within in one's own inner most abode where there is none to steal any of these things from you. They all belong to you and the very qualities become a part of you and ultimately you become these very qualities which are with God and you take from Him to become like Him.

—m—

19ᵀᴴ OCTOBER 1998   01 00 A.M.

Something snaps within me and sometimes a thought from within; and some other time a smell, a sound, a word or a movement of air, or movement of something even the external calm influences this snap and all of a sudden I loose myself from within and in the process the whole connection between me and the surrounding world including my own physical body separates from me. When I become aware of this condition, the surroundings and my own body look strange to me, beyond my knowledge in spite of my looking at them with innocence and ignorance; for I would not know to recognize them at all. Why and how it happens is beyond me. It just happens in spite of me. I cannot give any rational explanations nor do I understand its process. Thoughts slow down and only awareness of this condition remains. While in such a condition sometimes something urges me to start writing about this condition and pen is pushed into my hand without any effort or any demand from me, to write. And sometime, which is more often, I rather would remain in this condition without doing anything at all. And some other time while writing under this condition something stops me to write and the pen falls down from my fingers, automatically, without any desire to drop writing; probably because writing becomes more a burden to the condition I am in, at that particular point in time. I experience this condition mostly when I sit in my office than elsewhere for four to five times a day, lasting sometimes for half to one hour. While in this condition when one hand touches the other hand or any portion of the physical body the touching hands feels the softness of cotton, that touch will have no dimension, it feels as if a soft breeze has passed over, it looks as if the whole body is of cotton, loose cotton; still there is a type of magnetic force in that touch, interactive. I don't know whether this condition is a type of state of my mind or really happening, for I have no proof to say authentically and I have no way of knowing other than being aware of this condition. This condition is completely thoughtless and in deep silence and looks that I become aware of myself being beyond any external influences and further I feel that I am aware of my being in eternity and I feel as if I am nondestructive and had never had any birth nor death and an unchangeable one, remaining to have been both in the past and in the future while no such qualification is attached since the present seems to be the one eternal without either the past or the future; and I am always there as an entity separate from the external physical body world. This condition, rather this awareness looks as if I am the only one who has come to stay in this condition and I do not see any other person except myself in this external space and timeless world and thoughtless universe. It looks I am the only one beside and along with that Cosmic Being. There are no one else except we two in this part of the world.

—m—

18ᵀᴴ OCTOBER 1998   04 00 A.M.

The fundamental question is to question myself as to 'who am I'? But the answer—the correct answer, if any, is difficult to find. Many theories are promoted by many. Many might have experienced their own theories. To me, it does not looks to be an intelligent question, for it has no answer in the real sense. One may give elaborate and theoretical and equally convincing answer. That conviction shakes, many a times, the very person who convinces himself. To me, I am not a separate entity and the wholeness of this universe is me. Me, I etc are only expressions made in conversational ways. The Truth, as I understand, is that the whole universe, known and unknown, is one and the only one and everything is a part of the universe having all the required optimum qualities of the universe, whether these qualities are uttered differently by different people at different places and at different times. Everything, whether primordial or modern or ultra modern society is one and the same expression of this universe in different degrees, which we human beings consider ourselves, each as a separate entity and a separate intelligent being, different from the universal phenomenon, which, in fact, is not. But at the same time it becomes impossible to understand the whole universe in total and yet one can project one's understanding of the universe by understanding a part of it, for the part cannot be different, rather does not differ from the whole universe. It is a natural phenomenon without any bias towards any other events. It is the totality of all events at all times in the whole universe that makes the universe a complete one (*Sampoorna*). However, the whole is inclusive of a part of it.

—ɯ—

16ᵀᴴ OCTOBER 1998   03 30 A.M.

When scientists say that the brain is still a mystery to them, I feel that the whole Universe is a mystery to me. Nothing could be understood, at least I do not understand the functioning of this universe, I may theorize and all theories vary from time to time. The theories that are established about a century back or even decade ago may not hold good now. That which holds good now may not hold good after a few years. And yet, I feel, that there is something unchangeable, permanent, eternal, divine, pure in itself (not that pure which the human qualifies or quantifies as values) and natural beyond the dimensions of time, cause-effect and neither negative nor positive. Still it is a mystery to me. I feel that I know about this One since time immemorial and I am always with this One constant cosmic energy and yet it is beyond me, to say with full confidence, to understand This. To me It is still a mystery and yet I am one with this while I myself am a mystery to myself. Sometimes I feel that this cosmic energy is running all through my body encompassing every cell and I become energized and loose the awareness of my surroundings. Time stops and everything stops, the whole universe becomes a small place that could be held in the fist of my hand. So light it becomes, so mysterious it looks, so blissful, so wonderful are my experiences in such moments.

—ɯ—

11ᵀᴴ OCTOBER 1998   00.00 HOURS

The simplest thing is that 'my very existence is unknown to myself', if there is such a thing as 'myself'. Is there anything like 'me', an entity 'me'? The very title me, is very vague and equally looks to be nothing. The state of my own 'being' is impossible to define to myself, let alone to any outsider. Some desire creeps in from nowhere—the desire which has the past, the desire of what has been attained by someone and to attain it, to be someone other than what I am and the desire to arrive at some level other than at what level I am. This desire to be something different from 'what-I-am', at times grips my heart. And ultimately some type of realization comes to me that the very desire is 'me'; desire is not from outside but from inside which is a part of me and me itself. All knowledge, whether perceived or not, are within the realms of this universe. Am I not a part of this universe which is nothing but a pure energy? The energy which is equally functioning in and through me? This 'me' too is a part of this universal cosmic energy. Black holes, night, day, birth, life, death etc. are the part of this cosmic energy expressed in different manner at different times and in different degrees. Manifestation of this cosmic energy in different expressions creates different images. There cannot be any other way of expression than what is being expressed, rather I do not know the very expression of this energy in a particular function let alone my imagination of its being desired to be expressed differently. Imagination, desire are equally expressions of the same cosmic energy in a very subtle manner unknown to human being. Knowledge is also an expression of this energy and so the ignorance too is an expression of this energy, which is of the same kind but at different levels and in different degrees. I feel that this energy is functioning uniformly at its optimum level, perfectly all through the universe in every sphere. I would rather go still ahead and say that the whole universe is nothing but this cosmic energy and It is manifesting Itself in all the animate or inanimate objects, in all five elements etc. known and un-known. Everything is the expression of the same energy in different forms at different levels. And I am one of these expressions of the same cosmic energy, though very insignificant. Yet, I feel that everything that is functioning/ happening in all its forms is somehow connected to me and I love these happenings in response to all these happenings because I see myself in these happenings. I feel that I belong to this cosmic happening, being myself a part of this cosmic happening, eternally with neither past nor the future. It is one continuous process of happening from one present to another present. These happenings by themselves neither have past nor future. All past, present and future are only arbitrary measurements, which are timeless and have no cause and effect. They are simply happenings and that is how they function beyond the human understanding, but with precise cosmic intelligence.

I feel, as it were, that I should get out of this trap. I feel that I have trapped myself and some help also comes from me for my trapping, rather I help them to help me to trap myself. Nothing could ever be done to de-trap myself. If not this trap, some other trap will trap me. It is only a replacement of one by another. The only difference is the language, but meaning ultimately is the same—to get trapped somewhere. Universe, energy, cosmic dimensions are mere words without any understanding, there is nothing in the first instance to understand about 'out—there' not 'in here', because there is nothing that could be called as 'out' nor 'in'. They are all human concepts of comparative degrees when objectively looked at. There is neither spiritual, nor material, nor superior, nor inferior, nor sin, nor divine. It is all a degree in variance of the same kind. All talks of God looks to me to be mere words to make others to respect the man who talks about God and thus derive some sort of subtle power and ride over others. This gives pleasure to man who talks about God. It gives leverage of one over the other. The human nature being what it is, a man always wants to be 'somebody' other than what 'he is' and sometimes a 'special somebody'. The one, I feel, who is with himself does not wants to be a 'somebody' amongst his beings for that man does not stay with others but he stays with himself. This feeling of being 'somebody' comes with the knowledge of superiority in power either in wealth, beauty, knowledge, status etc. When this ego of superiority is lost naturally, but not killed artificially, then probably man does not remain to be a man physically, but someone with Cosmic Energy, both in body and mind together. One can never understand anyone operating independently without the complement of the other. Body, when functioning, functions equally through the mind in a very subtle manner. A person becomes entirely an isolated one mentally when one is with oneself away from the world of materials. Man gets powers and strength naturally when he is with himself without asking or desiring or even being aware of himself—like the light spreading when the day breaks which is natural and automatic, even when one desires it or not or when one ask for it or not. No one need to ask for the light during the day from the sun when one is in the day, so with himself. If he is away from himself darkness, fear, isolation encompasses him and he becomes an enemy to himself and as well to others and all deeds are committed during the darkness, for he looses himself, looses his rationality and the faculty of discrimination. In the end he stays with himself and with the Supreme Being who is his ultimate companion. One cannot function without the other. Whether man is aware of himself or not, he always remains with himself. Then God reflects Himself in the midst of man's life. The reflection will be clear and accurate when the mind is clear and clean without any blemishes and when the mind is pure. Otherwise there may not be any reflection at all and even if there is one it is very hazy and distorted. Every day and very often this mirror of mind requires cleaning, only then the God can reflect Himself in this mirror.

—–ɯ––

29ᵀᴴ Aᴜɢᴜsᴛ 1998   03 30 ᴀ.ᴍ.

I feel that I am being pushed to end the present life. In a way, the intense desire to understand, if at all such a machinery continuous to exist, what exactly it could be after the end, is one of the factors for me to push myself. However, whether I push it or not it will come only on the appointed day rather hour and even at that second and cannot pre-pone or postpone even by a second. The desire to be one with the whole cosmic energy, cosmic intelligence, and the universal cosmic consciousness—awareness of the entire universe and to be with it, to be a part part of it, is increasing within me. Sometimes, I feel that I am a stranger to myself and being a stranger to this world, I am feeling that I belong to the Cosmic Home with cosmic energy, the presence of which I feel deep within me and in very deep silence. Will such an intense desire hasten my going from this world? I wonder not. Calmness pervades me and prevails upon me. Deep down within me there is infinite and absolute silence, the silence, I feel, eternally exists along with me, while I am eternal to infinity having the companionship of the Cosmic Wonder. Nothing could be a wonder. Even the very God standing, if at all, before me or even He entering me could not be a great wonder, to be accounted for, irrespective of what meaning, what description, what definition or explanation others may give. To me, it would be the most natural phenomena if it could happen, if at all such a thing could happen either to me or to any one. Even if it does not happen, it is equally natural.

Why I am made to write all these things is a matter unknown to me. I am made to write naturally, because that is the thing to do now and may be that is how it should be too. Everything is happening in its own natural state and as it has to happen. It is the human mind with limited intelligence that gives values, that designates and that discriminates between these happenings and it is the very same human mind that desires the things to be otherwise. This desire to be otherwise than 'what is' is creating problem, the culprit for all mysteries in the human life. I feel sometimes even the mystery and sorrows too are natural phenomenon by themselves, but the human mind always wishes it be otherwise.

—w—

27ᵀᴴ AUGUST 1998   03 30 A.M.

It is a sudden jolt to me when I try to understand myself to know that there is no such a thing as 'me' or 'self', as a separate entity. Nothing comes to my understanding and comprehensions about this universe within which I am a part, may be the whole itself. May be the whole universe is incomplete without even an iota of dust on a grain of sand, it has no duality. Every bit of the universe is functioning naturally. It is the human mind that qualifies and names the various functions of the universe including the human mind, variously. Time makes no meaning in the order of the whole universal function such as birth, life and death which are natural phenomenon of the universe. And God is created and given life to and ultimately destroyed also by human concepts. Knowledge of God whether now or in the future, whether in existence and functioning now or whether existing but not functioning in the future, is a matter of conjecture of human mind. I feel, it is simply a hallucinating experience that is being given expression, to make the life of others too, hallucinating. It is a travelogue on the way of the movement of our life from birth to death. Present cannot be held to show that 'this is the present and so with the past and the future. Past is held in our memory and that memory is a thought process stored or retained through another thought and when desired that thought can be brought out from the store-house of memory. I do not qualify my state of mind which is just subjective. High waves of thoughts become a whirlpool within and take me down deep into a silence world of its own, where probably, consciousness will be watching or witnessing this state of silence to recall it as the experience it had witnessed earlier. Like a quick-sand it engulfs everything that comes within its boundary in a matter of seconds without leaving a trace of that object which it has gulped rather pushed into within itself. The quick-sand has no mind of its own to discriminate between the object it encompasses. So, God does not discriminate between any type of human being who comes within His influence, but simply takes everyone and everything to His inside bosom. But in the end everything looks to be very normal and natural. It is the human mind which desires otherwise, but only after the event.

—w—

30ᵀᴴ August 1998   03 00 a.m.

If God stands before me now, I would neither be happy nor unhappy. 'What if ?', would be my feelings? It would be natural, if at all, He appears before me. If not also, it is natural. I don't give any importance to anything and that does not mean I would be on any one side of myself. To me a saint or a sinner are the same natural beings irrespective of what part or physical position they are in, or psychological, or if we call it as spiritual level they are standing. I am on my own. I neither desires for God's blessings nor for his curses, as I stand. I just don't want to desire for anything either the so called spiritual power or any other power to be received from God, nor do I want that whatever the power is already there in me to be lost due to my refusal to receive any of the God's powers. I, as an individual, would be ready to undergo everything that I have to undergo without any desire to be otherwise.

—ɷ—

20ᵀᴴ August 1998   00.00 Hrs.

It becomes impossible to give any headings to certain writings or to certain deep feelings within, and it is best left without any heading for those who read and to give their own heading. Many a times, I experience the 'in-expressible'; which I recognize only after the event from out of the memory of that experience that has imprinted upon my mind. While experiencing, I am not aware of it or its qualities or its influences upon me. Time probably stops and everything stops while I become the very experience itself, for there is no 'I' when experiencing and there is no one who experiences. Time, cause-effect, qualifying things and the events are due to dualistic approach of one's mind. But, for these things by themselves have no approach at all, for they are natural phenomenon having nothing to do with the human mind of dualism. These very writings have no sense or meaning either to myself or to anyone else. I write because some inner urge, after having experienced something beyond my comprehension, something beyond my capacity, makes me to write. In writing, I feel that the quality of that experience is lost and yet I am urged to write and I write. Of late, I am feeling, that nothing matters, not even the God matters. Nothing makes any difference to me. I feel the naturalness of my own being having not had any dualistic qualities. I feel that I am a part of the whole universe functioning in my natural state without qualifications what-so-ever. Seeking has completely stopped, going to any place or hearing or reading anything about God from any source has no meaning to me. Sometimes even the knowledge of God has become a burden and bondage to me. Let alone the knowledge of the world except the knowledge to maintain the basic necessities of this physical body. All these things are happening to me from within under some mysterious force of energy that I am constantly aware of, which was latent hither to, has now come to express itself of its presence to me. With awareness of its presence other faculties are slowly withdrawing and may ultimately come to a naught and dissipate altogether. It is in the process of dissipation

—ɯɯ—

18ᵀᴴ AUGUST 1998   03 30 A.M.

Every type of knowledge is bondage and in turn burden, whether it is the knowledge of God or of science or of anything of this world. In deep silence there is no knowledge, no bondage, nothing is there, not even my own self exists in that deep silence because I become the very silence itself and I am one with the silence, about which I become aware of when I come out of that silence and from the impression it left behind on my mind. The mind belongs to me and so the thoughts are, but I am not both while they are mine; and still I cannot separate myself from my thoughts, or intellect, or my mind, or consciousness, or awareness. They become latent when 'me' becomes potent, similarly acquisition of every type of power, be it spiritual, or economic, or physical, or mental whatever you may name, is vicious and sinister, is a weakness in a way. To be oneself is the most difficult thing for a man who is struggling to be somebody. Being oneself is more natural than to be somebody. But being not one self is something imaginary and un-natural. Words, sweet words so called pure and divine words will not take us to heaven for there is no heaven while everything is here and now.

—ɯɯ—

30ᵀᴴ JULY 1998   03 00 A.M.   IT IS A MYSTERY

It is a mystery to me about my own self. I don't know anything about my own self. I even don't know whether there is such a thing as 'myself'—a separate entity, for I having not had any choice to this life, choice to be here in this physical body, choice to be born into a particular family. It was probably a chance that this so called myself is here in this physical body. I feel that I am conditioned to various systems and I am helpless but to go through this conditioned life, if at all it is to be called as my life. Everything, including the functioning of my physical body, is unknown to me. I have no way of knowing or experiencing the functioning of my own self or even my own physical body. It functions under its own laws; which I don't know what they are and why they are so and not otherwise. I feel, that not to desire, not to know, brings a kind of peace. Knowledge becomes a burden to the mind, which creates ego, another heavy burden, for that is not the knowledge but a projection of my own conditionings acquired and also inherited due to my birth in a particular family, caste, society, culture and nation. I feel and I think of universalisation of energy of 'self'—my energy is or may be a part of the universal cosmic energy, taking different shapes, different colors at different times. Time, a measurement, a dimension, a hypothetical convention of man's mind or a projection of movement, has its own phenomenon beyond the understandings of the human beings. It is the human nature to give values and term it as either negative or positive, while there is nothing like these qualifications in the order of the cosmic world. The cosmic world is just there, manifesting itself beyond any human rationalities or values or qualification or quantifications. The ego, a part of human nature that separates the human intelligence from the cosmic intelligence, the human energy from the cosmic energy, human consciousness from the cosmic consciousness, while every part is complete of the entirety and inseparable and yet looks to be separable and separate. It is this separation and comparability that makes the value system fortified and different systems are branched out and in the end it falls into one system or the other; or falls from one system to another system. Man is helpless. To understand this helplessness, to know that this helplessness is the reality, is in fact the realization. And in the end this realization hits the man in such a way that he is shattered into pieces and stands in no way to understand the nature of the universe as a whole. Man is an infinitesimal part of the cosmic energy and still a part of the same, but man does not recognize himself that he is a part of the cosmic energy. If man realizes that he is a part of the whole cosmic energy, then the man realizes that there is no such a thing as going (death) or coming back (birth) for, there is no place to go or place to come back. It is all a concept of man's egoistic intelligence.

29TH JULY 1998   **03 00 A.M.**

Deep down within me, of late, I am feeling the eternity of my life. I am a companion of that force which is eternal while the world moves in terms of birth, death etc. I feel that eternity within myself and of that universal energy, the Cosmic Being, who is my companion, known to each other from eternity. I feel that energy is present within me and I am within that energy. I really feel that I can touch It, talk to It and always feel to be with me and within me. My conscious expands and I feel my presence everywhere throughout the universe while death is not a matter of the fear or rather not a problem to me. I don't know how and why I feel the presence of something extraordinary, in deep silence, most intelligent and blissful along with me and inside me. I come to feel It whenever I need and this need increases day by day and I don't have to do a thing about It comes to me in a fraction of a second when I think about It. This is a fact, not an imagination or hallucination. Then immediately I become very calm, silent and dive myself deep into this phenomenon and hardly do I become aware of anything in spite of hearing I hear not, in spite of seeing I see not. And these hearing and seeing of me does not make any impression upon my mind and I do not recognize the hearing or seeing. Somehow, I feel the deep silence of eternity within me. Nothing matters to me in that status. Sometimes the very energy, which is central, makes no difference to me. I feel the feelings of 'what-if'? Even the very thing that gives me companionship matters not to me and does not influence or makes me wonder, while I take it to be very natural in the stride, as most naturally we are companions of each other from eternity to eternity. This, as I said, is increasing day by day. All these I did not realize till now. Now it looks meaningless, for I feel that I am in the companionship of the very Being Himself in every breath of me and hence either struggling or doing anything looks to be a child's play. While I feel that I can be in that state of being always and whenever I need, in a split of a second. In spite of this I am doing all the mundane talks and acts as naturally as any other ordinary human being does. The most important thing of all is: that I am with It and It is with me in split of a second.

—ᴕ—

10TH JULY 1998   **03 30 A.M.**

It is very difficult to comprehend somebody talking about 'giving-up' everything, stating that 'we have not brought anything while being born and we shall not take anything while being dead'. The whole universe being one, everything that is within the universe should necessarily be a part of the universe, how can I be separated from the universe, is a matter of conjecture. Birth and the death are just two faces of the same coin and one cannot exist separately from the other, so also all the materials including the physical body of any being within the manifestation of the whole universe. Talking about separation is a contradiction in terms. I feel everything, whatever one designates as positive or negative etc is in its very natural state. That is how everything is. To expect anything other than 'what-is', is an aberration. Even, I feel that the aberration is natural in its own ways. All such aberrations are part of the whole universe. Even the so called disease is perfectly operating in its own natural order though it looks to cause disturbance to the physical body system. That disturbance too is natural in its own ways. But we can never understand the functioning force of anything while we try to give explanatory utterances of external functions to the extent of our comprehensive intelligence which, in fact, I feel, is limited compared to the cosmic intellectual functioning of the whole universe.

—∞—

4ᴛʜ Jᴜʟʏ 1998   04 00 ᴀ.ᴍ.

Somehow, I feel completely different from the rest of the world, rather people and their life. I feel the permanency of my 'self' despite so many things happening around me. It looks as if I have nothing to do with anything about them, since I do not understand anything about time, cause-effect, and divine and sin etc. Things go on in spite of me. I am both a part and a separate entity of the universal cosmic activities. I neither can name the goings-on as activities nor as in—activities. They are simply happenings to which I have no explanations, for I do not understand anything of these happenings to give any explanations, however sweetly others may interpret them. I have no interpretation to make. Everything, whether you call them sin or divine, is in its own natural state of function to which we attribute qualities; the qualities which rather we perceive. But the happenings are beyond these qualities. Even cancer is natural; it is just that the functions of these cells are different from the functions of the other cells of the body. The state of my being untouched or unrelated to any of these worldly functions is something that I cannot understand myself. I go beyond myself, beyond everything and still feel that I am a part of them all, is really a strange phenomenon to me. I don't know why and how this happens. When I am in that condition, I am not aware of any other conditions and further, I become aware of that non-physical condition only when I come back to this physical condition and not when I am in that non-physical condition. In this physical condition it is the memory that brings a shadow, a hazy picture, a resultant of the left over of that condition. While in that condition I know not myself, but expand myself to the universal consciousness. It brings me the joy that no other joy brings me to; the bliss, no other thing in the world would bring me to, but, I feel, I become the very joy, the very bliss and I am not a separate entity from them but I become them. Separate entity becomes known to me when I turn back to them—the joy and bliss—then their shadows I see on this plane, on this conditioned mind. To become victorious, to become successful, to become glorious, is something which contradicts to say that 'I am sadly in joy'. But silence, total silence beyond sadness and joy, beyond any expressions, beyond any thought, beyond all dualities, is the real silence to me. That very silence should not be a thought, should not be an interpretation and should not be an explanation to me. In silence 'I' is not there, but 'I' becomes the very silence itself. And only when I come out of silence I become aware of 'I was there in silence' and not when I am that very silence itself. This is how I am; I become the very silence itself, though for a short period.

—⚬⚬—

10TH MAY 1998   03 30 A.M.

Which is the easiest profession, especially in India? I think it is selling God; and it is the most profitable business too, as no raw materials are required, no working capital is required, nothing is required to manufacture God, no men are needed to be engaged to work and most important is: no 'know-how', nor intelligence is needed except some pervert manipulative words of explanation would be sufficient to take the gullible public and equally some educated (qualified?) persons for a beautiful ride with sweet words and a mask to put on with a little show business, always talking about the negative side of human ways to which most of the general public are victims too and so, more susceptible for these sweet words of another man's, about God. Every person feels that he needs something that which he does not have. And that something which even this seller does not have for himself, but sells by mere sweet and beautiful worlds, copied from someone else's talks or writings, as if God is a special commodity belonging entirely and exclusively to that seller. I feel if I have any business with God let it be between me and Him without any media, however mighty that media be. Mere words or writings would not be the explanation of God. He, I feel, is beyond explanation or expression, but deep down experiencing of him comes within me. And God is purely the personal Being without anyone or anything coming in between. He belongs to me in full, so do I feel towards him. My God is from my personal experiences with Him and of Him, while the expressions of Him is the after effect, a memory spilled over out of that experience. No one can say or explain the nature, the quality and the characteristics of God. To each He is different, depending upon the state of mind of that individual. For sure, I cannot say that 'this is the God' and God for everyone else cannot be like the one I see Him. And God can neither be patented nor be promised nor be made a personal property of any individual or any institution. One type of God or one type of explanation cannot be universalized and He cannot be a monotype and be told that they have ultimately found God in His true form and character. These forms, qualities and characteristics of explaining God are the conceptual projection of a man in his own image. And still people sell God for they know not any other profession which is more profitable, more comfortable, more lazier but still brings more respect from the society. May be, they give up family life but I am not sure, since it is not physical but mental and know not, for sure to say, that very person is entirely free from their family life; for no one can get into the inner most thoughts of the other person, so also the very person himself cannot find out his subtle thoughts. So God is sold by these so called god-men who declare them-selves to be pure while looking into the other side of the people of the society as impure. God is expandable and also expendable, always treating God as a salable commodity exclusively by such god-men and the institution he builds up, while the God is available equally and individually to everyone irrespective of the sinner or the saint.

—⁓—

20ᵀᴴ March 1998   03 00 a.m.

What is silence? Is it to shut one's mouth? No. Then is it to shut both mouth and thoughts? One can shut one's mouth but how to shut one's thoughts? The very awareness of silence is not silence; it is the thought of silence, but not the silence itself. Is it possible to be thoughtless? I am afraid not. Probably, one with great trials may bring down the speed or rapidity of thought process but cannot stop thought altogether. The very effort to stop thought is in turn a thought itself.

When things that are already in knowledge and memory, if they cannot brought back when looked at or heard of that thing, probably that is 'not-knowingness', 'blankness', 'ignorance' and that may be called as 'silence'. The physical eyes may be seeing, the ears may be hearing and still having already had the knowledge and memory of what is seen or heard, is not understood and that means if that knowledge does not translate and if that hearing is not got back from the earlier stored memory and that leads to ignorance, of not knowingness, is probably the real silence. But I don't know what the real silence is. It is more a concept than the reality. Our ears and brain have been created to certain decibel of sound and even the circulation of blood in our body, though we hear not, has its own sound. They say that it is almost like a river in spate, but we don't hear a sound of circulation or for that matter any functions of any voluntary organs within our body. And that does not mean they are silent. So is about the physical silence. There is no such a thing as absolute physical silence. And still I go crazy to be in non-physical silence within me. I desired it so badly without which I feel that I shall not be my original. Only in non-physical silence can I know myself in my original and real form; because I face myself, I become a companion to myself. In that non-physical silence I become empty and some force of cosmic energy gets into me to fill up this emptiness within me. Only when I empty myself from everything I feel lightness of my body and then this very lightness becomes a strong current of energy flowing from cosmos into me while I am already a part of cosmos.

—m—

12ᵀᴴ MARCH 1998 03 30 A.M.

I feel that my conscious expands to the whole universe. I become the very universe itself, when the 'I' is lost. Time stops and all thoughts come to a naught. Still, I am aware of all these things and yet I understand nothing. 'Nothingness' encompasses me and I look at the universe with awe and ignorance and innocence like a just born baby. Energy fills me, light strikes me, dualistic concepts fall apart and I don't know what this stage is though I am there. Waves and waves of bliss is felt, never before having had that experience, heart sings and I enter into the eternal world beyond birth and death. Lot many a times such experiences takes me to great heights, still I sit and see everything through the physical eyes; but I don't know a thing about what I am looking at. There is no interpretation of what I see. What all I see become a part of Cosmic Universe, inseparable from each other having the same kind of energy expressing differently in different degrees and at different levels. And yet everything is bound to each other influencing each other and has no separate identity or entity by themselves. As my body is inter connected by various organs within and also without with almost three trillion cells, each cell having a nuclei within which DNA is hidden and that can never be the same in two persons. The total sum of all these DNAs intelligence that manifest with complete activities in rhythm and pattern beyond the understanding of science, is the real 'me' in gross at macro level; and at the same time I am also in one of the sub atomic particle of the DNA and in its life and intelligence at micro level. At both levels I represent myself while I am aware of macro, I am not aware of the micro. When once I become aware of my micro, probably my understanding and awareness considerably differs and I look at the whole universe as one which is at macro level and inter connected with all such micro entities. And then this conscious expands and becomes aware of the whole universe in that one cosmic consciousness. When such an expansion takes place, fear of what-so-ever does not stays any more. I become aware that death is to pass on to a different level of function—a movement of oneself from one level to another level. This function goes on eternally. It is only the limited human mind and limited intellect that questions the cosmic function. But no answer is received, because the cosmos does not answer any question, or clear any doubts, or interprets any of its functions. Universe with its own eternal energy and intelligence functions, as it were, without any deviation as human mind deviates. Ultimately everything, animate and inanimate objects of the universe including the human, being parts of the whole universe, is in reality the cosmic function with the same kind of energy but at different degree. So everything the universe holds is cosmic.

9ᵀᴴ MARCH 1998   03 00 A.M.

Many a times I am pervaded by that cosmic central energy emanating from the space into me and that energy reaches me and moves out in ripples of waves and spreads all around. I feel the pure energy reaching me and burning all my thoughts and further spreading out. May be, this is also my conceptual thought. And yet, I physically feel that energy entering me in a jet like column and beam, powerful rays converting themselves like a eddy current within me and spreading out in circle of waves like ether all round me reaching the inner remotest corners of the me. In this process I become only a media. I receive it, I feel, directly from the center of the universe which is the eternal self-generating source of the whole universe's energy. I only feel that a very fraction of this energy reaches me and only to the extent of this physical body could withstand, or otherwise this body would be burnt out. This Cosmic Being is the most intelligent of all the intelligences of the universe, or otherwise this universe could not be functioning in the precise manner, as it is functioning.

In spite of this, I know, I can never understand or even become aware of, as to how this energy functions. Probably, I need not know too and whatever I think I know may not be the correct and real understanding of the knowledge. My understanding and my knowledge are all contaminated and conditioned with pre-conceived notions from my culture, social up-bringing, from the books and hearings of others, apart from my being genetically coded, whether it is material or spiritual, since, for me there is neither of these two are absolute. To me, they are one and the same but differing with the angle of degree of perception and knowledge of understanding in limited capacity. I feel strongly, that I do not understand anything about this universal central energy point, but only perceive its functions and its presence both within and outside of me.

I feel the presence of this cosmic energy most of the times but more so when I am alone and isolated physically and mentally, especially between 03 and 04 a.m.

—m—

25ᵀᴴ FEBRUARY 1998   03 00 A.M.

There is nothing obsolete or dispensable in the universe. Everything is complete only when every particle, every atom is complete; one less makes it incomplete, And so with this universe. Even the less of a dry straw, a grain of sand makes this Universe incomplete. So making something dispensable, however minute it may be, has no completeness. It is only the conditioning of ourselves, based on value system, makes us to look into the direction of dispensability or indispensability. There is no separate entity to qualify the terms of the whole. You cannot separate materialism from spiritualism because they have no independent existence. It is we who qualify these things. But under the cosmic umbrella they are one and the same. The angle of our looking at them, the conceptual understanding of them varies. But in the end however beautifully, however rationally, however convincingly it looks at that point in time, we, at-least I, reach a point of 'not understanding' anything about anything. Honestly I do not understand anything even about myself as to how I am functioning. My understanding is only my concept and it varies from place to place, time to time and circumstances to circumstances. So my understanding is not true understanding, since that which is true is always true under every situation without any change whatsoever. But the fact is; that there is neither truth nor untruth. Everything is as 'they—are' without any qualifications, without any comparison and without any duality. It is the nature of the human intellect to give and attribute quality, to make comparison and to find duality; because the human mind is a split one, split in hundreds of parts and paths according to the directions of thoughts. However, it is very difficult to understand even our own thoughts; as they originate, then coming into the surface and melting away as past, while the past, present and future are the creations of thoughts, rather they are different waves of thought. Memory of past creates future; future is a conceptual projection of our thought. Time is one of the dimensions creating yesterday, today and tomorrow. So when there is no time, there is neither yesterday, nor today, nor tomorrow. In the end I find that nothing absolutely answers me, because I feel there are no answers to such questions and the questions are wrong, just like asking such questions as 'why there are no two suns in opposite directions to avoid darkness?'—

26ᵀᴴ FEBRUARY, 1998   03 00 A.M.

In spite of restlessness, the urge, a very strong urge, to find answers, grips me, and when the answer does not come from within or from any other sources, slowly mind reconciles to the answer-less-ness and the conscious expands to the whole universe and to everything the universe holds. It looks that everything is inside me and nothing lies outside of me. Suffering, pain, sorrow, pleasantness, happiness etc; and all dualities, merge and a kind of silence dawns wherein neither any question arises nor any answer given. This silence is a kind of happening of 'nothingness' and everything looks to be just happenings including myself being another wave of happening in the universe to which there is no 'why' or 'how' or 'where' or 'which' etc. This happening which leads to nothingness probably is the reality and the truth. Probably, this may be the ultimate truth, but I do not know whether it is. May be, there is another answer, which might be, the ultimate answer, but I don't know for sure.

23ʳᵈ FEBRUARY 1998   01 00 A.M.

Everything is just happening in the way they should. I don't know whether they are really happenings or just concepts of happenings. Something snaps within me all of a sudden and in a fraction of a second the understanding comes to me to mean that my very intellect, the thinking power, the thoughts, the mind are separate entities from me, but parts of the whole cosmos. There is no 'me' in me. The whole universe becomes 'me' and still I am not the universe—complete detachment from everything including to my own self engulfs me. All these happenings have no meanings or values. Meanings and values arise from that as to what 'should-be' and 'what-should-not-be'. Here there are no questions neither as to what 'should-be' nor what 'should-not-be'; but, everything is as 'they-are' with no meanings, qualities or qualifications that can be attributed to. All actions whether positive or negative in thought, words and deeds come to an end and with that, search also comes to an end, or there is nothing to search for, while all the time I am the one who was searching for myself. How can I search myself? While the searcher, the searched and searching all being myself. When this understanding comes by itself, not by imposition of anything from outside, and not with the help of any outside world, then the fear of death vanishes. Birth and death are only natural happenings of the cosmos, which is a movement from one phase to another phase. Rather birth and death do not exist at all—they being the continuous process, like waves on a sea shore. Nothing remains, no duality remains. I become a part of it and also the whole of it at the same time. 'Me' is lost. I become that very process of the happening without any quality or qualifications or characteristics and in the end nothing remains including 'me'. And when I come back to this physical plane, I feel I know nothing; I understand nothing, because there is nothing either to know or to understand, since to know and to understand two entities are required—the knower and the known. This creates the duality and the separate entity when there is neither 'me' nor 'that'; there the question of duality does not arise. There is neither incompleteness nor part, it is the whole. These are conceptual and conditioned thoughts of the human mind. The totality including all qualities of me is in the universe; as I am the totality of all my functions. Everything in universe has been happening in its own ways and any questions do not arise, they are just happenings, in-spite of our doubts. They, the happenings have nothing to do or untouched by any of the human interpretations of them, they are just happenings in spite of anything that the human intellect tries to interpret.

—〰—

15ᵀᴴ Fᴇʙʀᴜᴀʀʏ **1998**   03 30 ᴀ.ᴍ.

To know that there is nothing to know is the true knowledge. Why to struggle to know something that is projected by somebody who has set the ball rolling for you? You go after that ball and still that eludes you for there is no ball at all. It is like a mirage in a desert. You create thirst while there is neither the desert nor the mirage. This created thirst is artificial and you need only artificial quenching. You hallucinate yourself that you are in different world while there is no world at all. You are that very world itself in which everything is happening despite of you and in-spite of yourself. The Cosmic Energy which is omnipresent in the whole universe in which you are also a part, as such, you cannot seek yourself as sugar cannot taste itself and so sugar can never know the truth of its sweetness. Birth, life and death are the movements of the universal force which just happen and you are that happening. The question as to why it happens in the way it happens, does not arise, even if such questions arise there are no answers to such questions in the order of the functioning of the cosmic energy. It is the human limited knowledge that creates these questions and the human mind becomes agitated for want of answers to these questions. If you are searching for something you have the answer, since without any pre-knowledge of what you are searching, you would not be searching. Searching is to a have lost what you had and known to have had; which you don't have now. So, you have the knowledge about that which you had, while now, having lost, you are searching for the same, though you cannot explain in correct terms what that you had, but lost. Search comes to an end since you have not lost anything while you are that itself which is lost and you have to realize that you are everything that you are searching till now. This awareness strikes you like a thunder bolt of unimaginable energy and you will be shattered and burnt out and then stop every activities however wonderful, however divine it may look. These happenings have no rationality, no scientific reasons, even no spiritual reasons and nothing can be attributed to such happenings. They are just happenings beyond the human understanding. All talks, all attributions like divinity, purity etc. have no place in the order of these happenings because these qualities are the human conceptual projections for those which are not attainable by him. They are happenings of the cosmic movements and you are within it and you are one of these movements and you are that very movement itself. This is the only understanding and the only enlightenment. I am just a cosmic movement in the order of the whole cosmos without any beginning or an end beyond time, causation and space too. So ultimately you are the very cosmos itself in kind but of a lesser degree.

—ɯ—

12ᵀᴴ FEBRUARY 1998 03 00 A.M.

Lot many people say lot many things. But I am not influenced, they are mere words. Nothing more. I am my own self and I don't give easily to any of such utterances of others. I have my own personality uninfluenced by anybody's sayings. Sometimes I feel that even if God Himself comes and stands before me it makes no difference to me. The things are just happening in the way they should and no. body will have any say or control over any happenings. I am a happening to myself, I have no control whatsoever upon myself. When so, how come could I think to make something to happen and to control that happening? Everything is fine and happening in the way that it should according to its originality, of its nature. No qualifications, no reasons, howsoever rationalistic or scientific they may look to be. No definitions could ever be given to anything. All qualities attributed to such happenings are only a status of mind created and projected according to one's conditioned heritage, religion, culture etc. Nothing can be known as regards to functions of the happenings and nothing can be qualified, or quantified, or devised, or found, or gained, or lost. Everything is just as they are and as they should be. Everything is, in a way, a state of mind and in this process, I feel, I know nothing about anything because there is nothing to know. Everything functions according to its nature and capacity. I am functioning both mentally and physically according to my nature, my capacities and still I know not how and what my nature and capacities are. I don't know anything about myself but still I feel that I am a part of the whole cosmos, when so, how can I know myself? If I know myself I would know the WHOLE. In fact there is only WHOLE and as such there is no 'me'. 'ME' assumes a separate entity from the Whole. Knowledge becomes a mental burden. There is no coming or going, nothing, even the Supreme Being cannot come or go, He is everywhere, if at all such a Being is there. Universal force in which I am a part with all its qualities, which I know not what, is and can be perceived to be omnipresent, though it is in the center of the universe around which the whole universe go in cycle; as gravitational force is, though the origin is at the center of the earth, it can be perceived all around the earth's atmosphere up to thirty miles high above the sea level rotating with the earth; and that gravitational force is there whether we know it or not, for the simple reason your whole body is in one piece, because of this gravitational force. Everything within and outside the earth surface is subject to gravitational force and everything is in its proper place or else nothing could exist including the earth itself.

—⚍—

11ᵀᴴ FEBRUARY 1998   03 00 A.M.

Yes, I don't want anything to be other than me happening. I am myself is a happening beyond my creation and control as I desire. How can I be a separate entity from this universe? I am one with it and a part of it. Anything that is happening in terms of thoughts, words and deeds through me are not entirely mine, they belong to the whole universe rather the whole cosmos and I am a part of it. Nothing can be excluded, even me, however I may try, from the happenings. I am the very happening itself. I and the happenings to me are not different. There is nothing in a way to be called as 'me' or 'I' as a separate entity from this universe. Still, when I think deeply, which may or may not be mine, I slowly start realizing that I don't know anything about these happenings and knowing is beyond me. All, so called knowledge, look to be nothing to me, as they are. As the knowledge of bio-science is beyond my understanding, so this cosmic knowledge is beyond my understanding too. I do not like to struggle to understand. It becomes a burden and a strain to me. Not knowingness brings peace and tranquility. In the blankness and darkness I see the Light within me, the light of understanding of knowing of un-know-ability, understandability stares at me. I know that 'I don't know'. This knowledge of not knowingness, not being able to understand dawns upon me while all the while I was thinking that 'I knew'—what a sham it had been; what an ego I had, as to have had thought that 'I knew', while all the while I knew nothing about anything. This realization that I not only 'know nothing' but also 'there is nothing to know, has brought me to a new dimension of life, new knowledge and new understanding of ignorance leading to 'NOTHINGNESS"

I feel that I should stop everything. I am the totality of all my conditions of the past and the present. My frame of mind is the result of my upbringing through the religion, teachings, books I read, genetic, environmental and social conditions and values etc. that affect me both externally and internally and by myself. I should get free from all types of bondages even such bondage which promises bondage-less-ness. I feel ultimately there is nothing to be free from for I am a prisoner of my own physical body and thoughts, words and deeds and they just happen as any other happenings of this universe. Finally I understand that I am only one insignificant happening out of the trillions of happenings of the universe.

—ɯ—

08ᵀᴴ FEBRUARY 1998

03 00 A.M.

What Truth is? I don't know. Equally I don't know anything about false. Truth and false are synonym. And at the same time I understand nothing of these concepts. At least I know that I don't know and am incapable of understanding, due to great extent the functioning of this physical world, let alone the world beyond. Status, whether mundane or spiritual, makes no difference; but the very awareness of it makes a person egoistical. I feel everything is a state of mind. The existence or otherwise of God and the mundane pressures etc. are only a status of mind. But what mind is? I don't know. Even I also do not know what this so called 'I' is. Some times when I hear some one's sayings I feel that person's interpretation seems to be correct. But that would only be for a few moments and afterwards I come back to my original position of 'not knowingness'. And still I feel, sometimes, some type of agitations, knots, some uneasiness, some type of emptiness, wanting, dissatisfaction within me, I feel that I should arrive at, reach, get fulfilled and get completeness of something, but I do not know what that something is. Still I feel that there nothing to arrive at, to reach to, to be complete. May be this state of mind is due to my trainings, my conditionings of my mind. However I am sure that this span of existence—it is more an existence than living—is coming to an end and day by day I am approaching nearer and nearer to that end. And that this existence with a beginning has to have an end too which in-tern has to have a beginning of another phase, another term and another end, despite of myself. These are all happenings to me in their own natural ways. In the cosmic universe it is happening in the way it has to and I have no wanton part, but a part beyond my wanting, beyond my desires, beyond my understanding, is just happening over which neither I have control nor desire to be controlled or even freed from. Even if I desire to be freed from, I am afraid, it only remains as my wish or desire, but it would happen naturally and I am that very happening itself with no escape whatsoever for there is nothing to escape from or escape to.

The reality is; I am a happening beyond my wish or control. The desire to be something other than what I am is the cause for misery and that misery is the reality. For I cannot escape to be other than what I am and in the end I really don't know what I am and that is the Reality.

26TH JANUARY 1998   04 40 A.M.

I do not induce silence but it happens to me very naturally especially when I feel that I am on a journey through non-physical levitation which takes me to the Central Point of Cosmic energy. It is like a bottomless pit and I am somewhere at a point, but I do not know where, and start going up beyond words, deeds and thoughts and also beyond time, space, cause-effect etc. There in that plane, status of awareness is attained and 'I' is lost and 'I' becomes one with the universal consciousness; not confined to this galaxy, let alone to this solar system and also to this earth. These, our earth, our solar system and our galaxy are infinitesimal points lost on the vast plane of this universe. There are no limitations, no boundaries like these planets which we see around this galaxy. There are no galaxies there. It is the vastness in all directions—while there are no directions, there are no dimensions which we measure on this earth. Science is limited to man's intelligence, but there, in that plane I find that no science or the man's intelligence plays any part, except the awareness. I cannot perceive the light as I do here, since there is no darkness—which is almost a conceptual recognition of the normal working brain here. And still you find the soothing bright milky light , equally spread, everywhere, transparent and occupying the whole vastness. In this I am alone and yet I know that I am not alone since Someone stays all the way and also permanently there. I travel in this silence experiencing myself not in the speed I experience here on this earth. It has its own laws and functions; I cannot perceive them but only become aware of that point from where this vastness of light and energy emerges. Now the silence is complete. I become aware of that silence, the energy of that silence which has no parallel, which is incomparable, unimaginable but it is functioning most powerfully everywhere. Slowly I fill up myself with that energy deep into me. That silence of light engulfs me and I become that very silence, that peace, that purity and that divinity. In that silence the knowledge of the entire universe is stored, everything the universe holds is emerging from out of this silence. And ultimately I know that I have those qualities in myself rather I become the very qualities themselves loosing my separate entity. I am a part of that, rather as a grain of sugar is as sweet as a bag of sugar which is whole and complete. Then everything stops—this awareness also stops, for to be aware there should be 'I' and silence, as two separate entities, but in this state I and that silence are one and the same. And the experience of this silence is without the physical body and in the end I and that silence and the point from where that silence emanates become one.

—⁂—

18TH JANUARY 1998   03 00 A.M.

I am not surprised by anything. Even the presence of God does not surprise me,' what-if' and 'what-is-so-to-be-surprised' arises in me. There is nothing new and nothing makes me to wonder and stand in awe. Because I want nothing from God and I am what I am. I neither can give nor borrow anything from anybody that would change neither my life nor the life of others. That does not mean that I would disrespect any one however insignificant that person may be in the eyes of others, but that person is in par with me. But, at the same time, I would not make myself a slave to any person in any manner. I want to be away from every institution that tries to sell the God, in a way. If God is there I want to know and find out by myself alone and for myself, depending on no man's works or words, for that person may exploit me and in the end exposes himself as worthless as I am.

—m—

17TH JANUARY 1998   03 00 A.M.

It is the conditioning of one's society, religion upbringing and above all the genetic character that brings the concept of God and further the ambition or the desire to attain that God—head and reach by giving up every thing and by distinguishing between the material and spiritual world, while for me there is nothing to give-up for there is nothing to attain even. It is a mirage of oasis in a desert for a thirsty man. The thirst is artificial, the desert is also artificial and so the oasis too

The whole universe is one and I am part of it, less by me do make difference to the whole, so in a way by being a part I am one with it. When so, how can I be separated from the whole? How can I seek that whole while I am already in it and part of it? This is my concept of God

—m—

16TH JANUARY 1998   01 00

If there is God anywhere and if He has all those qualities the humans attribute to Him, can He be institutionalized? Can He be reached only through a method to be followed under instructions of that particular institution? Can

He be said to have instructed that particular institution to spread and advertise Him so that those who desire to seek God or to understand God have to necessarily come to that particular institution or otherwise people will have no way of understanding and seeking God? This way of thinking is a very difficult proposition for me. Somehow, I feel it will be an intellectual surrender and slavery to that institution. And if one once accepts their way of thinking and allow oneself to be brain-washed by them, one is hooked and one is exploited physically, mentally, intellectually and to a great extent financially too, because one is hungry for God. God is a perennial quencher to those who are really hungry and one can see God directly without any intervening mediums. If every one has to seek God directly all the institutions, temples etc. have to be closed down, then this society may go hay-wire. I am not proposing this but if a person is really hungry for God he can seek God directly and quench his thirst for God.

15ᵀᴴ JANUARY 1998   03 30 A.M.

I am neither a theist nor an atheist nor an agnostic, but I don't know what otherwise I am. I do not know about my own functioning and even do not know what I am really is. I have no way of knowing myself, when so, how can I know someone or something beyond me? Even I do not know how a tree functions; how it grows I don't know. I see the tree only externally and physically and that is how it is. When so, how can I know somebody whether living or dead have/had been or functioning? I am just a happening as anything is. Even that happening I cannot feel, but can only imagine and that is not the reality to me. The reality is that I just don't know anything about anything including the so called 'self'. I am no better than a small insignificant worm crawling but only with and at different pattern of physical body that go with its natural creation. As a human being, probably, I seek the companionship of other human beings and yet I will not allow anyone to influence me especially in the knowledge of God. I know, whatever I may do, will not take me there, for there is no 'there'. Everything is here and now, even the 'now' is not there. It is all past. I live in my memories of thoughts which are past, even the future is only a projection of the past memory. From the memory of the dead past I project the future, which when arrives turns to be the past, past stands permanently while the present and the future are misnomers.

9ᵀᴴ JANUARY 1998

03 30 A.M.

I don't know why I feel physically tired, which affects my mind. Or, is it the other way? I don't know. I would have no interest whatsoever especially in anything connected with God or spiritualism. Just blankness and emptiness encounters me. And still something deep within me functions very actively. I am aware of the activities within me. It is beyond my comprehension and rationalism. Time stops, all external activities stop and may be certain functions of my body slow down though not stop. Seeing I see not, hearing I hear not. I don't find the difference between one day or the next. Every day is the same, every night is the same. These, days and nights are natural phenomenon. They happen despite of everything most naturally without any change in them. It is the capacity of the human body which is also subject to natural phenomenon, that perceives these days, nights, temperature, time etc and with reference to the function of the human body these variations in nature are conceived. Otherwise they are just happenings without any bias or dualistic actions. Human body is restricted and has limited capacity in all its senses and functions. I feel I am becoming empty. Nothing is achieved in my life. May be there is something material for some to recon with. But, for myself, I earned nothing. I am totally empty.

Time is short. God did not come to me in spite of my time is ebbing away and in spite of my doing everything possible within my capacity. Coming of God, I mean, is to feel Him within me deeply. I look empty because I wanted all through to be 'somebody' while I had been myself—a 'nobody' other than what I am as myself. This desire to be and to become' somebody' where one is looked upon not by one but by many scores of people. 'Somebody', is a crazy idea for the one who can never become 'somebody' other than what or 'one— is'. The craze to be 'somebody' other than' one—is', is something that cannot be natural and ultimately drowns the life itself. To be satisfied, to be happy, to be content with what' one—is', should be cultivated for the well-being and health of oneself both in body and mind. Otherwise one becomes a thirsty person in a desert running after mirage. I do not compete with anybody or anything even the so called spiritual, however lofty, however divine it may look. I am trying to be myself within and without and be natural. This might lead to the Reality.

---

06 JANUARY 1998   03 30 A.M.

It is my experience that whatever I endeavor to undertake—of course having no eye for the selfishness of such benefit at the cost of others—by keeping myself along with the whole cosmic energy and become a part of that energy, which of course I am, I always succeed in such endeavors. Hardly did I meet any failures. My goal in the endeavors have been purely for others benefits not having any strings attached; or any bargain due to which any undue benefits are derived by me. Probably, this is due to His companionship with me; otherwise it would have been impossible. All sorts of things were happening to me from early 1960's and onwards, when I almost was to become an inmate of Sri Ramakrishna Ashram. Such things are not happening to me only since recently. They are not happening now but as I said, far earlier. I do not except that my not joining the Ramakrishna Ashram was a failure. There were no failures as such in my life though of some small percentage and they were mostly due to some sort of laxity of some type of self interest I had, probably. Not otherwise. Success and failures are mostly counted in terms of physical and mental benefits one derives from the outside world, spiritual success will only be gauged by an individual himself for he knows best and worst of himself.

Well, is not spiritual, apart of social behavior, is within oneself? I think it is, because no man is an island who lives by himself and without dependability. To me, there is no such a thing as independence. We are all conditioned and influenced all through our life from cradle to grave. No one can escape it. All we talk or do, are not our own original acts, may be certain scientific inventions are seems to be original. But, results of such inventions are also available in the Cosmos and only the scientists get it from their intellectual intuition from the cosmic intelligence while they are a part of cosmos. It is just the ego of man to think that he is a great inventor, whether material or spiritual, that he is the only one who saw and did what others did not see and do. When out his ego goes, then he becomes empty and almost a dead person, but in the end he being a part of the cosmic world, understands that by himself he knew nothing and he could not understand anything about anything. With this humility probably he may reach the reality.

05ᵀᴴ December 1997   03 00 A.M.

About God I have heard a lot, read a lot, participated a lot in discussions and they have only helped me to some extent. They have helped me to think whether my thoughts are real or unreal. However, there is no scale from which I could measure my knowledge about God. Is it possible to measure the God with reference to the majority opinions of those, so called as spiritually experienced persons? Are not these thoughts conditioned from what they learnt from others, by losing their freedom to think? First of all is there any such a thing that could be called as freedom? Freedom is a concept fed by those who feel that they are the prisoners and need some imaginary freedom, which is not there for them. In the whole cosmological universe, we the human beings with the best of our intelligence and knowledge are a speck of dust, changing at every second The time concept is only of human mind while there is no time concept in cosmic; neither is there any concept of 'cause and effect', everything is just as 'it-is, and 'as-it-should-be'. It is we who give reason and if there is none we invent one, which led the human being to coin a word 'God' and attribute all qualities that he desires to gain for himself from that coined word God. Ultimately we have subjected ourselves to this conceptual word of God and further man has exploited man in the name of this coined, conceptual and conditioned word God and some made others to be slaves to them and subjugated their mind to the so called spiritualism wearing different colored garb. Colors of clothes and language may be different but the goal of wanting to hold others in their fisted powers in any manner whether financially, intellectually or physically or even by so called spiritually. Everyone is hungry for power—to subjugate the other human to his wishes. To make another an intellectually bankrupt and to make him an intellectual slave. When so, why is it we are talking about freedom? I don't know. If we are not slaves to any other human being, at least we become slaves to the word God, because we desire to be comfortable, materially, mentally, physically and permanently also; and we are always afraid to lose any of these things, while definitely everything will be lost in the end, in spite of the so called God is, supposed to be, protecting us. God cannot save Himself, when so, how can He save any human being? God is bound by His duties. He has to perform to keep the whole universe in balance. In fact, there is nothing that we could be saved from and there is nobody to save and also there is nobody to be saved either. We don't know how to save ourselves, let alone the so called God saving us. Best would be to 'let-go' of everything including God in one go. Only that may bring the ultimate answer to all questions

—ᴍ—

06ᵀᴴ December 1997　　　　　　　　　　03 00 a.m.

Is there any possibility that one of these days He would visit me, not in my dreams but while I am awake to prove to myself that I have physically seen Him? Really, I know nothing about God. I feel completely empty within and without, these years of life have gone just like that. May be that is how it would go the remaining years too. I know not how many are still left. Nothingness and emptiness, not knowingness about anything of anything bring me immense peace. In this peace I become not only myself but the wholesome. A separate entity 'me' dies and I become a part of the whole universe. Time stops, all activities stop, whether mental or physical. In this state of mind I become a total emptiness. I become aware of that state only when I come out of it. It becomes a memory of the past experience, not the experience of present since while experiencing I know nothing of it. It is the impression from out of my memory that I read afterwards not while experiencing it. So, such experiences are always of the past. Past is dead and so the experiences are always dead experiences. We live in the past in the dead memory. There is nothing like tomorrow. It is just a word and a concept. Tomorrow is only an imagination projected from the experience of the dead yesterday. You just can't stop even a second to call it as present. The moment you utter present, every syllable of the present becomes the past and that is how we live in the present. So, practically we live in our past, in the dead yesterday or in the dead memory with the dead experience. With these dead ones as base we plan for the unknown tomorrow. As such we can say that we live beyond time. Once again a cause and effect lie within the framework of time. When the very 'time' has no meaning, so the' cause and effect' too has no meaning. The concept of time created the concept of space. When time becomes 'timeless' space becomes 'spaceless' cause becomes 'causeless' and effect becomes 'effectless', then everything becomes Nothing. Everything is with reference to a point—you. When this point goes, 'you' go too. Only One Centre Point-God—eternally stays. But how do you know that this Centre Point is God? You have no way of knowing it at all, because there is no point as 'you'. So you become a naught, a nothing. When you become nothing you become everything and you become the whole from nil. So be nothing to reach the reality which is 'timeless', 'space-less', 'causeless' and 'effect-less' and finally 'you-less'.

—m—

16ᵀᴴ NOVEMBER 1997 04 45 A.M.

How strange to think that I am a separate entity from this universe. The infinite and eternal universe is beyond the comprehension of these finite and temporary vibrations called human intellect. And yet, I can never be separated from the universe, I am a part of it and being a part of it I recognize the whole of it, through my conscious awareness rather than my imagination. What a narrow perspective it is of the human to think only about this globe and about his own physical body. Beyond the body and this globe there are innumerable globes of different kinds and dimensions with living intelligence of different types. Those intelligent living beings may not require necessarily air, water or food in the way we human beings of this globe require. Their physical bodies may not necessarily confirm to the beings of this globe. Everything might be totally different and unimaginable to us, even the intelligence may not be what we possess here on this globe. And yet everything this universe hold is within the realms of the fundamental law of this universe. What that law is, I don't know. I could only guess that it is the law of birth and death. May be after our death we may be reborn in any corner on any other such intelligent planet of this universe, or maybe that is the end of oneself. But I do not know. Wherever one may or one may not go after the so called death, one definitely always remains a part of this universal energy, may be in different form. Death may be a misnomer and so the life may be. Man wants to excel the cosmic intelligence and with his vanity he thinks he can do that and desire to conquer the whole universe let alone this solar system. I don't think he could do that. Time is running out, I think, for this body to be in the living condition. What next? I don't know. As I grow older the 'not knowingness' increases. Even I don't know whether the universe is in the form of what I see or what I imagine it is. I can never understand. I have no way of understanding the universe. But in reality I know nothing about anything including myself. That is how the universe is and that is how I am. It is my ego which thinks otherwise.

—m—

10ᵀᴴ NOVEMBER 1997 03 00 A.M.

I feel, I am a burden to myself. My knowledge is a burden to me. Even my feelings of emptiness in self becomes a burden. There is no such a thing that could be called as 'burden-less' or freedom. To seek freedom from something is to confirm to myself that I am the prisoner of my own mind and it turns to be a burden to me. Whether knowledge is mundane or spiritual does become burden. The very teachings I am conditioned to since birth are burden to me. Once again when I try to know what that burden is, I get the answer that it is a state of mind. The state of mind to some extent, I feel, is the force that results from the chemical changes on the functions of the brain. Can I separate the functions of my brain from my mind? Is there such a separate entity called mind from the functions of the brain? I don't know. I feel that the intellect, the mind, the thought etc. are the functions of my brain at different levels and vibrations. It is the brain that recognizes its own functions; it is both the spectator and the actor of its own functions. As long as my brain functions whether in normal or abnormal level, both in waking and deep sleep stage, I am alive and when the brain stops to function completely in spite of every other support, I think the death to the whole body sets in and different type of functioning starts, chemically, thereon wards—many types of worms, bacteria at micro and macro level start sprouting out of the so called dead body and that is how the eternity of life may be recognized. This is how the whole universe functions at different levels under different chemical and biological compositions and with different vibrations. This vibration, is a force, rather a part of the Universal Force, which keeps the entire universe in balance and in function. So my thoughts have no separate entity or function. My thoughts function in balance with the cosmic thoughts which is a universal vibration—a universal force. I am one within and part of the entire universal force which is eternal. So I am both the Universe and also eternal, as the Universe is.

6ᵀᴴ NOVEMBER 1997   03 30 A.M.

There is a strong urge to understand that which is said to be beyond understanding. But, to me, fundamentally, unless one knows It, one cannot say that It is beyond understanding. Knowing a thing is different from understanding the thing. Is it beyond understanding to all others except to those who say so? I am dissatisfied with everything other than That, but still I don't know what That is. In the end I feel there is nothing to understand. It is only a concept created by some who have called themselves as intellectuals to confuse the common man. Time just flies. Time, a hypothetical measurement as a dimension, created by man based on this earth's movement around the sun, while by itself this movement does not care whether man names it differently or not. Its nature law is to go around the sun and it is doing so even before the man came on the surface of this earth and continues even beyond the human race on this earth. And I feel I am one of the vibrations of this eternal movement and I come and go innumerable times at different frequencies while 'I' in me is constant at all its frequencies but only the intensity of vibration varies. There is cyclic movements in every aspects of the whole universe. It is dynamic, accurate and does act according to its nature and the vibrations it receives from the ultimate cosmic intelligence. Even this cosmic intelligence has its own perfect order to perform. It does not act quixotically. Everything is inter-connected and inter-dependent. No one particular iota of anything can act differently or independently. And man's intelligence can never reach the stage of understanding of this cosmic intelligence, since man's intelligence being limited within the realms and sphere of the cosmic intelligence as its part. How can a part understand the whole? My urge is my own conditioning taught to me by the society, by my so called religion and expanded by my ego to go beyond everything and still to be within my own prison of my own thoughts. My thought is my prisoned life. When thought dies, the prisoned 'I' is set free and with that my physical form dies. I don't know whether I die first or my thought dies first. I and my thought being one and the same, it is one death not two, that comes to both simultaneously and as such while I am eternal so the thoughts which are projected from the cosmic intelligence too is eternal. But thought goes to cosmic store to be retrieved to accompany me in my next birth according to the quality of my thoughts (which include my words and deeds of all my previous lives) (Prarabhda karma).

—m—

03ᴿᴰ NOVEMBER 1997   03 00 A.M.

Strange feelings engulf me. I am not myself. Neither I am 'I' nor somebody else. I feel no difference between me and all the other things surrounding me. I feel that I am all of them and all those things are me, I hardly feel that I am a separate entity myself. Time stops. It has no meaning in this state of mind. There is eternity and as well limitations in me. I get the feelings of naturalness in everything; there are no dualities, neither peculiar nor abnormal in anything. They are perfect in their naturalness, even the lowest voice or noise out there on the road. They are natural, the dust, the noise, the pollution etc. doing their best performance. May be they are not palatable to the human body, but they are perfect in their nature. Human body reacts chemically to them and so they become abnormal with reference to human body but by themselves they are perfect. Night is perfect, darkness is perfect, volcano is perfect, earthquake is perfect, destruction is perfect and death is perfect. And everything is perfect and natural. Why to otherwise qualify them? Is it only because they harm the functioning of the human body? Even this harmfulness to human body is natural and perfect. Neither do I see any good nor bad in any of these things. They are just natural and perfect. There are no dualities in them. Human being does not understand them in their perfect-ness and as such qualify them according to his concept of good and bad. Aging of this body is natural and so with everything that goes with aging of the body—the loss of physical and mental original capacity. Even the so called worrying about this is natural and perfect so far as that worry is concerned. Some—body who is not worrying or being of any concern is equally perfect and natural. So death and annihilation are perfect and natural. In this process the whole universe is inter-connected and inter-dependent which is perfect and natural too. Hence everything including human mind which is not a separate entity from the universe, is one with the whole process and order of this universe. I do not find anything to be called as going out and coming in. There is neither going nor coming. Everything is just there in their perfect natural order. There is no dimension such as distance, time etc. There are no reference points. Everything, every living being, however small, is a reference point by itself and at the same time has no reference point at all. When I have no reference point I have no radius and equally I have no circumference. So, I am limitless and I am eternal and beyond time, space and cause-effect. I am also beyond thoughts, words and deeds. Nothing affects me, I experience this limitlessness, timelessness, and causeless-ness and in turn effortlessness, but I am just 'I am' and I don't have to know to be a separate entity as to enquire 'who I am'? I am a perfect and natural universal force, a part of It without being a separate entity; but one with the whole universe. Finally when I am one with GOD, 'I' vanishes and only God remain

—m—

26ᵀᴴ Aᴜɢᴜsᴛ 1997   03 00 A.M.

Thyag (sacrifice) is a unique word that could be understood only by Indians. There is not an exact word in English that gives meaning to *Thyag.* It roughly means 'sacrifice' or 'give-up' on your own volition, something that you already have. What is it that we have and which needs to be sacrificed or be given up? To whom should we give it up? Everything that is capable of being given up, physical or mental, have to be given up. But, for what purpose? Is it to attain something else? If so, you replace one thing with the other and that is barter, a business. Today you are asked to give up certain materials physically and certain way of thinking and talking mentally, for something that you are promised in the future. When you give up where does it go? At least physical things go to someone else for whatever the purpose he/she or that organization may utilize such materials and money and whatever the sacred name they may give. It changes hands. I understand about thought. Thoughts are not yours. You receive them from the Cosmic Stores of thoughts which control the universe while you are a part of it. Well, you can control your thought to some extent and once again they have to chanalized in to certain ways that the other man or some scriptures or some so called divine lectures say about it. Here also you replace one kind of thought with another. Thoughtlessness is unthinkable, for that will be the death. As long this body is functioning thoughts are its food. It is through thought you are living, you recognize yourself and by yourself through your thoughts. So thoughts also cannot be given up. You can give up, with great training, one kind of thought but the other kind of thought will replace it and I don't know what type of training and how long it takes to arrive at such replacement. In the process you may break, and then probably you may fall into altogether a third kind of thought which I know not what kind. Thoughts by themselves are neither positive, nor negative, nor waste. It is the qualification that we give that make thought so.

As regards to talk (*vacha*), yes, you can control it and make it most sophisticated, urbanized and gentle and at the same time hypocritical, or you can keep quiet when you don't want to talk. You can replace certain types of talks with other types, probably this may buy you a lot of appreciation, applause, thereby you are encouraged and in the process you have learnt to talk more and more about less and less subjects. In the end when you face yourself you understand your own emptiness, hollowness and hypocrisy of your life.

So, the thing is to please others and yourself too; to earn your own appreciation about yourself—self appreciation

There is a new coin of word—'do the *thyaga* of *thyaga*', sacrifice the sacrifice.

'Why not give up your life for a cause?' they the fundamentalist ask. Every sacrifice is for a cause. The cause is to transform the whole human society, they say. I looked at it internally. What transformation they are talking about, I know not. Have you changed? Do you mean to change, not just because somebody says so? Do not compare yourself with any sayings with any one's utterances, however great, holy and utopian they may look. Ask yourself standing aside from all the conditioning that you are subjected to till this date, honestly and truly, 'do I need a change'? Have you understood yourself so far and if so, do you want to be different from what you are? And then try. Let God speed you. As for me, I am happy with myself and need no change, for I am influenced by myself not by anything from outside, so no word they say appeals to me.

—𝍃—

24ᵀᴴ August 1997   03 30 A.M.

'What is peace? I think it is a state of mind mostly influenced by external happenings either directly or indirectly connected to a person. Sometimes it is also an internal making of oneself. Is there an absolute state of mind having absolute peace? I am afraid not. Given under the similar situations two human beings may be in the opposite sides, one attaining or rather feeling peace and the other still wanting it. Wanting to be something other than what you are; and trying to attain by putting efforts, but not becoming 'that' makes a person peace-less. Some get it with less effort because their wants are limited while someone will never get it because his wants are never ending. Somewhere one has to draw the line of wants and say to himself 'this far and no further'. May be, this itself brings him peace or stops him from any more wants. 'Desire-less-ness' or 'wanting-less-ness'. is just a theory. Desires and wants are there only to keep the society moving. Otherwise the whole human race would have turned to a status of vegetables. Desires and wants have to be properly channeled so that both are fulfilled and at the same time peace is attained too. So, how to canalize desires and wants? I feel it is through proper knowledge of desires and wants. May be you would understand desires and wants when you have something other than material and mundane things to attain. That something may be illusory or imaginary. Be it so, but it is worth to go for it as long as peace is attained. Peace is necessary not only for our mental health but also for physical health. Health is the most wanted one by every person be he a hermit or a king; for he wants to live as long as he can, even on losing any or many limbs of his body. No one wants to die, that is primary. While living he wants to live in peace not only with him, but wish the whole society as such. And from the society's point of view it has taken care of, to some extent, by imposition of laws and policing it so that your neighbor should not rob you.

But as regards to his own individual peace it is for him to attain it. When one turns one's mind to within one's own being, one finds peace deep within oneself in abundance and unused energy. And slowly recognizing one's own different kinds of energy one have, one tries to awake them for one's own good and for the good of others. While doing so, one finds oneself to be a strange person. Then one tries to adopt oneself to this new situation drawing energy from Cosmic source and loses all fears of death. He knows now that this energy was always, within him. Slowly, peace sets on him. As he looks to himself on the grand panorama of the life and death hidden in a tiny nut-shell, all resultants of his *karmic* energies, as in a seed of a fruit bearing tree with roots, branches, leaves, flowers, fruits and again seeds of a huge tree potentially hidden in that small seed. Like a seed evolving to become a complete tree, it is manifested in a man when he dies and takes resultants of it along with him to the next life. So each life is the result of the past lives and there is a chain connection and chain reaction. Peace is one of such things that come to man from life to life provided such actions are being constantly taken in each life to be in peace. Peace is not attained just in one life. Peace is the result of accumulated effects of all the previous lives. It can be hastened in this life provided certain way is followed and that way has to be found by himself. May be, some external influences come to help him. The first and the foremost to attain peace is: to be 'true to oneself' and not to be a hypocrite. One must be a friend to oneself and not an enemy. To be a friend to oneself one has to do such *karmas* in thoughts, words and deeds that he can approve of them himself. That which is against his own conscious should not be undertaken, however utopian they may look, however beautifully they might be painted by others. What others say is not important. What he says to himself is the most important one and how he goes about them are equally important. If he neglects to answer himself positively to his own questions, to his own acts— either through thoughts or words or deeds, he cannot attain peace. May be certain circumstances bring him to act against his thought, but he has to take it up as if he is only an instrument and not directly responsible for such acts. That he is only a trustee to such acts and witness himself all his acts as if he is only an actor under the direction of someone beyond him. Probably, this witnessing one's act as a trustee leaving the result of such acts to its natural course with complete detachment would bring permanent peace. Further, he should forget that the whole act, however wonderful it might have been, immediately on its completion, as if it was not he who acted upon it, this would also bring peace. And this forms the foundation for peace. Detachment in all acts and their results are very important to attain peace. To so act there should not be even an iota of selfishness or self interest in the acts. When the self is not involved, self will not be influenced by such acts. An act becomes a separate thing from the self. Then the selfishness runs away. So when one witnesses one's own acts with complete detachment and selflessness, then that would lead to peace which becomes permanent in that person for lives to come. To act as such there cannot be a second thought. This life, not the next life, is the best part of all lives for one will not get a better chance for all the other lives, because one will, more or less, have lesser chances of actions and lesser chances of converting oneself from what one was to what one desires to become. This life has the golden opportunity for a man to attain that state hood of witnessing one's own actions in the most detached way and absolutely without any selfishness, treating himself only as an instrument in the hands of Someone beyond him.

Peace by itself brings the kind of life that one never expected. It brings in abundance the quality of life to enjoy mentally the long healthy life, useful life not only to himself but also to all those around him. By attaining peace he does a great service to humanity.

—ɯ—

22ND AUGUST 1997   03 30 A.M.

It is very difficult to define Purity. Is the definition of purity is purity? Definition is not. Definitions and concepts are not purity; they are just simply words about purity. Purity is the originality without any admixture or adulteration with anything other than its originality. Purity is an entity; it is an entity of thought, words and deeds and even of materialistic one's without any external influences, without anything foreign to it. It stands on its own; it is strength on its own. Neither it looks at others, nor influenced, nor attracted by others. It is neither positive nor negative. The moment you qualify it as positive the comparison starts from its negative qualities. Example—Sun. Sun has its own qualities, it is pure and original by itself and in itself. Neither does it gets mixed up nor allows anything to mix up. All chemical composition of helium and hydrogen burning in trillions of tons and bringing heat and light is the original quality of the sun. Sun does not seek anything external for its functioning. Sun functions by itself, this is the purity of Sun. So, you have to find out what your original qualities are without any bias or influence from anything external, but by your own self, that external thing be even God. God has His own original qualities. God is a universal measurement accepted by all for comparison while no one can become God; neither God can become me or you. May be our desire to attain God-hood, in His qualities, once again, I feel strongly, is our own projection of utopian thought. We extend our projection of these desired qualities to be ours. May be, they are conceptual and theoretical thoughts about God; and we in turn once again try to attain that which is not our own, but set goal of the qualities of God. It is we who qualify God, having not really known who the God is and what His qualities are, in spite of theoretically explaining all about Him or even from the so called experiences of Him, which, once again, is within the boundaries of our limited capacity with pre-conceived ideas of God, either taught or told to us, either orally or in the form of books etc. So, all these have, in a way, conditioned our mind to think and act in the way others wants us to do. God is not our own making, but rather, as others have told to us. So, God to us, in a way, becomes impure in theory because we are influenced by others about God and we accept what someone else says about God because that person who says so is respected by us as an elevated personality and that person is our icon. So, we are not icons to ourselves to find out by ourselves about God. We are influenced not only about God but also about our own thoughts of God. Anything that is influenced and conditioned is not pure. So, our thoughts of purity are impure because that measurement is set by somebody else and it is not our original thought. And further no thought of ours could be called as our original thought because it is the vibration of cosmic intelligence, that have already been stored with trillions of 'thoughts-vibrations' of every person so far, from the time of the creation of man. (May be, also thoughts of all other animate objects which are capable of thinking if at all, but cannot express by words unlike man). In the process, purity becomes a conceptual thought conditioned by the cosmic intelligence. Hence what we call as purity is not real purity but just an admixture of so many vibrations of thought. It is just a word coined for hallucinating ourselves.

Spiritualism is a contradiction is terms for there is nothing either like pure materialism or abstract philosophy. For us to realize God, or whatever it is, we need the body. It should also be functioning in perfect order both in its mental and physical forms, for us to realize God ourselves in our pure and original status. If we are to separate ourselves from this instrument of body calling ourselves as only *atmas* (soul), it is mere hypocritic than a rational fact.

It is impossible to realize the God only by the soul as a separate entity while the soul recognizes itself one with God having the same qualities of God and when so, the realization of oneself and one's own qualities does not arise because *atman* cannot be separated from its own functioning of realization. What is our original status apart from what has been told to us, we don't know it in fact. We just believe what has been told to us. But believing without intellectual and rational discretion is an intellectual slavery, surrendering our capacity to think freely, whether those thoughts are 'far' or 'against' the way the spiritualists think.

Now, what is self-realization? First we should be sure, in a rational way, that there is some separate entity called as 'Self'. Is there? I don't know. Just because I don't know, is it not irrational to believe that which the other person says as truth? Without finding out by my own self is it rational to believe him? May be he is right and what is right for him may not be so for me. So, he cannot insist that just because I like to be with him or with his other members while they are all gentleman of likeable characters, I should not believe and follow everything he says. I do not like to disturb any of his feelings or thoughts and do not like either giving opinion about what I think about his findings. Fine for me, to be with him and respect his findings but not necessarily accept and follow him

To me, nothing is strange, nothing is vice or virtue. Who am I to give qualifications to others behavior? To me, everything is the same. There is no absolute sin or absolute purity. Everything is just as they are and ought to be. Only because we human beings could be able to control an infinitesimal part of nature and other living beings through our intellectual powers, (which, in fact, come to us from the cosmic intelligence since our brain is only capable of catching the cosmic vibrations to a very limited extent from a cosmic intelligence while it is impossible to gauge or quantify and also qualify that cosmic intelligence.) we think we are 'know alls' of this universe. We know nothing as to how this universe and its different aspects are functioning. We will never know. Even we can never know how our physical body is functioning, what best we could say about it is, that the physical organs are functioning in the way they are to function in their normal conditions and that will be its pure nature of functioning. We don't have to qualify any of its natural functioning and we don't have to express any wonder at its natural functioning. We are totally ignorant of everything either of ourselves or inside of us. I am becoming a pure ignorant person about which I am aware of and 'not knowingness of anything' is encompassing me.

I do hear some voice and am hearing of late since about a year that there is less time left for me. End I could see, but I am not afraid of it, neither I am happy about it. It just comes unannounced and I am preparing to receive it and to accept it in its natural way. Just because I hear these intuitive feelings from deep within me, I do not have to assess what all I did in the life so far and I do not feel that there is still a lot to do. Neither there is anything to do nor anything not to do. As it was natural for me to have been born and so it is natural for me to depart too. I do not attach much importance either to my birth or to my so called life that I am presently leading or to the end of it. Everything seems to be natural for me. There is neither purity nor impurity in the life that I led for having been born and had to live till the end comes. If you call something impure and try to correct it for purity, it is a ritual and you do not know the end result. Why to fall into these dualistic, disturbing and argumentative thoughts? Leave everything to its own functioning and to my way of thinking to myself. Also leave God to Himself. I allow you to be left to yourself. And I desire to be free from the bondage of thoughts of God. And that is purity I think.

21ST AUGUST 1997   03 30 A.M.

What is it say that one has to turn to oneself and to where to? The mind is turned to know deep within as to what is going on within. Is it to judge, to understand and to discriminate what thoughts are born within and whether these thoughts are positive or not and to understand the impulses that come with the feelings? Feelings arise from within (*Anthahkaran*), from the depth of our heart, which are not thoughts but intuitions translated by thoughts. Feelings have no language, emotions have no language. It is the thought that translate and the intellect that compares such thoughts from the one's whose resultants are already stored within us, from the earlier conditioned thoughts. At the same time thoughts take us deep into our feelings and in deep feelings deep silence is felt. At that time everything stops, even to a great extent thoughts slow down, though not totally stop. In deep silence I see the bright light, inexpressible. Silence is not darkness, it is an extraordinary light. I was there experiencing this deep silence and the extraordinary light there-from, as a witness. And yet, it was my own deep silence I was experiencing and it was not something from outside. I became that very deep silence myself, though I was seeing through my physical eyes I could not recognize what I was seeing, so with my ears. My body was touching the seat and arms of the chair I was sitting on and still I was not in touch with anything at all.

My thoughts triggers and takes me to that inner depth as if I was submerging myself in a deep sea full of unique light beyond this mundane world, beyond everything this physical body experiences. There was no sound, still I could hear even in this deep silence, the most divine sound of communication between me and that extraordinary power of silence. Thoughts were divine which took me into this deep silence, then that silence too became divine. I enjoyed that extraordinary and unique power of silence. Estacy and joy came to me and I became a stranger to myself from within though not physically and externally.

I have been experiencing this deep silence whenever I turned myself inwardly. Sometimes some sound, some fragrance or some thought takes me to the depth of me. I have cultivated this habit since long, of going deep within me, especially when I am alone. But somewhere along the line I had dropped this habit. Now, I have once again could be able to do so on my own volition at a very mere thought, just in seconds

—m—

15ᵀᴴ AUGUST,1997   03 30 A.M.

While in deep, silence which is coming to me more often, though I have not fixed any particular time, all my idiosyncrasies fall out, all habits both acquired and inherited also fall out. And I become a stranger to myself because while I am functioning in my physical body certain characters and habits being a part of me of which I am aware of, will no more there when I turn deep within me and dive deep into that sea of silence. As I said, I came face to face with that unique and extra-ordinary silence which is very bright and soothing. An unimaginable power, inexpressible, was before me. I was aghast with wonder at the vastness of silence which encompassed me and there I was enjoying every second of my stay before that power of silence since it brings the power of joy, love and kindness. That power was not something separated from any of these qualities. That power was the very personification of these qualities and I knew. I had all those qualities, but yet I was insignificant before that power. I just did not want to depart from that power and still something took place within me and slowly I become aware of and finally I came back to where I had started my journey and afterwards I can chew the cuds of the results of my experiences and could give meaning, translating them in my own conceptual thought, either through the utterances or by writing. Till I take another journey I would be thinking of the experiences of the last journey which fades slowly and become a memory of the past. Slowly, but surely my journey transforms me differently from what I was. May be one day I would be completely a different person. Only time would tell.

—⁂—

10TH AUGUST 1997   03 00 A.M.

Once I was a voracious reader of books. I would choose a book and sit for two to three days continuously to complete that book. But not now. No more any book or any talk of any great person interest me. Nothing seems to interest me. Nothing draws me and nothing influences me. There is neither joy nor sorrow, neither peace nor disturbance. No duality draws me to them. Everything seems to be in their natural conditions. No qualifying takes place. Even my very thoughts seem to be natural to me. I don't want to qualify the thoughts either as good or bad or as normal. They are just there. The totality of 'me' is something that slips away from me and still I am the totality with different facets which are qualified and quantified by the preceptors of my personality. 'I', as such, do not have any separate personality. Even this very writing I desire to stop, since it does not make any difference either to me or to anybody else. However, somewhere in the corner of me there lies my own idiosyncrasies, acquired and inherited qualities, which of course have conditioned me to what I am today—which cannot be compared or qualified in any way. Honestly, I don't know what birth is or death is or even life is.

The more I think, the more vacuum is created in me. I feel, I am heading to be a big zero in every aspect leading me to 'Nothingness' May be, that is THE REALITY.

I feel why should I subordinate myself in even in my thoughts to God, and if at all such an entity called God exist? Why? Any surrendering is only with the pre-conceived notion to ultimately gaining power of any nature, whether spiritual or otherwise.

—⁂—

20ᵗʰ July 1997   03 30 A.M.

What is desire? It is a pleasurable want with a motivation to enjoy either with such things and thoughts that are either presently existing or making its existence in future, perhaps becomes possible, whether it is attainable or not. Sometime it may be mundane and some other times a mystic. Desire by itself has no qualification or character, it is we who qualify the desire and give a value to it according to our social and mental conditions which once again depends upon our conditioned thoughts and upbringing. Religion does play a great part in qualifying the desire. Desire to attain a status, to get richer or even to realize the so called God is almost the same. Desire by itself does not discriminate between God and dog. Totally desire may look selfish. There is nothing wrong to be selfish. That is one of the natural phenomenon of all living beings—man and animal. Attainment of God-hood is also a desire or going away from God-hood is also a desire. The failure, mostly it will be a failure to most of us that brings hallucination of having-attained God-hood, brings its own results or even not being satisfied fully, though not a complete failure, brings its own mental dissatisfaction which results in anger. So this in turn becomes an impediment, they say, to attain God-hood. It is a vicious circle. Anger, I feel, is equally a natural phenomenon of all living beings. It is not unnatural being angry. Whether this anger is in thoughts, words or deeds, it is always there, but only expression differs. Anger is one of the emotions. Emotion-less-ness is a state of being a vegetable, it is lifeless. A wall cannot express any emotion. I feel, thought too is another facet of emotion, whether you call it as good or bad, it is a value judgment, which differs not in kind but in degrees. Thoughtlessness is death. The very concept of death is a thought, because death cannot be experienced and subsequently explained since the very instrument that experiences death also dies. So, the root of desire is thought. Desirelessness is thoughtlessness which is death and which cannot be either experienced or expressed. Hence, 'desire-less-ness' is death, which cannot be experienced or expressed. To be 'desire-less' is also a 'desire'. To be 'anger-less' is a state of a subtle anger. To go beyond these emotions, go to the deep silence that helps, but still a thought will be lingering, witnessing and experiencing those emotions, which expresses themselves subsequently. So, even in dead silence desire continues to exists, hence, no living being can be 'desire-less'.

—ɯ—

16ᵀᴴ July 1997   03 30 A.M.

Who is God? I think, it is just phraseology of concept giving meaning according to one's own conditioning, both socially and intellectually. I knew nothing about God except what books have said or what others have said and how I was brought up in my earlier age. I was conditioned by all these including my religion to which I was born to or that which I may follow. By myself I do not belong to any particular religion or a particular Nation. To me, the whole universe looks be a home to everything—animate and inanimate objects in any form which are the creations and I am one of those created. So, neither can I claim any superiority or inferiority of myself, since this comparison is one of a degree but not of kind. There is nothing, even thoughts, ideas, concepts which can be called as superior or inferior—that the values, we, human intellectuals try to measure with our own scales. All that are created are just there without any qualifications. I don't understand anything of these creations. The thought, the idea, the concept are not independent but are part of the entire creation and the whole cosmos is intelligence itself, from which each individual draws his intelligence according to his capacity to receive—rather an individual's intelligence does not exist but he is a part of that cosmic intelligence.

There is no such a thing as change—rather it is a happening on its own which we human beings try to understand, but fail, since we give our own meanings and reasons with our limited intelligence while the whole cannot be perceived by a part. The eternal cannot be understood by the limited, finite. The omnipotent cannot be understood or measured by the weak, let alone the so called impotent.

—ɱ—

10ᵀᴴ July 1997   03 00 A.M.

Of late, probably since last September when I was in deep silent meditation continuously for twenty one days, I have been feeling a sort of tightness and stiffness, as if some energy is concentrating with pressure, between my two eyes, on the forehead. I feel, as if it is expressing to burst—out. This happens unnoticed and unexpectedly and particularly when I just sit and go into silence—which I do quite often, even amidst my working in the office, unaware of my own self, let alone the surroundings. The deep silence takes me off from this world to unknown spheres and some type of unique way of contentment and inexpressible happiness and peace descends on me and occupies my whole being. Silence, deep silence, brings immense peace and peace in turn brings happiness unparalleled. I become a childlike personality. Knowing, I feel the sense of 'not knowingness'. This sense of not knowingness unburdens me of all the past knowledge, of all the past days of this life, may be even the previous lives, if at all such lives were lived. Sense of lightness, both in respect of weight and illumination, is felt within me and that leads to the feeling of 'not-caring' to any of the ways of the world, a complete detachment from my own self is experienced. But still, this bodily stiffness between the eyes on the forehead continues, when I become aware of my body. One of these days it may burst out or ooze out of me. But this concentration of pressure brings me its own pleasure and happiness as if my whole body is at that particular point concentrating and I become that point itself; but I do not know how and why. This is real and physical, not mental or intellectual imagination. When I touch that point I feel it to be very soft, as if there is no bone at all. I could feel the throb of it. Of course, yesterday I could be able to perceive that on my forehead an elliptical marble like shining thing. It was transparent and uniformly white, white like cotton. Was it my soul I saw? May be. I have seen such white patches between the eye brows of many persons, whether they could be able to feel it themselves I don't know. Still I feel all these experiences are of no consequences to me and may not bring me nearer to God.

Irrespective of whether I am with Him or not, I go to such a state of silence very naturally and whenever I desire. Just a thought is enough to bring me to that state without any efforts. There are occasions when I sit for a long time and I will be happy at the state of silence to which I arrive at which ultimately I become myself, that silence.

—ɯ—

16ᵀᴴ JUNE 1997   03 30 A.M.

What is desire? It is to possess something for oneself. It may be physical or mental. Why to possess? It is to enjoy, to get pleasure and to get security and safety. Security and safety, for whom and from what? For one-self? What is one-self? It is the combination of my physical body and my inner being and also my thoughts. I am not other than my thoughts. Even my 'soul' is the creation of my thought. What is thought? I don't know. 'Not knowing' is also a thought.

There is nothing like 'desire-less-ness'. The very thought of being 'desire-less', is also a 'desire'. I desire to be 'desire-less'. The basic of desire, even of God, heaven etc; is to seek a status, a position, a pleasure, may be even spiritual, safety, security and permanence. Why do we want to be nearer to God? Is it to receive His grace? But, why? Is it to have some of His powers in us? What do we do with that power we get from God? Use it? Use it for what purpose? To enhance oneself in further acquiring power of God and other qualities of God that He is described to hold. But still I do not understand why we should have God's powers or his qualities. Well, that does not mean that we should have other qualities, the so called negative thoughts. How about shunning or discarding the both the positive and negative thoughts? While one is the worldly thought, to some extent existing physically and becomes a fact of day to day living, the other is a mental projection, a concept conditioned by sayings of others either orally or though books. But it does not help me. I don't know whether it could help others. To me, it might have influenced but did not help me. Because the very 'help' is a desire that seeks from outside something what you want and that you don't have. Somehow, to me, nothing has any meaning, for I don't go to give any meaning to anything. Absolutely and very frankly 'I know nothing', for, I think, there is 'nothing to know'. Everything is just there. It is the human ego, the intellectual ego that tries to give meaning to everything as if it is being his creation, while his race is just a cog in the whole wheel of the universe and of course a necessary cog—a part of the wheel, not a separate entity, but at the same time not the wheel itself. To seek, to become is already to conceptualize what is seeked, what is to become. To give meaning to the objects of what is sought. Neither the life nor the death makes any difference to any such meanings. I feel that there is nothing like life nor death nor birth. They are simple egoistical projections of man's intellectual ways of giving meanings to the movements of the universe. If someone asks me 'whether I am living or dead?' I would say I don't know. How do I know that 'I know' or 'I know nothing', I just know that I know nothing, but I cannot explain. Better not, to think, or contemplate, or to question these. These are simply intellectual somersaulting. Let me put a full—stop to all these enquiries. In conclusion I can never be without desire. Desire and hope are the sustenance of life.

14ᵀᴴ JUNE 1997   03 00 A.M.

Blankness and strangeness occupy me. I recognize them. Time becomes meaningless and so the life. I don't know what the life is. I don't know what I am or who I am. Individuality comes to a dead stop. Recognition of me by myself stops. It is impossible to express my status of being. Everything looks to be just there, the earth, the living beings, plants everything including the atmosphere, the sun, the moon, stars etc. I don't know what they are in reality. It is just a name that we give to understand one another. It has no meaning if this body is called by some name or another. It is only to recognize and to communicate, a name or a word and its meaning to recognize that particular object or a person, is given. Other than that it has no other objective or usefulness. Everything is just simply there. No meaning need be given to it. Sun is there to give light and heat. Light and heat are reference points of this body. This body needs light and heat at a particular level of its tolerance. Beyond that it makes difference. Light, darkness, heat, cold etc. are always measured with reference to human body's normal tolerances. All are with reference to certain tolerances which in turn is its naturalness, as human body needs or rather tolerates certain degree of light and heat, but for animals it is different and for different animals it varies and so also from objects to objects. To me everything looks normal and natural including the feelings of oneself. Thoughts by themselves have no meaning unless they are translated to words or deeds. Thoughts do create certain imagination of physical being or physical actions. Man, who speaks, gives meanings to these words through expression, but I don't know how animals think or whether they think at all. Animals are very natural, they have no knowledge of light or night, or time or space, or cause-effect, they only feel and understand their physical necessities. They would never kill their own species in spite of fighting between themselves. It is the man who kills the other man for power, money, jealousy etc. In spite of my being a man I feel that I need very less of these, of course, when I am hungry I need food, physical protection from pain etc. But other things I don't understand. Even hunger is natural to the physical body according to the circumstances and chemical changes that take place within the body which is also natural.

Ignorance encompasses me stronger and stronger, day by day. I am feeling ignorant and hardly understand anything of these concepts. Just to be in the society, I am functioning in the way I do superficially, but from within I am not functioning at all. I know not what functioning is, in reality. I am part of the universe and I am not different from the universe and I don't know whether the functioning of the universe can be qualified in any other way. I do not find either the beginning or the end of this functioning. The whole universe functions eternally under its own natural law in which we, human beings find changes but in the universe, by itself there is no change. Our concept, our thought, feels the changes in the universe. But the universe goes on, on its own natural path eternally with no beginning or end and I am one with it. No other meaning can be given and I don't know any other meaning to this functioning, called as life.

—w—

7ᵀᴴ JUNE 1997   03 30 A.M.

When I sit at this hour my thought waves go very deep within me and time stops and the thought waves slow down. What is that 'me' or every other thing that I perceive around? Are they not my thoughts, I exist and function through my thoughts while I am completely unaware of the functions of my body except when it suffers from pain. Even the pain, I think, is my thought. Then, is there any condition that is thoughtlessness? I am afraid not. Thoughtlessness is annihilation of thought which in turn brings annihilation of body. The thought projected within me, brings 'my-ness'. The moment 'my-ness' comes; a separate entity is created, in fact there is nothing like 'me' being separate from the whole. I am part of this whole and I cannot be separated from the whole, while being in 'my' form. And still I feel that I don't know any of these things. As days pass on, weeks, months, years, decades and centuries roll-by., I feel that I am growing in ignorance and proportionately becoming light in body and mind. So called knowledge becomes a burden and so the God too. All types of fears lead to God. Fear of destruction, fear of annihilation, fear of losing identity which on the contrary craves for permanency and continuity of self in this very physical body, brings the concept of God and as a self-ramification, auto suggestion, self-brain-washing and may be, to some extent, self-hypnotism for the thought to be in tranquility and in sober state. Meditation, concentration of thought on one particular subject brings chemical changes in the brain matrix and a lot of un thinkable and unknowable, un imaginable things flashes on our brain, which, it is said, can easily be attained through drugs like LSD, marijuana, brown sugar etc. that brings chemical changes to the brain matrix. So a particular chemical change in the body brings or drives the imagination to different plane, different level, and different legion and different region. Can we call these as realities? I don't think so, and still I don't know. These experiences may leave a deep mark on our brain but still they are really artificially created experiences which have no real meaning to the physical world we live in. Experiences may come in many ways, induced, imaginary physical and by dreams. All leave back marks on the brain and the brain craves for repetition of such experiences, and so with the spiritual experiences too.

—ɱ—

1ˢᵀ June 1997   03 00 a.m.

Man creates God in his own conceptual image, uses that word for his advantage and equally abuses the word, God, to meet his selfish thinking that he is the only person who knows God. God is the most saleable commodity and available in plenty and perpetually, sold and resold and it is perennial and unexhausted, for nobody can hold God and show to the purchasers that 'this is the God'. God slips away the moment a person tries to hold it, for God cannot be held by anyone. God is a commodity available to anyone and not to any one particular person. Every person from a saint to a sinner, from a king to a beggar can use and abuse the word God in any manner he desires. There is no one who could stop another using God and yet nobody can use or get God in full. It is a universally conceptualized word without any patent rights. God to me is cosmic energy, cosmic intelligence and cosmic vibration. It can be experienced by any one who desires to receive the vibration of this cosmic centrally located energy. As the sun is located at a particular place without any movement and yet we, moving around the sun, feel the energy and heat of the sun through its vibratory rays.

I do not as an individual understand or have desire to know why this creation is for. It is just there including me. It has no answer. Nature does not answer any questions from the limited intelligence and concept of man. In the process of being, there is nothing to become, but just to be in being. However I may struggle, how-so-ever I may use all my intelligence at my command, the only realization is; 'that I can never know anything about anything'.

12ᵀᴴ MAY 1997   03 30 A.M.

Sometimes, I wonder at my own position in life. I do not recognize and also do not feel the duality in me. There is neither disturbance nor peace, neither hate nor love, neither attachment nor detachment, neither happiness nor unhappiness, no dual feelings, rather no feelings at all, as being qualified by the others as positive or negative. Nothing is there; I am just there with the whole universe about which I cannot comprehend. The basic question is: as to why should I try to understand the universal Being? Is it come to the status of being a vegetable to understand that being? Nothing of the two extremes touches me. The physical hurt does pain me. It is the physical and natural phenomenon of the physical working body to feel pain when physically hurt. We cannot start giving qualifications to that by saying 'do you feel the physical pain when the body is hurt?' Sure, I do. That is natural. But why should that be a controversial one when comes to spiritualism? When it comes I do suffer. Does the so called spiritualist not feel the physical pain? I think they do, may be they have better resisting power through their mind when such a mind is said to be turned towards God. I don't know. It is fine for me if they say so. To me it makes no difference that one person suffer more and the other person less when in physical pain of same intensity. Every argument has a counter-argument, but I have no argument either with the theists or atheist since I understand neither of them and I would rather not like to understand any of them.

To me, neither the past nor the future makes any difference, while the present makes no meaning to me. Then one may ask 'how are you functioning'? 'I don't know', I would say. I do not know whether I am functioning and further what functioning is? I am not sad of not knowing it. It is not a melancholy. I don't know what the mind is. Everything looks to me mere words. No meaning comes to me. Well, to exist, I have to do certain job and that is being done. I have to know certain things as regards to money and other physical necessities for the physical function and existence. At the same time I do not know what the spiritual life is. I do not know anything about them. I am in this state now. Why should I be born to my parents in a particular family and community and in a nation? I do not belong to any particular geographical area or to any particular religion. I am universal. I am just 'I-am'; and at the same time I do not know who 'I-am'. And still the caste to which I am born might have influenced me, both externally and internally to be what I am. I have no hero to worship, I have no icons. Neither I condemn nor praise anyone who says that he has God with him, because I do not know who God is. Each person has a right to think and behave in any particular way he deems fit provided his behavior does not impediments the rights of others and each person is a unique personality of his own individuality. Personality of an individual can never be compared, can never be qualified nor quantified while it is impossible to know what is the personality is of oneself let alone of others. The desire to know 'what-is' is impossible to achieve. The very desire to reach, to attain is an impediment to the reachable and attainable, for there is nothing, so far as I am concerned, either to reach or to attain. It is just a concept given by someone who claims to have reached or attained, while from within he knows for sure that he does not know for himself whether he has reached or attained and he does not know in reality 'The Reality'; and whether he has, or has not reached or attained. How does one can be so sure that he has reached or attained. To me, it looks beyond my understanding. I just don't know myself and to know something beyond me is impossible for me. I understand nothing. I give-up to understand, to reach or to attain. Sometimes, I wonder myself whether I am an individual entity because there seems to be no duality in me. I become one with the whole cosmic consciousness, one with the whole creation and loose my individuality, my 'self-personality' if I have any, which I very much doubt I have. Physically, at sometimes, when I see something I see not, and when I hear something I hear not, because I cannot comprehend what I saw or heard. They are blank within me. I, in the end, become completely blank and in that deep silence, despite of lot of activities going on physically outside, I dive into it and loose myself completely and there is no 'me' there and I am lost to this Silence. I become that very Cosmic vast eternal Silence Itself.

—ᵚᵚ—

6ᵀᴴ May 1997   01 00 a.m.

There is neither moroseness nor happiness within me. Somehow I feel that it is slowly coming to be my natural state. No dualistic problem arises. Nothing moves me. To call happiness as a 'state of mind' and to recognize that 'state', I feel, it is physical. Mental cannot exist on its own unless it is born with physical birth. How a 'mental state' can stand by itself without its origin—the physical? So, 'mental' is both a supplement and a complement to the physical. The death or the end of physical is the death or the end of mental too. One can never be sure that the resultant or the mental state continues even after accumulating or eliminating certain '(Karmas)' of the physical or the mental actions. Greed, hunger etc are natural phenomenon of physical body and as long as physical body functions these emotions too function though not with the same intensity, as the physical body withers so these emotions too wither and it is natural. They are neither good nor bad, neither positive nor negative, but they are natural. God is a sociological problem; He is not a problem to an individual either physically or mentally. It is the society that imposed God on man.

Sometimes, I feel that I am already dead from within, an emotionless and a desire less person. From this I feel the deep silence within me which in turn brings me immense peace and I am with myself. Not with God or with any such concept of being with some other person different from me, is there. Deep silence, deep peace I become. Psychologist may term me as a negative personality. It is fine with me, because I never value either the positive or the negative qualifications. I just want to be in this state where I am in timelessness, space-les-ness and beyond cause-effect phenomenon. Nothing touches me. But physical pain does bring me its own woe upon me to some extent. And it may influence sometimes my state of mind when I am not so effectively in silent mind. What is mind? I don't know what it is. Thought too, I don't know. I know very well that I don't know a lot of things. I always feel that not to know is very very peaceful. It brings harmony in me. When I am in silence I become the very silence itself, the very peace itself. Silence and peace are not different from me. They are I and I am they.

—☙—

03ʳᵈ MAY 1997   03 00 A.M.

If at all there is such a thing called God and seeking Him or to be one with Him by any method, I feel, is in a way, a selfish desire. Why should one seek Him? Is it to protect oneself from something? How do you protect yourself? Your self is a projection of your physical and mental body. Body and soul are complementary to each other. Soul cannot function without the physical body and the body is dead without the soul. So through body only you have to seek God. That goes to show that to a great extent you have to preserve your body whether the present one or the one that you would take in the future—taking is a concept of rebirth, is considered and accepted. You want to save your soul. But from what? From sin? What is sin? Is it not a principle of dualistic social order which, in fact, differs from geographical place, time, social stigma and religion etc? So, to seek God is to seek protection, safety, durability, permanency. But, all these for what? I feel these are your own making. There is nothing to get protected from. Every seeking, be it in the name of God or materialism, is selfishness. Everything is a way of life. Devils—people who are a burden to this society—are given the elusive God for them to mend them-selves so that they will have no time to deal otherwise in society. To that extent some rouge-hours are reduced to the society and social burden is lessened. God is elusive, a mirage, a conceptual thought, running non stop always, and to seek such a God, is to die in the process. Probably, even to the last breath of their life they may not realize that what they perused all their life was only a mirage. Or, may be, they may feel joy, for no one knows what a person in his / her last breath of life feels, because no one has come back to explain. All explanations of 'after death' are hypothetical and imaginary ones. No arguments can be made on the subject of death for the simple reason that both the sides are ignorant of 'after-death', or may be, both are right and the third person who judges them may be ignorant about it. When we know nothing about death, we would know nothing about life too, since both death and life are the two faces of the same coin. With the death life is born and with the birth of the life death is also born. I feel that coin is only an imaginary one since neither we are born nor we would die. However, I feel we know nothing about the functioning of this phenomenon including the functioning of the body, let alone the functioning of our so called soul. This very writing of mine has no meaning in the order of things of this Universe, because, whatever I may write, it is once again my concept, may be very far from the truth about which I do not know. I am really conditioned in all manners and ways from my idiosyncrasies that have had its information and knowledge I was fed with, sometimes fed by me to myself and some other times fed to me from by the outside world. My thoughts, my concepts and my very existence are conditioned. And I cannot help myself but being conditioned. There is nothing like freedom, absolute freedom from my own self. I am really a prisoner of my own thoughts and it cannot be otherwise. From this prison, I seek freedom, mentally. But still my thoughts are not mine, but conditioned by many thoughts of others, present and past. In these conditioned thoughts, I perceive the movement, that dynamism of the inner silence in me. I am part of it and only my thoughts seek separation. But, separation from what? And why? In what way can I be important than a fig or a dried or a small streak of leaf of a small plant? Everything perceivable and beyond makes the whole. A point is also the whole.

There are no escapes, no regrets, no desires either of being at low ebb or at the elevated pinnacle and just I am in my natural state of mind.

—ɯ—

19ᵀᴴ Aᴘʀɪʟ 1997

It is 3.15 AM now. I always, till some time past, use to think very deeply contemplating upon so many things and especially upon God, life beyond etc. But, I feel, having been slowly trying to know or rather trying to understand these concepts and coming to a firm conclusion that however I may try I can never know anything about these concepts. They remain just words or thoughts because I can never know for sure what these are, for I am either here or there because there is no 'half-way home.'

In spite of all knowledge, all the so called experiences, all that one could boasts of, one is always afraid and really afraid of one sure thing and that is—'death'. We are not afraid of somebody's death. But when we think that it will come to us one day, we become all of a sudden panicky from inside of us at our sub-conscious level. This is the Reality. And every other thing is a theory and to escape from this fear of the un-known, we just take shelter at our own mental concept of God. We don't want to talk or write about death since it brings to the mind and catches our whole being with fear. Probably, I feel, that this fear of death has created God to combat the reality of death and also to live in peace with others who is more stronger than us intellectually, economically, physically and sociologically by putting fear of death (rather God) into him so that he will subdue himself, for the simple reason that such a so called strong man is equally rather much more afraid of his coming to an end by death. This is 'hypocritical intelligence' of a person who has not any of these strengths, except his so called intelligence through which he wants to dominate the other and survive, being afraid of himself or of the death, within himself.

So, to me, everything looks that the whole world lives in fear and to assure oneself that one is not afraid of death, one takes to God to put up a brave façade. To me the greatest mystery is, why at all a person has to take up God? The answer to me is 'Escapism' Person wants to escape from everything including from himself. But still that mystery of concept of God remains to be a mystery only for we know not what God is. To me it is an empty slogan of escapists and probably, I am one of them.

11ᵀᴴ MARCH 1997   03 30 A.M.

It is the human nature to give meanings to everything irrespective of whether such meanings are apt or otherwise. Either it is positive or negative or waste, such is the qualified meanings, while they have no part of definitions in that meaning, they just happen beyond the understanding of the human beings and in spite of human efforts. We only give reasons from our limited knowledge and co-relate our own qualified values conditioned by our acquired cultural and social values, which change from society to society and in the same society from time to time and at the same time from situation of situation.

The universal energy, the one cosmic energy, does not get affected by our values. Values are required for the society to be held in control or otherwise there would be chaotic atmosphere and anarchy and slavery will survive, which, in fact, is so even now, to a great extent, because the fabric of the social values are being torn at every second; and it may not be late before the whole social fabric is torn apart. But in the order of the things of the Universe, it cares not whether the human race, a spec on the vast panorama of the cosmic, survives or not. The universe goes on as it were, as it is, as it would be, without being touched or influenced even by an iota of human value system. The whole universe is a complete consciousness of oneness. Everything just happens and we human beings are only a small expression of this whole cosmic energy. We try to make too much of ourselves and bring great importance to ourselves and think that this universe will come to a naught at the annihilation of the human race; but I am afraid not. When I connect myself completely with this one Cosmic Energy, my consciousness expands and I become one with the Universe and the whole spectrum looks as if it is made up of one energy only but with different expressions. Different expressions are not different entities but, have different functions. They are all, may be, in different degrees of expression but of only one in kind, as there are different kinds of cells in a human body while the pattern and characteristics of DNA in all cells are the same; and the manifestation of all these cells makes the human body a whole and so the manifestation of different expressions of this Cosmic Energy is in the totality with that of THE ONE AND THE ONLY OMNIPOTENT, OMNIPRESENT AND OMNISCIENT UNIVERSAL COSMIC ENERGY, WHICH MAY BE CALLED AS GOD.